The Four Steps to the Epiphany

Successful Strategies for Products that Win

Steve Blank

Fifth Edition

Published 2013
Printed by Quad/Graphics

ISBN 0 989200 5 07
$39.95

Table of Contents

The Hero's Journey

A legendary hero is usually the founder of something—the founder of a new age, the founder of a new religion, the founder of a new city, the founder of a new way of life. In order to found something new, one has to leave the old and go on a quest of the seed idea, a germinal idea that will have the potential of bringing forth that new thing.
— Joseph Campbell, Hero with a Thousand Faces

Joseph Campbell popularized the notion of an archetypal journey that recurs in the mythologies and religions of cultures around the world. From Moses and the burning bush to Luke Skywalker meeting Obi wan Kenobi, the journey always begins with a hero who hears a calling to a quest. At the outset of the voyage, the path is unclear, and the end is not in sight. Each hero meets a unique set of obstacles, yet Campbell's keen insight was that the outline of these stories was always the same. There were not a thousand different heroes, but one hero with a thousand faces.

The hero's journey is an apt way to think of startups. All new companies and new products begin with an almost mythological vision–a hope of what could be, with a goal few others can see. It's this bright and burning vision that differentiates the entrepreneur from big company CEOs and startups from existing businesses. Founding entrepreneurs are out to prove their vision and business are real and not some hallucination; to succeed they must abandon the status quo and strike out on what appears to be a new path, often shrouded in uncertainty. Obstacles, hardships and disaster lie ahead, and their journey to success tests more than financial resources. It tests their stamina, agility, and the limits of courage.

Most entrepreneurs feel their journey is unique. Yet what Campbell perceived about the mythological hero's journey is true of startups as well: However dissimilar the stories may be in detail, their outline is always the same. Most entrepreneurs travel down the startup path without a roadmap and believe no model or template could apply to their new venture. They are wrong. For the path of a startup is well worn, and well understood. The secret is that no one has written it down.

Those of us who are serial entrepreneurs have followed our own hero's journey and taken employees and investors with us. Along the way we've done things our own way, taking good advice, bad advice, and no advice. On about the fifth or sixth startup, at least some of us began to recognize there was an emerging pattern between our successes and failures. Namely, there is a true and repeatable path to success, a path that eliminates or mitigates the most egregious risks and allows the company to grow into a large, successful enterprise. One of us decided to chart this path in the following pages.

Discovering the Path

"Customer Development" was born during my time spent consulting for the two venture capital firms that between them put $12 million into my last failed startup. (My mother kept asking if they were going to make me pay the money back. When I told her they not only didn't want it back, but were trying to see if they could give me more for my next company, she paused for a long while and then said in a very Russian accent, "Only in America are the streets paved with gold.") Both venture firms sought my advice for their portfolio companies. Surprisingly, I enjoyed seeing other startups from an outsider's perspective. To everyone's delight, I could quickly see what needed to be fixed. At about the same time, two newer companies asked me to join their boards. Between the board work and the consulting, I enjoyed my first-ever corporate "out-of-body experience."

No longer personally involved, I became a dispassionate observer. From this new vantage point I began to detect something deeper than I had seen before: There seemed to be a pattern in the midst of the chaos. Arguments I had heard at my own startups seem to be repeated at others. The same issues arose time and again: big company managers versus entrepreneurs, founders versus professional managers, engineering versus marketing, marketing versus sales, missed schedule issues, sales missing the plan, running out of money, raising new money. I began to gain an appreciation of how world-class venture capitalists develop pattern recognition for these common types of problems. "Oh yes, company X, they're having problem 343. Here are the six likely ways that it will resolve, with these probabilities." No one was actually quite that good, but some VCs had "golden guts" for these kinds of operating issues.

Yet something in the back of my mind bothered me. If great venture capitalists could recognize and sometimes predict the types of problems that were occurring, didn't that mean the problems were structural rather than endemic? Wasn't something fundamentally wrong with the way everyone organizes and manages startups? Wasn't it possible the problems in every startup were somehow self-inflicted and could be ameliorated with a different structure? Yet when I talked to my venture capital friends, they said, "Well, that's just how startups work. We've managed startups like this forever; there is no other way to manage them."

After my eighth and likely final startup, E.piphany, it became clear there is a better way to manage startups. Joseph Campbell's insight of the repeatable patterns in mythology is equally applicable to building a successful startup. All startups (whether a new division inside a larger corporation or in the canonical garage) follow similar patterns—a series of steps which, when followed, can eliminate a lot of the early wandering in the dark. Startups that have thrived reflect this pattern again and again and again.

So what is it that makes some startups successful and leaves others selling off their furniture? Simply this: Startups that survive the first few tough years do not follow the traditional product-centric launch model espoused by product managers or the venture capital community. Through trial and error, hiring and firing, successful startups all invent a parallel process to Product Development. In particular, the winners invent and live by a process of customer learning and discovery. I call this process "Customer Development," a sibling to "Product Development," and each and every startup that succeeds recapitulates it, knowingly or not.

This book describes the "Customer Development" model in detail. The model is a paradox because it is followed by successful startups, yet articulated by no one. Its basic propositions are the antithesis of common wisdom, yet they are followed by those who succeed.

It is the path that is hidden in plain sight.

Introduction

Think Different
— Steve Jobs

When I wrote *The Four Steps to the Epiphany* over a decade ago, I had no idea I would be starting the Lean Startup revolution. Newly retired, with time to reflect on what I had learned from my 21 years as an entrepreneur, I was struggling to reconcile the reality of my experience with the then-common advice about how to start a company. Investors, VCs and educators all taught entrepreneurs to use the same process used in an established company. To be successful, you wrote a plan, raised money and then executed to the plan, all in a very linear direction.

My experience suggested that they were all wrong.

I spent several years working through a different approach to building startups. This became the Customer Development process and the idea of Market Types. In hindsight, I now realize that while educators and startup investors had adapted tools and processes useful for *executing* a business model, there were no tools and processes to *search* for a business model. It seemed obvious to me that *searching* is what startups actually do, but it was a pretty lonely couple of years convincing others.

Over time necessity – not investors or educators -- drove the adoption of the Customer Development process. The emerging web, mobile and cloud apps, built with small teams already using agile development, needed a much faster process to acquire customer feedback. This new generation of entrepreneurs were rapid early adopters of customer development as it helped them reduce the odds of failing – by getting them out of the building to get early customer feedback -- as they built their product incrementally and iteratively.

About a decade ago, after *The Four Steps* was published, I began teaching the Customer Development process as a full-semester course at U.C. Berkeley. A student in my first Berkeley class, Eric Ries, became the first practitioner and tireless evangelist of the process at IMVU, iterating and testing the process as I sat on his board. His insight coupled customer development to the emerging agile engineering practice, and together the two methodologies helped founders to rapidly iterate their products, guided by customer feedback.

A few years later, Alexander Osterwalder's business model canvas provided the Customer Development process with a much-needed front end to organize all of a startup's hypotheses into a simple framework that serves as a baseline and a scorecard for teams as they move through Customer Development.

These new ideas have coalesced into what has today become the Lean Startup movement. And hundreds of thousands of books later, the core ideas of *The Four Steps* have spread from startups to large corporations and the Lean Startup methodology has become the standard for commercializing scientific research in the U.S. It's taught in most major universities and in thousands of entrepreneurial programs around the world.

And it all started with this one book.

Who would've thought?

This third edition of The Four Steps to the Epiphany is substantively the same as the 2003 version. A few typos were corrected and unfinished sentences completed. The "update" to The Four Steps is The Startup Owner's Manual, published in 2012 with Bob Dorf. While The Four Steps remains the uber text, The Startup Owner's Manual builds on that work with a step-by-step process for building great companies using the business model canvas and the Customer Development process.

CHAPTER 1

The Path to Disaster:
The Product Development Model

... for the gate is wide and the road broad that leads to destruction, and
those who enter through it are many.
— Matthew 7:13

EVERY TRAVELER STARTING A JOURNEY MUST decide what road to take. The road well traveled seems like the obvious choice. The same is true in the search for startup success: Following a path of common wisdom—one taken by scores of startups before—seems like the right way. Yet for most startups, the wide road often leads straight to disaster. This chapter looks at how and why this is so.

Let me begin with a cautionary tale. In the heyday of the dot-com bubble, Webvan stood out as one of the most electrifying new startups, with an idea that would potentially touch every household. Raising one of the largest financial war chests ever seen (over $800 million in private and public capital), the company aimed to revolutionize the $450 billion retail grocery business with online ordering and same-day delivery of household groceries. Webvan believed this was a "killer application" for the Internet. No longer would people have to leave their homes to shop. They could just point, click, and order. Webvan's CEO told Forbes magazine Webvan would "set the rules for the largest consumer sector in the economy."

Besides amassing megabucks, the Webvan entrepreneurs seemed to do everything right.

The company raced to build vast automated warehouses and purchased fleets of delivery trucks, while building an easy-to-use website. Webvan hired a seasoned CEO from the consulting industry, backed by experienced venture capital investors. What's more, most of their initial customers actually liked their service. Barely 24 months after the initial public offering, however Webvan was bankrupt and out of business. What happened?

It wasn't a failure of execution. Webvan did everything its board and investors asked. In particular, the company religiously followed the traditional Product Development model commonly used by startups, including "get big fast," the mantra of the time. Its failure to ask, "Where Are the Customers?" however, illuminates how a tried-and-true model can lead even the best-funded, best-managed startup to disaster.

The Product Development Model

Every company bringing a new product to market uses some form of Product Development Model (Figure 1.1). Emerging early in the 20th century, this product-centric model described a process that evolved in manufacturing industries. It was adopted by the consumer packaged goods industry in the 1950s and spread to the technology business in the last quarter of the 20th century. It has become an integral part of startup culture.

At first glance, the diagram appears helpful and benign, illustrating the process of getting a new product into the hands of waiting customers. Ironically, the model is a good fit when launching a new product into an established, well-defined market where the basis of competition is understood, and its customers are known.

The irony is that few startups fit these criteria. Few even know what their market is. Yet they persist in using the Product Development model not only to manage Product Development, but as a roadmap for finding customers and to time their sales launch and revenue plan. The model has become a catchall tool for every startup executive's schedule, plan, and budget. Investors use the Product Development model to set and plan funding. Everyone involved uses a roadmap designed for a very different location, yet they are surprised when they end up lost.

The Product Development Model (Figure 1.1)

To see what's wrong with using the Product Development model as a guide to building a startup, let's first look at how the model is currently used to launch a new product. We'll view the actions at each step in two ways: in general practice and in the specific example of Webvan, which managed to burn through $800 million in three years. Then we will dissect the model's toxic consequences for startups.

What's wrong with the old model in general, and how did Webvan compound those wrongs in their billion-dollar implosion? Let's look at the model stage-by-stage.

Concept and Seed Stage

In the Concept and Seed Stage, founders capture their passion and vision for the company and turn them into a set of key ideas, which quickly becomes a business plan, sometimes on the back of the proverbial napkin. The first thing captured and wrestled to paper is the company's vision.

Next, issues surrounding the product need to be defined: What is the product or service concept? Is it possible to build? Is further technical research needed to ensure the product can be built? What are the product features and benefits?

Third, who will the customers be and where will they be found? Statistical and market research data plus potential customer interviews determine whether the ideas have merit.

Step four probes how the product will ultimately reach the customer and the potential distribution channel. At this stage companies start thinking about who their competitors are and how they differ. They draw their first positioning chart and use it to explain the company and its benefits to venture capitalists.

The distribution discussion leads to some basic assumptions about pricing. Combined with product costs, an engineering budget, and schedules, this results in a spreadsheet that faintly resembles the first financial plan in the company's business plan. If the startup is to be backed by venture capitalists, the financial model has to be alluring as well as believable. If it's a new division inside a larger company, forecasts talk about return on investment. Creative writing, passion, and shoe leather combine in hopes of convincing an investor to fund the company or the new division.

Webvan did all of this extremely well. Founded in December 1996, with a compelling story, and a founder with a track record, Webvan raised $10 million from leading Silicon Valley venture capitalists in 1997. In the next two years, additional private rounds totaling an unbelievable $393 million would follow before the company's IPO (initial public offering).

Product Development

In stage two, Product Development, everyone stops talking and starts working. The respective departments go to their virtual corners as the company begins to specialize by functions.

Engineering designs the product, specifies the first release and hires a staff to build the product. It takes the simple box labeled "Product Development" and using a Waterfall development process makes detailed critical path method charts, with key milestones. With that information in hand, Engineering estimates delivery dates and development costs.

Meanwhile, Marketing refines the size of the market defined in the business plan (a market is a set of companies with common attributes), and begins to target the first customers. In a well-organized startup (one with a fondness for process) the marketing folk might even run a focus group or two on the market they think they are in and prepare a Marketing Requirements Document (MRD) for Engineering. Marketing starts to build a sales demo, writes sales materials (presentations, data sheets), and hires a PR agency. In this stage, or by alpha test, the company traditionally hires a VP of Sales.

In Webvan's case, Engineering moved along two fronts: building the automated warehouses and designing the website. The automated warehouses were a technological marvel, far beyond anything existing grocery chains had. Automated conveyors and carousels transported food items off warehouse shelves to workers who packed them for delivery. Webvan also designed its own inventory management, warehouse management, route management, and materials handling systems and software to manage the customer ordering and delivery flow processes. This software communicated with the Webvan website and issued instructions to the various mechanized areas of the distribution center to fulfill orders. Once a delivery was scheduled, a route-planning feature of the system determined the most efficient route to deliver goods to the customer's home.

At the same time, planning began for a marketing and promotion program designed to strengthen the Webvan brand name, get customers to try the service in the first target market, build customer loyalty, and maximize repeat usage and purchases. The plan was to build Webvan's brand name and customer loyalty through public relations programs, advertising campaigns, and promotional activities.

Alpha/Beta Test

In stage three, alpha/beta test, Engineering works with a small group of outside users to make sure the product works as specified and tests it for bugs. Marketing develops a complete marketing communications plan, provides Sales with a full complement of support material, and starts the public relations bandwagon rolling. The PR agency polishes the positioning and starts contacting the long lead-time press while Marketing starts the branding activities.

Sales signs up the first beta customers (who volunteer to pay for the privilege of testing a new product), begins to build the selected distribution channel, and staffs and scales the sales organization outside the headquarters. The venture investors start measuring progress by number of orders in place by first customer ship.

Hopefully, somewhere around this point the investors are happy with the company's product and its progress with customers, and the investors are thinking of bringing in more money. The CEO refines his or her fund-raising pitch, and hits the street and the phone searching for additional capital.

Webvan began to beta-test its grocery delivery service in May 1999 to approximately 1,100 people. At the same time, the marketing buzz started with a PR blitz as hundreds of articles appeared touting the newest entrant in the online grocery business. Private investors poured hundreds of millions of dollars into the company.

Product Launch and First Customer Ship

Product launch and first customer ship mark the final step in this model, and what the company has been driving for. With the product working (sort of), the company goes into "big bang" spending mode. Sales is heavily building and staffing a national sales organization; the sales channel has quotas and sales goals. Marketing is at its peak. The company has a large press event, and Marketing launches a series of programs to create end-user demand (trade shows, seminars, advertising, email, and so on). The board begins measuring the company's performance on sales execution against its business plan (which typically was written a year or more earlier, when the entrepreneur was looking for initial investments).

Building the sales channel and supporting the marketing can burn a lot of cash. Assuming no early liquidity (via an IPO or merger) for the company, more fund raising is required. The CEO looks at the product launch activities and the scale-up of the sales and marketing team, and yet again goes out, palm up, to the investor community. (In the dot-com bubble economy, investors used an IPO at product launch to take the money and run, before there was a track record of success or failure.)

If you've ever been involved in a startup, the operational model no doubt sounds familiar. It is a product- and process-centric model used by countless startups to take their first product to market.

Webvan launched its first regional Webstore in June 1999 (just one month after starting beta test) and filed for its public offering 60 days later. The company raised $400 million and had a market capitalization of $8.5 billion the day of its IPO—larger than the top three grocery chains combined.

What's Wrong With This Picture?

Given that the Product Development model is used by almost every organization launching a new product, asking what's wrong with it might seem as heretical as asking "What's wrong with breathing?" Nevertheless, for Webvan and thousands of other startups, it has failed miserably.

The first hint lies in its name. The Product Development model is not a marketing, sales hiring, customer acquisition, or even a financing model. Yet startup companies have traditionally used a Product Development model to manage and pace all these non-engineering activities. In fact, there are 10 major flaws to using the Product Development model in a startup.

1. Where Are the Customers?

To begin with, the Product Development model ignores the fundamental truth about startups and all new products. The greatest risk—and hence the greatest cause of failure—in startups is not in the development of the new product but in the development of customers and markets. Startups don't fail because they lack a product; they fail because they lack customers and a proven financial model. This alone should be a pretty good clue about what's wrong with using the Product Development model as the sole guide to what a startup needs to be doing. Look at the Product Development model and ask, "Where are the customers?"

2. The Focus on First Customer Ship Date

Using the Product Development model forces sales and marketing to focus on the first customer ship date. Most competent sales and marketing executives look at the first customer ship date, look at the calendar, and then work backwards figuring out how to do their job in time so the fireworks start the day the product is launched.

The flaw in this thinking is that "first customer ship" is only the date when Product Development thinks they are "finished" building the product. The first customer ship date does not mean the company understands its customers or how to market or sell to them. (Read the preceding sentence again. It's a big idea.) Yet in almost every startup, ready or not, the sales, marketing, and business development people are busy setting their departmental watches to the first customer ship date. Even worse, a startup's investors are managing their financial expectations by this date as well.

Investors say: "Why of course that's what you do. Getting the product to market is what sales and marketing people do in startups. That's how a startup makes money." This is deadly advice. Ignore it. Focusing only on first customer ship results in a "Fire, Ready, Aim" strategy. Obviously, your new division or company wants to get a product to market and sell it, but that cannot be done until you understand who you are selling your product to and why they will buy it. The Product Development model is so focused on building and shipping the product that makes the fundamental and fatal error of ignoring the process I call Customer Discovery.

Think about every startup you've been in or known about. Haven't the energy, drive, and focus been on finishing the product and getting it to market? Think about what happens after the first customer ship party is over, the champagne is flat, and the balloons are deflated. Sales now must find the quantity of customers the company claimed it could find when it first wrote its business plan. Sure, Sales may have found a couple of "beta" customers, but were they representative of a scalable mainstream market? (A mainstream market is where the majority of people in any market segment reside. They tend to be risk-averse, pragmatic purchasers.) Time after time, only after first customer ship, do startups discover their early customers don't scale into a mainstream market, the product doesn't solve a high-value problem, or the cost of distribution is too high. While that's bad enough, these startups are now burdened with an expensive, scaled-up sales organization getting increasingly frustrated trying to execute a losing sales strategy, and a marketing organization desperately trying to create demand without a true understanding of customers' needs. And as Marketing and Sales flail around in search of a sustainable market, the company is burning through its most precious asset—cash.

At Webvan, the dot-com mania may have intensified their inexorable drive to first customer ship, but its single-minded focus was typical of most startups. At first customer ship, Webvan had close to 400 employees. It hired over 500 more during the next six months. By May 1999 the company opened its first $40 million distribution center, built and scaled for a customer base it could only guess at, and had committed to 15 more distribution centers of the same size. Why? Because the Webvan business plan said that was the goal—regardless of whether the customer results agreed.

3. An Emphasis on Execution Instead of Learning and Discovery

In startups the emphasis is on "get it done, and get it done fast." So it's natural that heads of Sales and Marketing believe they are hired for what they know, not what they can learn. They assume their prior experience is relevant in this new venture. They assume they understand the customer problem and therefore the product that needs to be built and sold. Therefore they need to put that knowledge to work and execute the product development, sales and marketing processes and programs that have worked for them before.

This is usually a faulty assumption. Before we can build and sell a product, we have to answer some very basic questions: What are the problems our product solves? Do customers perceive these problems as important or "must-have"? If we're selling to businesses, who in a company has a problem our product could solve? If we are selling to consumers how do we reach them? How big is this problem? Who do we make the first sales call on? Who else has to approve the purchase? How many customers do we need to be profitable? What's the average order size?

Most entrepreneurs will tell you, "I know all the answers already. Why do I have to do it again?" It's human nature that what you think you know is not always what you know. A little humility goes far. Your past experience may not be relevant for your new company. If you already know the answers to the customer questions, the Customer Development process will go quickly and reaffirm your understanding.

A company needs to answer these questions before it can successfully ramp up sales. For startups in a new market, these are not merely execution activities; they are learning and discovery activities critical to the company's success or failure.

Why is this distinction important? Take another look at the Product Development model. Notice it has a nice linear flow from left to right. Product Development, whether it is intended for large companies or consumers, is a step-by-step, execution-oriented process. Each step happens in a logical progression that can be PERT charted (a project management technique for determining how much time a project takes to complete), with milestones and resources assigned to completing each step.

Yet anyone who has ever taken a new product out to a set of potential customers can tell you a good day in front of customers is two steps forward and one step back. In fact, the best way to represent what happens outside the building is with a series of recursive circles—recursive to represent the iterative nature of what actually happens in a learning and discovery environment. Information and data are gathered about customers and markets incrementally, one step at a time. Yet sometimes those steps take you in the wrong direction or down a blind alley. You find yourself calling on the wrong customers, not understanding why people will buy, not understanding what product features are important. The ability to learn from those missteps is what distinguishes a successful startup from those whose names are forgotten among the vanished.

Like all startups focused on executing to plan, Webvan hired a vice president of merchandising, a vice president of marketing and a vice president of product management—to head three groups oriented around executing a sales strategy, not learning and discovering customer needs. Sixty days after first customer ship these three groups employed over 50 people.

4. The Lack of Meaningful Sales, Marketing and Business Development Milestones

The one great thing you can say about Product Development using a Waterfall methodology is that it provides an unambiguous structure with clearly defined milestones. The meaning of requirements documents, functional specifications, implementation, alpha test, beta test, and first customer ship are obvious to most engineers. If the product fails to work, you stop and fix it. In stark contrast, sales and marketing activities before first customer ship are ad hoc, fuzzy, and absent measurable, concrete objectives. They lack any way to stop and fix what's broken (or even to know if it is broken, or how to stop at all).

What kind of objectives would a startup want or need? That's the key question.

Most sales executives and marketers tend to focus on execution activities because these are measurable. For example, in sales, revenue matters most. Sales uses revenue as its marker of progress in understanding customers. Some startup sales execs also believe hiring the core sales team is a key objective. Others focus on acquiring early "lighthouse" customers (prominent customers who will attract others). Marketers believe creating corporate presentations, data sheets, and collateral are objectives. Some think hiring a PR agency, starting the buzz and getting on the covers of magazines at launch are objectives.

In reality none of these is the true objective. Simply put, a startup should focus on reaching a deep understanding of customers and their problems, their pains, and the jobs they need done discovering a repeatable roadmap of how they buy, and building a financial model that results in profitability.

The appropriate milestones measuring a startup's progress answer these questions: How well do we understand what problems customers have? How much will they pay to solve those problems? Do our product features solve these problems? Do we understand our customers' business? Do we understand the hierarchy of customer needs? Have we found visionary customers, ones who will buy our product early? Is our product a must-have for these customers? Do we understand the sales roadmap well enough to consistently sell the product? Do we understand what we need to be profitable? Are the sales and business plans realistic, scalable, and achievable? What do we do if our model turns out to be wrong?

Webvan had no milestones saying "stop and evaluate the results" (2,000 orders per day versus 8,000 forecasted) of its product launch. Before any meaningful customer feedback was in hand, and only a month after the product started shipping, Webvan signed a $1 billion deal (yes, $1,000,000,000) with Bechtel. The company committed to the construction of up to 26 additional distribution centers over the next three years.

Webvan leapt right over learning and discovery in its rush to execution. There is a big difference between a process that emphasizes getting answers to the fundamental questions I've listed above and a process using the Product Development model to keep early sales and marketing activities in sync with first customer ship. To see what I mean, consider the Product Development model from the perspective of people in sales and marketing (Figure 1.2).

5. The Use of a Product Development Methodology to Measure Sales

Using the Product Development Waterfall diagram for Customer Development activities is like using a clock to tell the temperature. They both measure something, but not the thing you wanted.

Figure 1.2 shows what the Product Development model looks like from a sales perspective. A VP of Sales looks at the diagram and says, "Hmm, if beta test is on this date, I'd better get a small sales team in place before that date to acquire my first 'early customers.' And if first customer ship is on this date over here, then I need to hire and staff a sales organization by then." Why? "Well, because the revenue plan we promised the investors shows us generating customer revenue from the day of first customer ship."

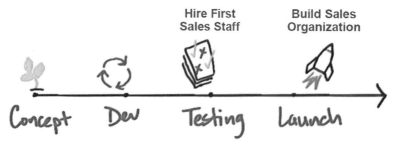

Hire First Sales Staff

Build Sales Organization

Concept   Dev   Testing   Launch

The View from the Sales Organization (Figure 1.2)

I hope this thinking already sounds inane to you. The plan calls for selling in volume the day Engineering is finished building the product. What plan says that? Why, the business plan, which uses the Product Development model to set milestones. The consequence of selling isn't predicated on discovering the right market or whether any customers will shell out cash for your product. Instead the Product Development model times your readiness to sell. This "ready or not, here we come" attitude means you won't know if the sales strategy and plan actually work until after first customer ship. What's the consequence if your stab at a sales strategy is wrong? You've built a sales organization burning cash, cash that needs to be redirected in a hurry. No wonder the half-life of a startup VP of Sales is about nine months post-first customer ship. "Build it and they will come," is not a strategy; it's a prayer.

Webvan had this problem in spades. After first customer ship, Webvan had a nasty surprise waiting for it. Customers refused to behave the way the Webvan business plan said they would. Six months after Webvan's June 1999 launch, the average daily volume of orders was 2,500. Sounds pretty good? Not bad for a startup? It was. Unfortunately, the Webvan business plan had forecast 8,000 orders per day, a number necessary for the company to achieve profitability. This meant the distribution center (designed to process product volumes equivalent to approximately 18 supermarkets) was operating at less than 30% of capacity. Oops.

6. The Use of a Product Development Methodology to Measure Marketing

The head of Marketing looks at the same Product Development Waterfall diagram and sees something quite different (see Figure 1.3). For Marketing, first customer ship means feeding the sales pipeline with a constant stream of customer prospects. To create this demand, marketing activities start early in the Product Development process. While the product is being engineered, Marketing starts creating corporate presentations and sales materials. Implicit in these materials is the "positioning" of the company and product. Looking ahead to the product launch, the marketing group hires a public relations agency to refine the positioning and begin generating early "buzz" about the company. The PR agency helps the company understand and influence key industry analysts, luminaries, and references. All this leads up to a flurry of press events and interviews geared to the product launch date. (During the Internet bubble, one more function of the marketing department was to "buy" customer loyalty with enormous advertising and promotion spending to create a brand.)

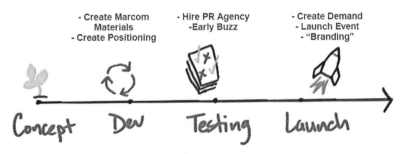

The View from the Marketing Organization (Figure 1.3)

At first glance this process may look quite reasonable, except for one small item: All this marketing activity occurs before customers start buying—that is, before Sales has had a chance to test the positioning, marketing strategy, or demand-creation activities in front of real customers. In fact, all the marketing plans are made in a virtual vacuum of real customer feedback and information. Of course, smart marketers have some early interaction with customers before the product ships, but if they do, it's on their own initiative, not as part of a well-defined process. Most first-time marketers spend a large part of their time behind their desks. This is somewhat amazing, since in a startup no facts exist inside the building, only opinions. Yet even if we get the marketing people out from behind their desks and into the field, the deck remains stacked against their success. Look at the Product Development model. When does Marketing find out whether the positioning, buzz, and demand creation activities actually work? After first customer ship. The inexorable march to this date has no iterative loop that says, "If our assumptions are wrong, maybe we need to try something different."

This "marketing death march" happened at Webvan. In its first six months of business, Webvan acquired an impressive 47,000 new customers. However, in those six months 71% of the 2,000 orders coming in per day were from repeat customers. This meant Webvan needed more new customers, and it needed to reduce the number of customers who ordered once and never used the service again.

These facts contradicted the marketing assumptions in the original business plan. As happens in most startups, those assumptions were wrong. Yet Webvan had scaled its spending (particularly on building and operating large distribution centers) on these unverified guesses.

7. Premature Scaling

Having Sales and Marketing believe that by first customer ship, come hell or high water, they need fully staffed organizations leads to another disaster: premature scaling.

Startup executives have three documents to guide their hiring and staffing: a business plan, a Product Development model and a revenue forecast. All are execution documents – they document spending and hiring as if success is assured. As mentioned earlier there are no milestones saying, "Stop or slow down hiring until you understand customers." Even the most experienced executives succumb to the inexorable pressure to hire and staff to "plan" regardless of early customer feedback.

In Webvan's case premature scaling was an integral part of the company culture and the prevailing venture capital "get big fast" mantra. Webvan spent $18 million to develop proprietary software and $40 million to set up its first automated warehouse before it had shipped a single item. Premature scaling had dire consequences since Webvan's spending was on a scale that ensures it will be taught in business school case studies for years to come.

As customer behavior continued to differ from the predictions in Webvan's business plan, the company slowly realized it had overbuilt and over-designed. The business model made sense only at the high volumes predicted on the spreadsheet. The average daily volume of orders was significantly below the capacity the company needed to achieve profitability. To have any hope of achieving favorable gross margins, Webvan had to find a way to substantially increase its volume, number of customers, number of orders placed by its customers, and average order size.

8. Death Spiral: The Cost of Getting Product Launch Wrong

Premature scaling is the immediate cause of the Death Spiral. Premature scaling causes the burn rate to accelerate. Sales, salaries, facilities, infrastructure costs, recruiting fees, and travel expenses start cutting into the company's cash flow. The pressure for revenue grows exponentially. Meanwhile the marketing department is spending large sums on creating demand for the sales organization. It is also spending "credibility capital" on positioning and explaining the company to the press, analysts, and customers.

By the time of first customer ship, if the company does not understand its market and customers, the consequences unfold in a startup ritual, almost like a Japanese Noh play. What happens when you fully staff sales and marketing and you haven't nailed who your customers are and why they should buy your product? Sales starts missing its numbers. The board gets concerned. The VP of Sales comes to a board meeting, still optimistic, and provides a set of reasonable explanations. The board raises a collective eyebrow. The VP goes back to the field and exhorts the troops to work harder.

Meanwhile, the salespeople start inventing and testing their own alternatives— different departments to call on, different versions of the presentations. Instead of following a methodology of learning and discovering, the sales team has turned into a disorganized and disgruntled mob burning lots of cash. Back in the home office, the product presentation slides are changing weekly (sometimes daily) as Marketing tries to "make up a better story" and sends out the latest pitch to a confused sales organization. Morale in the field and in Marketing starts to plummet. Salespeople begin to believe, "This product cannot be sold; no one wants to buy it."

By the next board meeting, the sales numbers still aren't meeting plan. The VP of Sales looks down at his shoes and shuffles his feet. Now the board raises both eyebrows and looks quizzically at the CEO. The VP of Sales, forehead bathed in sweat, leaves the board meeting and has a few heated motivational sessions with the sales team. By the next board meeting, if the sales numbers are still poor, the writing is on the wall. Not only haven't the sales numbers been made, but now the CEO is sweating the company's continued cash-burn rate. Why? Because the company has based its headcount and expenditures on the expectation Sales will bring in revenue according to plan. The rest of the organization started to burn more cash, expecting Sales to make its numbers. Now the company is in crisis mode. Here two things typically happen. First, the VP of Sales is toast. At the final board meeting no one wants to stand next to him. People move their chairs to the other side of the room. Whether it takes three board meetings or a year is irrelevant; the VP of Sales in a startup who does not make the numbers is called an ex-VP of Sales (unless he was a founder, and then he gets to sit in a penalty box with a nebulous VP title).

Next, a new VP of Sales is hired. She quickly concludes the company did not understand its customers and how to sell to them. She decides the company's positioning and marketing strategy were incorrect. Now the VP of Marketing starts sweating. Since the new VP of Sales was brought on board to "fix" sales, the marketing department has to react and interact with someone who believes whatever was created earlier in the company was wrong. The new VP of Sales reviews the original strategy and tactics and comes up with a new sales plan. She gets a few months' honeymoon from the CEO and the board. Meanwhile, the original VP of Marketing tries to come up with a new positioning strategy to support the new Sales VP. Typically this results in conflict, if not outright internecine warfare. If the sales aren't fixed in a short time, the next executive to be looking for a job is not the new VP of Sales (she hasn't been around long enough to get fired), it's the VP of Marketing—the rationale being, "We changed the VP of Sales, so that can't be the problem. It must be Marketing's fault."

Sometimes all it takes is one or two iterations of finding the right sales roadmap and marketing positioning to get a startup on the right track of finding exuberant customers. Unfortunately, more often than not, this marks the beginning of an executive death spiral. If changing the sales and marketing execs doesn't put the company on the right sales trajectory, the investors start talking the "we need the right CEO for this phase" talk. This means the CEO is walking around with an unspoken corporate death sentence. Moreover, since the first CEO was likely to have been one of the founders, the trauma of CEO removal begins. Typically, founding CEOs hold on to the doorframe of their offices as the investors try to pry their fingers off the company. It's painful to watch and occurs in more than half of the startups with first-time CEOs.

In flush economic times the company may get two or three iterations around a failed launch and bad sales numbers. In tougher times investors are tighter with their wallets and make the "tossing good money after bad" calculations with a frugal eye. A startup might simply not get a next round of funding and have to shut down.

In Webvan's case, the Death Spiral was public and messy, since none of this was occurring in the intimate enclosure of a private company. The consequence of going public was the sea of red ink was printed quarterly for all to see. Rather than realize the model was unrealistic and scale back, the company continued to invest heavily in marketing and promotion (to get more customers and keep the ones they had) and distribution facilities (building new ones in new parts of the country to reach more customers). By the end of 2000 Webvan had accumulated a deficit of $612.7 million and was hemorrhaging cash. Seven months later, it was bankrupt.

9. Not All Startups Are Alike

A fundamental truth about startups ignored in the Product Development model is they are not all alike. One of the radical insights guiding this book is that startups fall into one of four basic categories:

- Bringing a new product into an existing market
- Bringing a new product into a new market
- Bringing a new product into an existing market and trying to resegment that market as a low-cost entrant
- Bringing a new product into an existing market and trying to resegment that market as a niche entrant

These differences will be developed in detail in subsequent chapters. What's important to know now is the traditional Product Development model at times succeeds in getting a product out the door into a known market with known customers (first category). Executing past practices in this Market Type may work if the market is similar to that of past experiences. However, since most startups are not going after known markets (falling into the second and third categories), they don't have a clue where their customers are.

Webvan fell into the fourth category—bringing a new product (online grocery ordering and same-day delivery) into an existing market (the grocery business), and trying to create a niche of that market. One could even argue that Webvan's idea was so radical the company fell into the second category of startups—bringing a new product into a completely new market. In either case, Webvan's ability to predict customer acceptance and widespread usage was not based on facts, just untested business plan hypotheses. (Modeling customer adoption rates using traditional quantitative models like Bass Curve are impossible at first customer ship for category 2 and 3 companies. There aren't sufficient initial sales data to make valid sales predictions.)

Here's the point: Since the four types of startups have very different rates of customer adoption and acceptance, their sales and marketing strategies differ dramatically. Even more serious, each Market Type has radically different cash needs. A company creating a new market might be unprofitable for five or more years, while one in an existing market might generate cash in 12-18 months. As a result, the Product Development model is not only useless, it is dangerous. It tells the finance, marketing and sales teams nothing about how to uniquely describe and sell for each type of startup, or how to predict the resources needed for success.

10. Unrealistic Expectations

The Product Development model leads to fundamental and often fatal errors in the first year or two of a startup's life. We can sum up these errors in terms of three unrealistic expectations:

- The Product Development model can be relied upon to guide activities that have nothing to do with Product Development—namely, finding customers, a market, and a viable business model.
- Customer Development will move on the same schedule as Product Development.

- All types of startups and all new products will achieve acceptance and deployment at the same rate, namely starting at First Customer Ship.

In addition to these three errors, there is another consideration: Startups face enormous pressure from their investors to become profitable. Sometimes, to get funded, these new ventures make unrealistic financial assumptions—about market size, growth or by simply ignoring the consequences of the Market Type they have chosen. These optimistic expectations become the plan of record, forcing execution toward unrealistic and unachievable goals.

Webvan made all these mistakes, visibly and publicly. Yet most observers wrote off its failure as just one of the many "dot-com busts," attributing the venture's demise to something related to the Internet. The reality is more profound and germane. Webvan's failure and the entire dot-com collapse resulted from falling victim to the three expectations I've just described; "build it and the customers will come" (regardless of the number of dollars raised) is not a successful strategy.

So What's The Alternative?

If the Product Development model isn't an appropriate roadmap for startups, what is? To some, the phrase "thoughtful startup sales and marketing process" is an oxymoron. However, there are entrepreneurs who have been searching for a template for success with customers and markets.

Since the early 1990s, the closest thing to a Holy Grail for sales and marketing activities in startups has been the Technology Life Cycle Adoption Curve and the notion of The Chasm.

The Technology Life Cycle Adoption Curve

The Technology Life Cycle Adoption Curve (see Figure 1.4) was developed by Everett Rogers and popularized and refined with Geoff Moore's notion of the "chasm." It introduces entrepreneurs to five thought-provoking ideas:

- Technology is adopted in phases by distinct groups: technology enthusiasts, visionaries, pragmatists, conservatives, and skeptics.

- The first two groups—technology enthusiasts and visionaries—are the "early market." The next two groups—pragmatists and conservatives—are the "mainstream market."
- The shape of the overall market for any product approximates a bell curve. The early market starts small and grows exponentially into the mainstream market.
- There is a "chasm" between each of the different groups, with the largest chasm between the early and mainstream markets. These chasms are caused by the different product needs and buying habits of each group.
- The biggest problem in crossing the chasm is that few of the hard-won early marketing and selling lessons and successes can be leveraged into the mainstream market, as mainstream customers do not find early adopters to be credible customer references. Therefore, completely new marketing and sales strategies are necessary to win over this next, much larger group of customers.

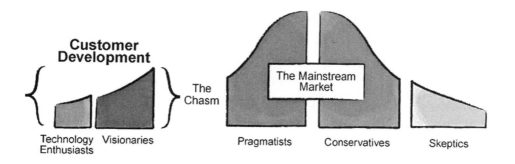

The Technology Life Cycle Adoption Curve *(Figure 1.4)*

Let's briefly consider why this notion doesn't provide a good roadmap for early-stage startups. With this last piece in place, we'll be ready to consider the alternative path this book describes, and I assert all successful startups follow. An entrepreneur on day one of a startup looks longingly at the graceful bell curve depicted in Figure 1.4, and dreams of marching her company to the pinnacle, determined to avoid those fearsome chasms. OK, this all sounds good. Now what? Take a good long look at the Technology Life Cycle Adoption Curve. Is it informative? Interesting? Does it lead you to think profound and wonderful thoughts about strategy? Well, forget it. If you are just starting your company this is the last time you are going to see this curve, at least for the next year. The problems you face occur much earlier than any chasm. In fact, you should be so lucky to be dealing with chasm-crossing activities, for they are a sign of success.

The Technology Life Cycle Adoption Curve provides true insight, because there are different types of customers in a company/product life cycle. However, this seductive curve leads early-stage entrepreneurs to four bad conclusions:

First, the curve naturally leads entrepreneurs to entertain dreams of glory in the mainstream market. In the early stages of building a company, those dreams are best forgotten. Not forever, but for now. Why? The sad reality is if you don't get the first part of early Customer Development right, you won't be in the mainstream. You'll be out of business.

Second, the curve invites us to think of technology enthusiasts as one part of the customer adoption curve. On the curve they look like just an early set of customers, but in reality they are not. Technology enthusiasts exist as one of those sales puzzles on the path to finding "real" paying early customers and a repeatable sales process. You need to deal with them and understand their influence in the sales roadmap, but they very rarely buy anything.

Third, the notion that a startup's customer base will grow in a smooth, continuous curve invites the tempting and dangerous idea that customer adoption is simply a sales execution problem. Even when the notion of a chasm is added, along with the observation that early-market customers and mainstream customers are different, only in entrepreneurs' dreams and business school cases does this take the form of an adoption curve. As we will see, the actual transition from one type of customer to another is at best a step function (and dependent on Market Type).

Fourth, the Technology Life Cycle Adoption Curve, along with the books written about it, emphasize "execution and adoption." That's all fine and good, but as my grandmother used to say, "You should be so lucky to have that problem." In the early stages of a startup, focusing on "execution" will put you out of business. Instead, you need a "learning and discovery" process so you can get the company to the point where you know what to execute.

So instead of dreaming up ways to cross the chasm, the first step for a startup is to focus on learning and discovery processes, from starting the company to scaling the business. Through trial and error, hiring and firing, startups that succeed have invented a parallel process to Product Development that is customer- and market-centric. I call it "Customer Development."

Customer Development: Common Sense Meets the Product Development Model

It's interesting to imagine what would happen if a startup told its venture capital backers it had hired the world's best engineering team, but it wasn't going to use any process or methodology to get the product out the door. Can you imagine saying, "Nah, we don't need no stinking Product Development methodology. We'll just go by the seat of our pants?" Only in your dreams. Startups use a Product Development methodology to measure the progress of their development team, control their cash-burn rate and time their product launch. Yet we don't think twice when we hire the best marketing, sales, and business development talent, toss them into a startup and say, "Go figure out who wants to buy this, and quickly sell a whole bunch. Let us know when you are done, but keep it vague and wave your hands a lot when we ask you how much progress you are making." Seems silly doesn't it? Yet that's the state of the startup today. There is no recognized process with measurable milestones for finding customers, developing the market, and validating the business model.

The Customer Development model of a startup starts with a simple premise: Learning and discovering who a company's initial customers will be, and what markets they are in, requires a separate and distinct process from Product Development. The sum of these activities is Customer Development. Note I am making a concerted effort not to call Customer Development a "sales process" or a "marketing process." The reason will become clearer as we talk about how to organize the team for the Customer Development process in a later chapter. However, early on, we are neither selling nor marketing. Before any of the traditional functions of selling and marketing can happen, the company must prove a market could exist, verify someone would pay real dollars for the solutions the company envisions, and then go out and create the market. These testing, learning, and discovery activities are at the heart of what makes a startup unique, and they are what makes Customer Development so different from the Product Development process.

The Customer Development model is intended to be everything the Product Development model is not. Where Product Development is focused on first customer ship, the Customer Development model moves learning about customers and their problems as early in the development process as possible. In addition, the model is built on the idea that every startup has a set of definable milestones no amount of funding can accelerate. More money is helpful later, but not now. The Internet Bubble was the biggest science experiment in this area. You cannot create a market or customer demand where there isn't any customer interest. The good news is these customer and market milestones can be defined and measured. The bad news is achieving these milestones is an art. It's an art embodied in the passion and vision of the individuals who work to make their vision a reality. That's what makes startups so exciting.

The ironic postscript to the Webvan story is that another company, Tesco, raced past pioneers such as Webvan to become the largest online grocer in the world. The people at Tesco did not raise a huge financial war chest to launch their service. They learned and discovered what customers wanted, and found a financial model that worked. They started their online grocery service by using their retail stores in the UK as the launching pad. By 2002 they had created a profitable online business handling 85,000 orders per week and had racked up more than $559 million in sales. Tesco could set up its online grocery business for a fraction of the investment of Webvan because it was able to build off its existing infrastructure of over 929 stores. In June 2001 online grocery shopping returned to the United States when Tesco moved into the market, purchasing a 35% investment in Safeway's online grocery service.

Explicitly or implicitly, Tesco understood the process embodied by the Customer Development model. The next chapter describes this model in detail.

His fledgling business was starting to take wing; now he wanted to raise serious venture capital funding to grow the company.

"No problem," I said. Pulling out my Rolodex and dialing for dollars, I got Rob in to see some of the best and brightest venture capitalists on Sand Hill Road in Silicon Valley. In each case, Rob went through his presentation and pointed out there was a $17.5 billion business-to-business market for high-quality, well-designed furnishings. He demonstrated that the current furniture distribution system was archaic, fragmented, and ripe for restructuring, as furniture manufacturers faced a convoluted system of reps, dealers, and regional showrooms preventing direct access to their customers. Consumers typically waited four months for product and incurred unnecessary markups of up to 40%. Listening to Rob speak, it was obvious he had identified a real problem, had developed a product that solved that problem, and had customers verifying he had the right solution by buying from him.

The presentation was so compelling that it was a challenge to identify any other industry where customers were so poorly served. Yet the reaction from the venture capital firms was uniformly negative. "What, no website? No e-commerce transactions? Where are the branding activities? We want to fund Web-based startups. Perhaps we'd be interested if you could turn your catalog furniture business into an e-commerce site." Rob kept patiently explaining his business was oriented to what his customers told him they wanted. Design professionals wanted to leaf through a catalog at their leisure in bed. They wanted to show a catalog to their customers. While he wasn't going to ignore the Web, it would be the next step, not the first, in building the business.

"Rob," the VCs replied sagely, "Furniture.com is one of the hottest dot-coms out there. Together they've raised over $100 million from first-tier VCs. They and other hot startups like them are selling furniture over the Web. Come back when you rethink your strategy."

I couldn't believe it: Rob had a terrific solution to sell and a proven business model, and no one would fund him. The tenacious entrepreneur that he was, he stubbornly stuck to his guns. Rob believed the dot.com furniture industry was based on a false premise that the business opportunity was simply online purchasing of home furnishings. He believed the underlying opportunity was to offer to a select audience high-quality products that were differentiated from those of other suppliers, and to get those products to customers quickly. A select audience versus a wide audience, and high-quality furniture versus commodity furniture, were the crucial differences between success and massive failure.

Ultimately, Rob was able to raise money from friends and family and much later got a

CHAPTER 2

The Path to Epiphany:
The Customer Development Model

How narrow the gate and constricted the road that leads to life. And
those who find it are few.
— Matthew 7:14

THE FURNITURE BUSINESS DOES NOT STRIKE many people as ripe for innovation. Yet during the halcyon days of dot-com companies (when venture capitalists could not shovel money out the door fast enough), the online furnishing market spawned a series of high-profile companies such as Furniture.com and Living.com. Operating on the James Dean School of Management (living fast and dying young), companies like these quickly garnered millions of dollars of investors' capital and just as swiftly flamed out. Meanwhile, a very different startup by the name of Design Within Reach began building its business a brick at a time. What happened, and why, is instructive.

At a time when the furniture dot-coms were still rolling in investor money, the founder of Design Within Reach, Rob Forbes, approached me to help the company get funding. Rob's goal was to build a catalog business providing easy access to well-designed furniture frequently found only in designer showrooms. In his 20 years of working as a professional office designer, he realized one of the big problems in the furniture industry for design professionals and businesses such as hotels and restaurants was that high-quality designer furniture took four months to ship. Customers repeatedly told Rob, "I wish I could buy great-looking furniture without having to wait months to get it." On a shoestring, Rob put together a print catalog of furniture (over half the items were exclusive to his company) that he carried in stock and ready to ship. Rob spent his time listening to customers and furniture designers. He kept tuning his catalog and inventory to meet designers' needs, and he scoured the world for unique furniture.

small infusion of venture capital. At its peak, Design Within Reach was a $180 million public company. It had both retail stores and an e-commerce website. Its brand was well-known and recognized in the design community. Furniture.com? It's been relegated to the dustbin of forgotten failures.

Why did Design Within Reach succeed, when extremely well-funded startups like Furniture.com fail? What did Rob Forbes know or do that made the company a winner? Can others emulate his success?

The Four Steps To The Epiphany

Most startups lack a process for discovering their markets, locating their first customers, validating their assumptions, and growing their business. A few successful ones like Design Within Reach do all these things. They succeed by inventing a Customer Development model.

The Customer Development model, depicted in Figure 2.1, is designed to solve the 10 problems of the Product Development model enumerated in Chapter 1. Rigor and flexibility are its strengths. The model separates out all the customer-related activities in the early stage of a company into their own processes, designed as four easy-to-understand steps: Customer Discovery, Customer Validation, Customer Creation, and Company Building. These steps mesh seamlessly and support a startup's ongoing Product Development activities. Each results in specific deliverables to be described in subsequent chapters.

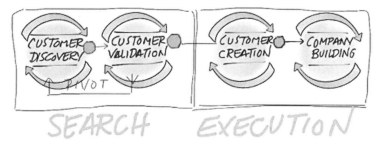

The Customer Development Model (Figure 2.1)

The Customer Development model is not a replacement for the Product Development model, but a companion to it. Broadly speaking, Customer Discovery focuses on testing whether a company's business model is correct, specifically focused on whether the product solves customer problems and needs (this match of product features and customers is called Product/Market fit.) Customer Validation develops a sales model that can be replicated, Customer Creation on creating and driving end-user demand, and Company Building on transitioning the organization from one designed for learning and discovery to a well-oiled machine engineered for execution. As I discuss later in this chapter, integral to this model is the notion that Market Type choices affect how the company will deploy its sales, marketing and financial resources.

Notice a major difference between this model and the traditional Product Development model is that each step is drawn as a circular track with recursive arrows. The circles and arrows highlight the iterative nature of each step. That's a polite way of saying, "Unlike Product Development, finding the right customers and market is unpredictable, and we will screw it up several times before we get it right." Experience with scores of startups shows that only in business school case studies does progress with customers happen in a nice linear fashion. The nature of finding a market and customers guarantees you will get it wrong several times. Therefore, unlike the Product Development model, the Customer Development model assumes it will take several iterations of each of the four steps. It's worth pondering this point for a moment, because this philosophy of "It's OK to screw it up if you plan to learn from it" is the heart of the methodology presented in this book.

In a Product Development diagram, going backwards is considered a failure. No wonder most startup businesspeople are embarrassed when they are out in the field learning, failing, and learning some more. The diagram they've used to date says, "Go left to right and you're a success. Go right to left, and you'll get fired." Consequently, startup sales and marketing efforts tend to move forward even when it's patently obvious they haven't nailed the market. (Imagine trying that philosophy in Product Development for pacemakers or missiles.)

In contrast, the Customer Development diagram says going backwards is a natural and valuable part of learning and discovery. In this new methodology, you keep cycling through each step until you achieve "escape velocity" and generate enough success to carry you out and into the next step.

Notice the circle labeled Customer Validation in Figure 2.1 has an additional iterative loop, or pivot, going back to Customer Discovery. As you'll see later, Customer Validation is a key checkpoint in understanding whether you have a product customers want to buy and a roadmap of how to sell it. If you can't find enough paying customers in the

Customer Validation step, the model returns you to Customer Discovery to rediscover what customers want and will pay for.

An interesting consequence of this process is that it keeps a startup at a low cash-burn rate until the company has validated its business model by finding paying customers. In the first two steps of Customer Development, even an infinite amount of cash is useless, because it can only obscure whether you have found a market. (Having raised lots of money tempts you to give products away, steeply discount to buy early business, etc., all while saying, "We'll make it up later." It rarely happens that way.) Since the Customer Development model assumes most startups cycle through these first two steps at least twice, it allows a well-managed company to carefully estimate and frugally husband its cash. The company doesn't build its non-Product Development teams (sales, marketing, business development) until it has proof in hand (a tested sales roadmap and valid purchase orders) that it has a business worth building. Once proof is obtained, the company can go through the last two steps of Customer Creation and Company Building to capitalize on the opportunity it has found and validated. The Customer Development process represents the best practices of winning startups. Describe this model to entrepreneurs who have taken their companies all the way to a public offering and beyond, and you'll get heads nodding in recognition. It's just until now, no one has ever explicitly mapped their journey to success. Even more surprising, while the Customer Development model with its iterative loops/pivots may sound like a new idea for entrepreneurs, it shares many features with a U.S. war-fighting strategy known as the "OODA Loop" articulated by John Boyd[1] and adopted by the U.S. armed forces in the second Gulf War. (You'll hear more about the OODA Loop later.)

The next four chapters provide a close-up look at each of the four steps in the model. The following overview will get you oriented to the process.

Step 1: Customer Discovery

The goal of Customer Discovery is just what the name implies: finding out who the customers for your product are and whether the problem you believe you are solving is important to them. More formally, this step involves discovering whether the problem, product and customer hypotheses in your business plan are correct. To do this, you need to leave guesswork behind and get "outside the building" in order to learn what the high-value customer problems are, what about your product solves these problems, and who specifically are your customer and user (for example, Who

[1] P Air War College, John R. Boyd, "Patterns of Conflict" and "A Discourse on Winning and Losing"

has the power to make or influence the buying decision and who will use the product on a daily basis?). What you learn will also help shape how you will describe your unique differences to potential customers. An important insight is that the goal of Customer Development is not to collect feature lists from prospective customers, nor is it to run lots of focus groups. In a startup, the founders and Product Development team define the first product. The job of the Customer Development team is to see whether there are customers and a market for that vision. (Read this last sentence again. It's not intuitively obvious, but the initial product specification comes from the founders' vision, not the sum of a set of focus groups.)

The basic premise of Furniture.com and Living.com was a good one. Furniture shopping is time-consuming, and the selection at many stores can be overwhelming. On top of that, the wait for purchased items can seem interminable. While these online retailers had Product Development milestones, they lacked formal Customer Development milestones. At Furniture.com the focus was on getting to market first and fast. Furniture.com spent $7 million building its website, e-commerce and supply chain systems before the company knew what customer demand would be. Once the website was up and the supply chain was in place, it began shipping. Even when it found shipping and marketing costs were higher than planned, and brand-name manufacturers did not want to alienate their traditional retail outlets, the company pressed forward with its existing business plan.

In contrast, at Design Within Reach Rob Forbes was the consummate proponent of a customer-centric view. Rob was talking to customers and suppliers continually. He didn't spend time in his office pontificating about a vision for his business. Nor did he go out and start telling customers what products he was going to deliver (the natural instinct of any entrepreneur at this stage). Instead, he was out in the field listening, discovering how his customers worked and what their key problems were. Rob believed each new version of the Design Within Reach furniture catalog was a way for his company to learn from customers. As each subsequent catalog was developed, feedback from customers was combined with the sales results of the last catalog and the appropriate changes were made. Entire staff meetings were devoted to "lessons learned" and "what didn't work." Consequently, as each new catalog hit the street the size of the average customer order and the number of new customers increased.

Step 2: Customer Validation

Customer Validation is where the rubber meets the road. The goal of this step is to build a repeatable sales roadmap for the sales and marketing teams that will follow later. The sales roadmap is the playbook of the proven and repeatable sales process that has been field-tested by successfully selling the product to early customers. Customer Validation proves you have found a set of customers and a market that react positively to the product. A customer purchase in this step validates lots of polite words from potential customers about your product.

In essence, Customer Discovery and Customer Validation corroborate your business model. Completing these first two steps verifies your market, locates your customers, tests the perceived value of your product, identifies the economic buyer, establishes your pricing and channel strategy, and checks out your sales cycle and process. If, and only if, you find a group of repeatable customers with a repeatable sales process, and then find those customers yield a profitable business model, do you move to the next step (scaling up and crossing the Chasm).

Design Within Reach started with a hypothesis that its customers fit a narrow profile of design professionals. It treated this idea like the educated guess it was, and tested the premise by analyzing the sales results of each catalog. It kept refining its assumptions until it found a repeatable and scalable sales and customer model.

This is where the dot.com furniture vendors should have stopped and regrouped. When customers did not respond as their business models predicted, further execution on the same failed plan guaranteed disaster.

Step 3: Customer Creation

Customer Creation builds on the success of the company's initial sales. Its goal is to create end-user demand and drive that demand into the company's sales channel. This step is placed after Customer Validation to move heavy marketing spending after the point where a startup acquires its first customers, thus allowing the company to control its cash-burn rate and protect its most precious asset.

The process of Customer Creation varies with the type of startup. As I noted in Chapter 1, startups are not all alike. Some startups enter existing markets well-defined by their competitors, some create new markets where no product or company exists, and some attempt a hybrid of the first two, resegmenting an existing market either as a low-cost entrant or by creating a niche. Each of these Market Type strategies requires a distinctive set of Customer Creation activities.

In Furniture.com's prospectus, the first bullet under growth strategy was "Establish a powerful brand." Furniture.com launched a $20 million advertising campaign that included television, radio and online ads. It spent $34 million on marketing and advertising, even though revenue was just $10.9 million. (Another online furniture startup, Living.com, agreed to pay electronic-commerce giant Amazon.com $145 million over four years to be featured on Amazon's home page.) Brand building and heavy advertising make lots of sense in existing markets when customers understand your product or service. However, in a new market this type of "onslaught" product launch is like throwing money down the toilet. Customers have no clue what you are talking about, and you have no idea if they will behave as you assume.

Step 4: Company Building

Company Building is where the company transitions from its informal, learning and discovery-oriented Customer Development team into formal departments with VPs of Sales, Marketing and Business Development. These executives now focus on building mission-oriented departments exploiting the company's early market success.

In contrast to this incremental process, premature scaling is the bane of startups. By the time Furniture.com had reached $10 million in sales, it had 209 employees and a burn rate that would prove to be catastrophic if any of its business plan assumptions were incorrect. The approach seemed to be to "spend as much as possible on customer acquisition before the music stops." Delivering heavy furniture from multiple manufacturers resulted in unhappy customers as items got damaged, lost, or delayed. Flush with investors' cash, the company responded the way dot-coms tend to respond to problems: by spending money. It reordered, and duplicates began piling up in warehouses. The company burned through investor dollars like cheap kindling. Furniture.com went from filing for a public offering in January to pulling its IPO in June 2000 and talking with bankruptcy lawyers. The company was eventually able to raise $27 million in venture funding, but at a lower valuation than the last time it raised money. In a bid for survival, Furniture.com furiously slashed costs. The company, which had been offering free shipping for delivery and returns, began charging a $95 delivery charge. Then it laid off 41% of its staff. But it never answered the key question: Is there a way to sell commodity furniture over the Web and ship it cost-effectively when you don't have a nationwide network of stores?

At Design Within Reach, Rob Forbes ran the company on a shoestring. The burn rate was kept low, first as a necessity as he scraped together financing, and then by plan as his team was finding a sales roadmap that could scale. Rob was finding a way to sell furniture without a network of stores - it was called a catalog.

The Four Types Of Startup Markets

Since time immemorial the postmortem of a failed company has typically included, "I don't understand what happened. We did everything that worked in our last startup." The failure isn't due to lack of energy, effort or passion. It may simply be not understanding there are four types of startups, each of them needing a very different set of requirements to succeed:

- Startups that are entering an existing market
- Startups that are creating an entirely new market
- Startups that want to resegment an existing market as a low-cost entrant
- Startups that want to resegment an existing market as a niche player

("Disruptive" and "sustaining" innovations, eloquently described by Clayton Christensen, are another way to define new and existing Market Types.)

As I pointed out in Chapter 1, thinking and acting as if all startups are the same is a strategic error. It is a fallacy to believe the strategy and tactics that worked for one startup should be appropriate in another. That's because Market Type changes everything a company does.

As an example, imagine it's October 1999 and you are Donna Dubinsky, CEO of a feisty new startup, Handspring, in the billion dollar Personal Digital Assistant (PDA) market. Other companies in the 1999 PDA market were Palm, the original innovator; as well as Microsoft and Hewlett Packard. In October 1999 Donna told her VP of Sales, "In the next 12 months I want Handspring to win 20% of the Personal Digital Assistant market." The VP of Sales swallowed hard, turned to the VP of Marketing and said, "I need you to take end-user demand away from our competitors and drive it into our sales channel." The VP of Marketing looked at all the other PDAs on the market and differentiated Handspring's product by emphasizing expandability and performance. End result? After 12 months Handspring's revenue was $170 million.

This was possible because in 1999 Donna and Handspring were in an existing market. Handspring's customers understood what a Personal Digital Assistant was. Handspring did not have to educate them about the market, just why their new product was better than the competition – and they did it brilliantly.

For comparison, now rewind the story three years earlier, to 1996. Before Handspring, Donna and her team had founded Palm Computing, the pioneer in Personal Digital Assistants. Before Palm arrived on the scene the Personal Digital Assistant market did not exist. (A few failed science experiments like Apple's Newton had come and gone.) Imagine if Donna had turned to her VP of Sales at Palm in 1996 and said, "I want to get 20% of the Personal Digital Assistant market by the end of our first year." Her VP of Sales might had turned to the VP of Marketing and said, "I want you to drive end-user demand from our competitors into our sales channel." The VP of Marketing might have said, "Let's tell everyone about how fast the Palm Personal Digital Assistant is." If they had done this there would have been no sales. In 1996 no potential customer had heard of a Personal Digital Assistant. No one knew what a PDA could do, there was no latent demand from end users, and emphasizing its technical features would have been irrelevant. Palm needed to educate potential customers about what a PDA could do for them. By our definition (a product that allows users to do something they couldn't do before), Palm in 1996 created a new market. In contrast, Handspring in 1999 was in an existing market.

The lesson? Even with essentially identical products and team, Handspring would have failed if it had used the same sales and marketing strategy used successfully at Palm. And the converse is true: Palm would have failed, burning through all its cash, using Handspring's strategy. Market Type changes everything -- how you evaluate customer needs and customer adoption rate, how the customer understands his needs and how you would position the product to the customer. Market Type also changes the market size, as well as how you launch the product into the market. Table 2.1 points out what's different.

Customer	Market	Sales	Finance
Needs	Market Size	Distribution channel	On going capital
Adoption Rate	Cost of entry	Margins	Time to profitability
Problem Recognition	Launch Type	Sales cycle	
Positioning	Competitive Barriers		

Market Type Affects Everything (Table 2.1)

Before any sales or marketing activities can begin, a company must keep testing and asking, "What kind of a startup are we?" To see why, consider the four possible "Market Types."

A New Product in an Existing Market

An existing market is easy to understand. You are in an existing market if your product offers higher performance than what is currently offered. Higher performance can be a product or service that runs faster, does something better or substantially improves on what is already on the market. The good news is the users and the market are known, but so are the competitors. In fact, competitors define the market. The basis of competition is therefore all about the product and product features.

You can enter an existing market with a cheaper or repositioned "niche" product, but if that is the case we call it a resegmented market.

A New Product in a New Market

Another possibility is to introduce a new product into a new market. A new market results when a company creates a large customer base that couldn't do something before. This happens because of true innovation, creating something brand-new; dramatically lower cost, creating a new class of users; or because the new product solves availability, skill, convenience, or location issues in a way no other product has. Compaq's first portable computers allowed business executives to take their computers with them, something simply impossible previously. Compaq created a new market, the portable computer market. With Quicken, Intuit offered people a way to manage their finances on their personal computers, automating check writing, maintaining a check register and reconciling monthly balances -- things most people hated to do and few could do well. In doing so, Intuit created the home accounting market. (By "created the market" I do not mean "first-to-market"; I mean the company whose market share and ubiquity are associated with the market.)

In a new market the good news is your product features are at first irrelevant because there are no competitors (except other pesky startups). The bad news is the users and the market are undefined and unknown. If you're creating a new market, your problem isn't how to compete with other companies on product features but how to convince a set of customers your vision is not a hallucination. Creating a new market requires you to understand whether there is a large customer base that couldn't do this before, whether these customers can be convinced they want or need your new product, and whether customer adoption occurs in your lifetime. It also requires rather sophisticated thinking about financing—how you manage the cash-burn rate during the adoption phase, and how you manage and find investors who are patient and have deep pockets.

A New Product Attempting to Resegment an Existing Market: Low Cost

Over half of startups pursue the hybrid course of attempting to introduce a new product that resegments an existing market. Resegmenting a market can take two forms: a low-cost strategy or a niche strategy. (Segmentation is not the same as differentiation. Segmentation means you've picked a clear and distinct spot in customers' minds that is unique, understandable, and, most important, concerns something they value and want and need now.)

Low-cost resegmentation is just what it sounds like—are there customers at the low-end of an existing marketing who will buy "good enough" performance if they could get it at a substantially lower price? If you truly can be a low-cost (and profitable) provider, entering existing markets at this end is fun, as incumbent companies tend to abandon low-margin businesses and head up-market.

A New Product Attempting to Resegment an Existing Market: Niche

Niche resegmentation is slightly different. It looks at an existing market and asks, "Would some part of this market buy a new product designed to address their specific needs? Even if it cost more? Or worse performance in an aspect of the product irrelevant to this niche?'

Niche resegmentation attempts to convince customers some characteristic of the new product is radical enough to change the rules and shape of an existing market. Unlike low-cost resegmentation, niche goes after the core of an existing market's profitable business.

Both cases of resegmenting a market reframe how people think about the products within an existing market. In-n-Out Burger is a classic case of resegmenting an existing market. Who would have thought a new fast-food chain (now with 200 company-owned stores) could be a successful entrant after McDonald's and Burger King owned the market? Yet In-n-Out succeeded by simply observing the incumbent players had strayed from their original concept of a hamburger chain. By 2001 McDonald's had over 55 menu items and not one of them tasted particularly great. In stark contrast, In-n-Out offered three items: all fresh, high-quality and great tasting. They focused on the core fast-food segment that wanted high-quality hamburgers and nothing else.

While resegmenting an existing market is the most common Market Type choice of new startups, it's also the trickiest. As a low-end resegmentation strategy, it needs a long-term product plan that uses low cost as market entry to eventual profitability and up-market growth. As a niche resegmentation, this strategy faces entrenched competitors who will fiercely defend their profitable markets. And both require adroit and agile positioning of how the new product redefines the market.

Market Type and the Customer Development Process

As a company follows the Customer Development process the importance of Market Type grows in each step. During the first step, Customer Discovery, all startups, regardless of Market Type, leave the building and talk to customers. In Customer Validation, the differences between type of startup emerge as sales and positioning strategies diverge rapidly. By Customer Creation, the third step, the difference between startup Market Types is acute as customer acquisition and sales strategy differ dramatically between the types of markets. It is in Customer Creation that startups that do not understand Market Type spend themselves out of business. Chapter 5, Customer Creation, highlights these potential landmines.

The speed with which a company moves through the Customer Development process also depends on Market Type. Even if you quit your old job on Friday and on Monday join a startup in an existing market producing the same but better product, you still need to answer these questions. This process ought to be a snap, and can be accomplished in a matter of weeks or months.

In contrast, a company creating a new market has an open-ended set of questions. Completing the Customer Development processes may take a year or two, or even longer.

Table 2.2 sums up the differences among Market Types. As you'll see, the Customer Development model provides an explicit methodology for answering "What kind of startup are we?" It's a question you'll return to in each of the four steps.

	Existing Market	Resegmented Market	New Market
Customers	Existing	Existing	New/New usage
Customer Needs	Performance	1. Cost 2. Perceived need	Simplicity & convenience
Performance	Better/faster	1. Good enough at the low end 2. Good enough for new niche	Low in "traditional attributes", improved by new customer metrics
Competition	Existing incumbents	Existing incumbents	Non-consumption / other startups
Risks	Existing incumbents	1. Existing incumbents 2. Niche strategy fails	Market adoption

"Market Type" Characteristics (Table 2.2)

Synchronizing Product Development And Customer Development

As I suggested in Chapter 1, Customer Development is not a substitute for the activities occurring in the Product Development group. Instead, Customer Development and Product Development are parallel processes. While the Customer Development group is engaged in customer-centric activities outside the building, the Product Development group is focused on the product-centric activities taking place internally. At first glance, it might seem there isn't much connection between the two. This is a mistake. For a startup to succeed, Product and Customer Development must remain synchronized and operate in concert.

However, the ways the two groups interact in a startup are 180 degrees from how they would interact in a large company. Engineering's job in large companies is to make follow-on products for an existing market. A follow-on product starts with several things already known: who the customers are, what they need, what markets they are in, and who the company's competitors are. (All the benefits of being in an existing market plus having customers and revenue.) The interaction in a large company between Product Development and Customer Development is geared to delivering additional features and functions to existing customers at a price that maximizes market share and profitability.

In contrast, most startups can only guess who their customers are and what markets they are in. The only certainty on day one is the product vision. It follows, then, the goal of Customer Development in a startup is to find a market for the product as spec'd, not to develop or refine a spec based on a market that is unknown. This is a fundamental difference between a big company and most startups.

Put another way, big companies tailor their Product Development to known customers. Product features emerge by successive refinement against known customer and market requirements and a known competitive environment. As the product features get locked down, how well the product will do with those customers and markets becomes clearer. Startups, however, begin with a known product spec and tailor their Product Development to unknown customers. Product features emerge by vision and fiat against unknown customer and market requirements. As the market and customers get clearer by successive refinement, product features are driven by how well they satisfy this market. In short, in big companies, the product spec is market-driven; in startups, the marketing is product-driven.

In both cases, Product and Customer Development must go hand in hand. In most startups the only formal synchronization between Engineering and the sales/marketing teams is when they line up for contentious battles. Engineering says, "How could you have promised these features to customers? We're not building that." Sales responds, "How come the product is missing all the features you promised would be in this release? We need to commit these other features to get an order." A goal of a formal Customer Development process is to ensure the focus on the product and the focus on the customer remain in concert without rancor and with a modicum of surprise. The emphasis on synchronization runs through the entire Customer Development process. A few examples of synchronization points are:

- In each step—Customer Discovery, Customer Validation, Customer Creation and Company Building—the Product Development and Customer Development teams hold a series of formal "synchronization" meetings. Unless the two groups agree, Customer Development does not move forward to the next step.
- In Customer Discovery, the Customer Development team strives to validate the product spec, not come up with a new set of features. Only if customers do not agree there's a problem to be solved, think the problem is not painful, or don't deem the product spec solves their problem, do the Customer and Product Development teams reconvene to add or refine features.

- Also in Customer Discovery, when customers have consistently said that new or modified product features are required, the VP of Product Development goes out with the team to listen to customer feedback before new features are added.
- In Customer Validation, key members of the Product Development team go out in front of customers as part of the pre-sales support team.
- In Company Building, the Product Development team does installations and support for initial product while training the support and service staff.

Summary: The Customer Development Process

The Customer Development model consists of four well-defined steps: Customer Discovery, Customer Validation, Customer Creation, and Company Building. As you will see in succeeding chapters, each of these steps has a set of clear, concise deliverables giving the company and its investors incontrovertible proof that progress is being made on the customer front. Moreover, the first three steps of Customer Development can be accomplished with a staff that can fit in a phone booth.

While each step has its own specific objectives, the process as a whole has one overarching goal: proving there is a profitable, scalable business for the company. This is what propels the company from nonprofit to moneymaking endeavor.

Being a great entrepreneur means finding the path through the fog, confusion and myriad of choices. To do that, you need vision and a process. This book gives you the process. Its premise is simple: If you execute the four steps of Customer Development rigorously and thoroughly, you increase the odds of achieving success, and you can reach the epiphany.

CUSTOMER DISCOVERY STEP-BY-STEP

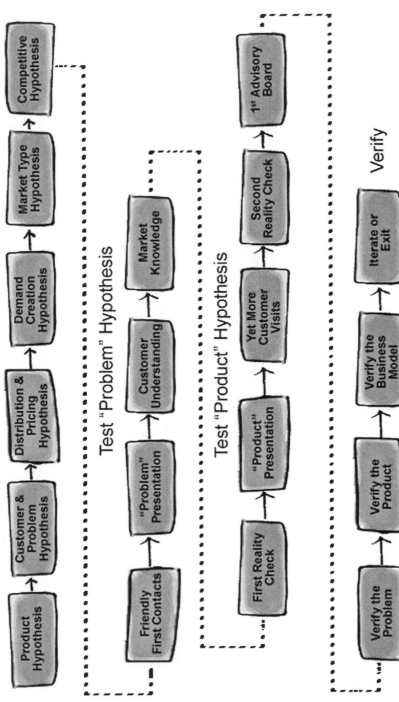

State Your Hypotheses

Product Hypothesis → Customer & Problem Hypothesis → Distribution & Pricing Hypothesis → Demand Creation Hypothesis → Market Type Hypothesis → Competitive Hypothesis

Test "Problem" Hypothesis

Friendly First Contacts → "Problem" Presentation → Customer Understanding → Market Knowledge

Test "Product" Hypothesis

First Reality Check → "Product" Presentation → Yet More Customer Visits → Second Reality Check → 1st Advisory Board

Verify

Verify the Problem → Verify the Product → Verify the Business Model → Iterate or Exit

CHAPTER 3

Customer Discovery

A journey of a thousand miles begins with a single step.
— Lao-tzu

IN 1994, STEVE POWELL HAD AN IDEA for a new type of home office device. Capitalizing on the new high-speed phone connection called ISDN, Steve envisioned creating the Swiss Army knife of home office devices. His box would offer fax, voicemail, intelligent call forwarding, email, video and phone all rolled into one. Initially Steve envisioned the market for his device would be the 11 million people with small offices or home offices (the SOHO market).

Steve's technical vision was compelling, and he raised $3 million in the first round of funding for his company, FastOffice. Like most technology startups, FastOffice was first headed by its creator, even though Steve was an engineer by training. A year after he got his first round of funding, he raised another $5 million at a higher valuation. In good Silicon Valley tradition, his team followed the canonical Product Development diagram, and in 18 months he had first customer ship of his product called Front Desk.

There was just one small problem: Front Desk cost $1395, and at that price, customers were not exactly lining up at FastOffice's door. Steve's board had assumed that, as with all technology startups, first customer ship meant FastOffice was going to ramp up sales revenues the day the product was available. Six months after first customer ship, the company had missed its revenue plan and the investors were unhappy.

It was at about this time I met Steve and his management team. His venture firm asked me to come by and help Steve with his "positioning." (Today when I hear that request I realize it's code for, "The product is shipping, but we're not selling any. Got any ideas?") When I got a demo of Front Desk, my reaction was, "Wow, that's really an innovative device. I'd love to have one at home. How much is it?" When Steve told me it was $1400, my response was, "Gosh, I wouldn't buy one, but can I be a beta site?" I still remember Steve's heated reply: "That's the reaction everyone has. What's wrong? Why wouldn't you buy one?" The stark reality was FastOffice had built a Rolls Royce for people with Volkswagen budgets. Few—unfortunately, very few—small home businesses could afford it.

Steve and his team made one of the standard startup mistakes. They had developed a great product, but neglected to spend an equivalent amount of time developing the market. The home office market simply had no compelling need that made Front Desk a "must-have," especially at a high price. FastOffice had a solution in search of a problem.

When Steve and his team realized individuals were simply not going to shell out $1400 for a "nice–to-have peripheral," they needed a new strategy. Like all startups faced with this problem, FastOffice fired its VP of Sales and came up with a new sales and marketing strategy. Now, instead of selling to individuals who worked at home, the company would sell to Fortune 1000 corporations that had a "distributed workforce"— salespeople who had offices at home. The rationale was that a VP of Sales of a large corporation could justify spending $1400 on a high-value employee, and the "new" product, renamed HomeDesk, could make a single salesperson appear like a large corporate office.

While the new strategy sounded great on paper, it suffered from the same problem as the first: The product might be nice to have, but it did not solve a compelling problem. Vice Presidents of Sales at major corporations were not going to bed at night worrying about their remote offices. They were worrying about how to make their sales numbers.

What ensued was the startup version of the ritualized Japanese Noh play I mentioned in Chapter 1. Faced with the failure of Plan B, FastOffice fired the VP of Marketing and came up with yet another new strategy. The company was now on the startup Death Spiral: The executive staff changed with each new strategy. After the third strategy didn't work either, Steve was no longer CEO and the board brought in an experienced business executive.

What's interesting about the FastOffice story is that it's very common. Time and again, startups focus on first customer ship, and only after the product is out the door do they learn customers aren't behaving as expected. By the time the company realizes sales revenues won't meet expectations, it's already behind the proverbial eight ball. Is this the end of the story? No, we'll revisit FastOffice after we explain the Customer Discovery philosophy.

Like most startups, FastOffice knew how to build a product and how to measure progress toward the product ship date. What the company lacked was a set of early Customer Development goals that would have allowed it to measure its progress in understanding customers and finding a market for its product. These goals would have been achieved when FastOffice could answer four questions:

- Have we identified a problem a customer wants solved?
- Does our product solve these customer needs?
- If so, do we have a viable and profitable business model?
- Have we learned enough to go out and sell?

Answering these questions is the purpose of the first step in the Customer Development model, Customer Discovery. This chapter explains how to go about it.

The Customer Discovery Philosophy

Let me state the purpose of Customer Discovery a little more formally. A startup begins with a vision: a vision of a new product or service, how the product will reach its customers, and why lots of people will buy it. But most of what a startup's founders initially believe about their market and potential customers are just educated guesses. A startup is in reality a "faith-based enterprise" on day one. To turn the vision into reality and the faith into facts (and a profitable company), a startup must test those guesses, or hypotheses, and find out which are correct. So the general goal of Customer Discovery amounts to this: turning the founders' initial hypotheses about their business model, market and customers into facts. And since the facts live outside the building, the primary activity is to get in front of customers, partners and suppliers. Only after the founders have performed this step will they know whether they have a valid vision or just a hallucination.

Sounds simple, doesn't it? Yet for anyone who has worked in established companies, the Customer Discovery process is disorienting. All the rules marketers learn about product management in large companies are turned upside down. It's instructive to enumerate all things you are not going to do:

- Understand the needs and wants of all customers
- Make a list of all the features customers want before they buy your product
- Hand product development a features list of the sum of all customer requests
- Hand product development a detailed marketing requirements document
- Run focus groups and test customers' reactions to your product to see if they will buy

Instead, you are going to develop your product iteratively and incrementally for the few, not the many. Moreover, you're going to start building your product even before you know whether you have any customers for it.

For an experienced marketing or product management executive, these statements are not only disorienting and counterintuitive, they are heretical. Everything I say you are not supposed to do is what marketing and product management professionals have been trained to do well. Why aren't the needs of all potential customers important? What is it about a first product from a new company that's different from follow-on products in a large company? What is it about a startup's first customers that makes the rules so different?

Develop the Product for the Few, Not the Many

In a traditional product management and marketing process the goal is to develop a Marketing Requirements Document (MRD) for engineering. The MRD contains the sum of all the possible customer feature requests, prioritized in a collaborative effort among Marketing, Sales and Engineering. Marketing holds focus groups, analyzes sales data from the field, and looks at customer feature requests and complaints. This information leads to requested features that are added to the product specification, and the engineering team builds these features into the next release.

While this process is rational for an established company entering an existing market, it is folly for startups. Why? In established companies, the MRD process ensures engineering will build a product that appeals to an existing market. In this case the customers and their needs are known. In a startup, the first product is not designed to satisfy a mainstream customer. No startup can afford the engineering effort or the time to build a product with every feature a mainstream customer needs in its first release. The product would take years to get to market and be obsolete by the time it arrived. A successful startup solves this conundrum by focusing its development on building the product incrementally and iteratively and targets its early selling efforts on a very small group of early customers who have bought into the startup's vision. This small group of visionary customers will give the company the feedback necessary to add features into follow-on releases. Enthusiasts for products who spread the good news are often called evangelists. But we need a new word to describe visionary customers—those who will not only spread the good news about unfinished and untested products, but also buy them. I call them earlyvangelists.[2]

Earlyvangelists: The Most Important Customers You'll Ever Know

Earlyvangelists are a special breed of customer willing to take a risk on your startup's product or service because they can envision its potential to solve a critical and immediate problem—and they have the budget to purchase it. Unfortunately, most customers don't fit this profile. Here's an example from the corporate world:

Imagine a bank with a line around the block on Fridays as customers wait an hour or more to get in and cash their paychecks. Now imagine you are one of the founders of a software company whose product could help the bank reduce customers' waiting time to 10 minutes. You go into the bank and tell the president, "I have a product that can solve your problem." If his response is "What problem?" you have a customer who does not recognize he has a pressing need you can help him with. There is no time in a startup's first two years of life that he will be a customer, and any feedback from him about product needs would be useless. Customers like these are traditional "late adopters" because they have a "latent need."

Another response from the bank president could be, "Yes, we have a terrible problem. I feel very bad about it, and I hand out cups of water to our customers waiting in line on the hottest days of the year." In this case, the bank president is the type of customer who recognizes he has a problem but hasn't been motivated to do anything more than paper over the symptoms. He may provide useful feedback about the type of problem

---

[2] There's a great body of work on the area of "Lead Users" popularized by Eric Von Hippel of MIT. Also see Enos 1962, Freeman 1968, Shaw 1985, Lilen & Morrison 2001.

he is experiencing, but more than likely he will not be first in line to buy a new product. Since these types of customers have an "active need," you can probably sell to them later, when you can deliver a "mainstream" product, but not today.

If it's a good day, you may run into a bank president who says, "Yes, this is a heck of a problem. In fact, we're losing over $500,000 a year in business. I've been looking for a software solution that will cut down our check cashing and processing time by 70 percent. The software has to integrate with our bank's Oracle back end, and it has to cost less than $150,000. And I need it delivered in six months." Now you're getting warm; this customer has "visualized the solution." It would be even better if the president said, "I haven't seen a single software package that solves our problem, so I wrote a request for our IT department to develop one. They've cobbled together a solution, but it keeps crashing on my tellers and my CIO is having fits keeping it running."

You're almost there: You've found a customer who has such a desperate problem he has had his own homegrown solution built out of piece parts.

Finally, imagine the bank president says, "Boy, if we could ever find a vendor who could solve this problem, we could spend the $500,000 I've budgeted with them." (Truth be told, no real customer has ever said that. But we can dream, can't we?) At this point, you have found the ultimate customer for a startup selling to corporate customers. While consumer products usually don't have as many zeros in them, earlyvangelist consumers can be found by tracing out the same hierarchy of needs.

Earlyvangelists can be identified by these customer characteristics (see Figure 3.1):

- The customer has a problem
- The customer understands he or she has a problem
- The customer is actively searching for a solution and has a timetable for finding it
- The problem is painful enough the customer has cobbled together an interim solution
- The customer has committed, or can quickly acquire, budget dollars to solve the problem

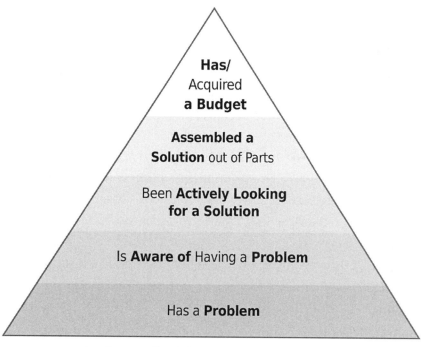

Has/ Acquired *a Budget*

Assembled a Solution out of Parts

Been **Actively Looking for a Solution**

Is **Aware of** Having a **Problem**

Has a **Problem**

Earlyvangelist Characteristics (Figure 3.1)

You can think of these characteristics as making up a scale of customer pain. Characterizing customers' pain on this scale is a critical part of Customer Discovery. My contention is that earlyvangelist customers will be found only at points 4 and 5: those who have already built a homegrown solution (whether in a company by building a software solution, or at home by taping together a fork, light bulb and vacuum cleaner) and have or can acquire a budget. These people are perfect earlyvangelist candidates. You will rely on them for feedback and for your first sales; they will tell others about your product and spread the word the vision is real. Moreover, when you meet them, you mentally include them on your list of expert customers to add to your advisory board (more about advisory boards in Chapter 4).

Start Development Based on the Vision

The idea that a startup builds its product for a small group of initial customers, and builds the product iteratively, rather than devising a specification with every possible feature for the mainstream, is radical. What follows is equally revolutionary.

On the day the company starts, there is very limited customer input to a product specification. The company doesn't know who its initial customers are (but it may think it knows) or what they will want as features. One alternative is to put Product Development on hold until the Customer Development team can find those customers. However, having a product you can demonstrate and iterate is helpful in moving the Customer Development process along. A more productive approach is to proceed with Product Development, with the feature list driven by the vision and experience of the company's founders.

Therefore, the Customer Development model has your founding team take the product as spec'd and search to see if there are customers—any customers—who will buy the product exactly as you have defined it. When you find those customers, you tailor the first release of the product so it satisfies their needs.

The shift in thinking is important. For the first product in a startup, your initial purpose in meeting customers is not to gather feature requests so you can change the product; it is to find customers for the product you are already building.

If, and only if, no customers can be found for the product as spec'd do you bring the features customers requested to the Product Development team. In the Customer Development model, then, feature request is by exception rather than rule. This eliminates the endless list of requests that often delay first customer ship and drive your Product Development team crazy.

If Product Development is simply going to start building the product without customer feedback, why talk to customers at all? Why not just build the product, ship it, and hope someone wants to buy it? The operative phrase is "start building the product." The job of Customer Development is to get the company's customer knowledge to catch up to the pace of Product Development—and in the process, to guarantee there will be paying customers the day the product ships. An important side benefit is the credibility the Customer Development team accrues internally within your organization. Product Development will be interacting with a team that understands customer needs and desires. Product Development no longer will roll their eyes after every request for features or changes to the product, but instead understand they come from a deep understanding of customer needs.

As the Customer Development team discovers new insights about the needs of this core group of initial customers, it can provide valuable feedback to the Product Development group. As you'll see, these Customer Development/Product Development synchronization meetings ensure once key customer information becomes available it is integrated into the product's future development .

To sum up the Customer Discovery philosophy: In sharp contrast to the MRD approach of building a product for a wide group of customers, a successful startup's first release is designed to be "good enough only for our first paying customers." The purpose of Customer Discovery is to identify those key visionary customers, understand their needs, and verify your product solves a problem they are willing to pay to have solved—or not. Meanwhile, you start development based on your initial vision, using your visionary customers to test whether that vision has a market. And you adjust your vision according to what you learn.

If FastOffice had understood this philosophy, it could have avoided several false starts. As it happens, there was a happy ending (at least for some later-stage investors), as the company survived and lived to play again. The new CEO worked with Steve Powell (who became the chief technical officer) to understand the true technical assets of the company. The new leadership terminated the sales and marketing staff and pared the company back to the core engineering team. What they discovered was their core asset was in the data communications technology that offered voiceover data communications lines. FastOffice discarded its products for the home, refocused, and became a major supplier of equipment to telecommunications carriers. The Customer Discovery process would have gotten the company there a lot sooner.

Overview Of The Customer Discovery Process

I've already touched on some of the elements of the philosophy behind this first step in the Customer Development model. Here's a quick overview of the entire process.

As with all the steps in Customer Development, I divide Customer Discovery into phases. Unlike subsequent steps, Customer Development has a "Phase 0." Before you can get started, you need buy-in from your board and executive staff. Four more Customer Discovery phases follow (see Figure 3.2).

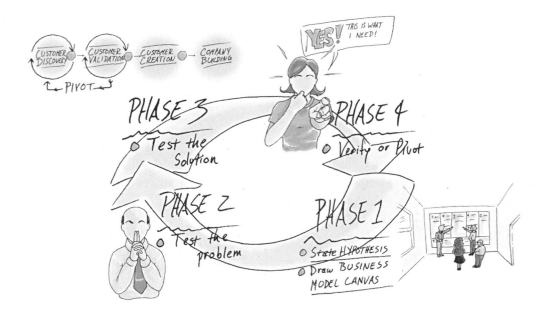

Customer Discovery: Overview of the Process (Figure 3.2)

Phase 1 is a rigorous process of writing a series of briefs that capture the hypotheses embodied in your company's vision and business model. These hypotheses are the assumptions about your product, customers, pricing, demand, market, and competition you will test in the remainder of this step.

In Phase 2 you qualify those assumptions by testing them in front of potential customers. At this point you want to do very little talking and a lot of listening. Your goal is to understand your customers and their problems, and arrive at a deep understanding of their business, workflow, organization, and product needs. You then return to your company, integrate all you learned, update Engineering with customer feedback, and jointly revise your product and customer briefs.

In Phase 3 you take your revised product concept and test its features in front of customers. The goal is not to sell the product but to validate the Phase 1 hypotheses by having customers say, "Yes, these features solve our problems."

At the same time you've been testing the product features, you've been also testing a bigger idea: the validity of your entire business model. A valid business model consists of customers who place a high value on your solution, and find the solution you offer is (for a company) mission-critical, or (for a consumer) a "have-to-have" product (product/market fit.) In front of potential buyers, you test your pricing, channel strategy, sales process and sales cycle, and discover who is the economic buyer (the one with a budget). This is equally true for consumer products where a sale to a teenager might mean the economic buyer is the parent while the user is the child.

Finally, in Phase 4 you stop and verify you understand customers' problems, that the product solves those problems, customers will pay for the product, and that the resulting revenue will result in a profitable business model. This phase culminates in the deliverables for the Customer Discovery step: a problem statement document, an expanded product requirement document, an updated sales and revenue plan, and a sound business and product plan. With your product features and business model validated, you decide whether you have learned enough to go out and try to sell your product to a few visionary customers or whether you need to go back to customers to learn some more. If, and only if, you are successful in this step do you proceed to Customer Validation.

That's Customer Discovery in a nutshell. The remainder of this chapter details each of the phases I have just described. The summary chart at the end of the chapter captures this step in detail along with the deliverables that tell you whether you've succeeded. But before you move into the details of each phase, you need to understand who is going to be doing the work of Customer Development. Who comprises the Customer Development team?

The Customer Development Team

The Customer Development process gives up traditional titles and replaces them with more functional ones. As a startup moves through the first two steps of the process, it has no Sales, Marketing or Business Development organizations or VPs. Instead, it relies on an entrepreneurial Customer Development team (see Appendix A for the rationale for the Customer Development team concept).

At first, this "team" may consist of the company's technical founder who moves out to talk with customers while five engineers write code (or build hardware, or design a new coffee cup, etc.). More often than not it includes a "head of Customer Development" who has a product marketing or product management background and is comfortable moving back and forth between customer and Product Development conversations. Later, as the startup moves into the Customer Validation step, the Customer Development team may grow to several people including a dedicated "sales closer" responsible for the logistics of getting early orders signed.

But whether it is a single individual or a team, Customer Development must have the authority to radically change the company's direction, product or mission and the creative, flexible mindset of an entrepreneur. To succeed in this process, the team members must possess:

- The ability to listen to customer objections and understand whether they are issues about the product, the presentation, the pricing, or something else (or the wrong type of customer)
- Experience moving between the customer and Product Development team
- The ability to embrace constant change
- The capacity to put themselves in their customers' shoes, understand how they work and what problems they have

Complementing the Customer Development team is a startup's product execution team. While Customer Development is out of the building talking with customers, the product team is focused on creating the product. Often this team is headed by the product visionary who leads the development effort. As you will see, regular communication between Customer Development and product execution is critical.

Phase 0: Get Buy-In

Phase 0 consists of getting buy-in from all the key players on several fundamentals, including the Customer Development process itself, the company's mission, and its core values.

Customer Development as a separate process from Product Development is a new concept. Not all executives understand it. Not all board members understand it. Market Type is also a new concept and integral to several key Customer Development decisions. Consequently, before your company can embark on Customer Development as a formal process, you must get all the players educated. There must be agreement between investors and founders about the process, key hires, and values. You must make sure all the players—founders, key execs, and the board—understand the differences among Product Development, Customer Development and Market Type, and that they buy into the value of differentiating between them.

The Product Development process emphasizes execution. The Customer Development process emphasizes learning, discovery, failure, iterations and pivots. For this reason you want to ensure there is enough funding for two to three passes through the Customer

Discovery and Customer Validation steps. This is a discussion the founding team needs to have with its board early on. Does the board believe Customer Development is iterative? Does the board believe it is necessary and worth spending time on?

Unique to the process is the commitment of the Product Development team to spend at least 15% of its time outside the building talking to customers. You need to review these organizational differences with your entire startup team and make sure everyone is on board.

You also want to articulate in writing both the business and product vision of why you started the company. Called a mission statement, at this point in your company's life this document is nothing more than "what we were thinking when we were out raising money." It can be no more complicated than the two paragraphs used in the business plan to describe your product and the market. Write these down and post them on the wall. When the company is confused about what product to build or what market you wanted to serve, refer to the mission statement. This is called mission-oriented leadership. In times of crisis or confusion, understanding why the company exists and what its goals are will provide a welcome beacon of clarity.

Over time, a company's mission statement changes. It may change subtly over a period of months, or dramatically over a week, but a wise management team will not change it with the latest market or product fad.

Finally, next to the mission statement post the founding team's core values. Unlike mission statements, core values are not about markets or products. They are a set of fundamental beliefs about what the company stands for that can endure the test of time: the ethical, moral, and emotional rocks on which the company is built. A good example of a long-lasting set of core values is the Ten Commandments. It's not too often that you hear someone say, "Hey, maybe we should get rid of the second commandment." More than 4,000 years after they were committed to paper—well, tablets—these values are still the rock on which Judeo-Christian ethics rest.

To take an example closer to our purpose, the founding team of a pharmaceutical company articulated a powerful core value: "First and foremost, we believe in making drugs that help people." The founders could have said, "We believe in profits first and at all costs," and that, too, would be a core value. Neither is right or wrong, so long as it truly expresses what the company believes in.

When the company's mission or direction is uncertain, the core values can be referenced for direction and guidance. For core values to be of use, a maximum of three to five should be articulated.[3]

[3] The seminal book on the subject of core values is *Built to Last*, by James C. Collins and Jerry I. Porras.

Phase 1: State Your Hypotheses

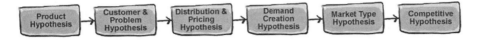

Once the company has bought into Customer Development as a process in Phase 0, the next phase of Customer Discovery is to write down all of your company's initial assumptions, or hypotheses. Getting your hypotheses down on paper is essential because you will refer to them, test them, and update them during the entire Customer Development process. Your written summary of these hypotheses will take the form of a one- or two-page brief about each of the following areas:

- Product
- Customer and their problem
- Channel and pricing
- Demand creation
- Market Type
- Competition

Initially, you may lack the information to complete these hypotheses. In fact some of your briefs may be shockingly empty. Not to worry. These briefs will serve as an outline to guide you. During the course of Customer Discovery, you will return to these briefs often, to fill in the blanks and modify your original hypotheses with new facts you have learned as you talk to more and more customers. In this first phase, you want to get down what you know (or assume you know) on paper and create a template to record the new information you will discover.

A. State Your Hypotheses: The Product

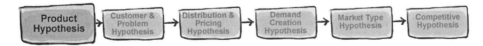

Product hypotheses consist of the founding team's initial guesses about the product and its development. Something like these were part of the company's original business plan.

First Product Development/Customer Development Synchronizaton Meeting

Most of the product brief is produced by the Product Development team. This is one of the few times you are going to ask the head of product execution and his or her partner, the keeper of the technical vision, to engage in a paper exercise. Getting your product hypotheses down on paper and turning them into a product brief, agreed to by all executives, is necessary for the Customer Development team to begin its job.

The product brief covers these six areas:

- Product features
- Product benefits
- Intellectual property
- Dependency analysis
- Product delivery schedule
- Total cost of ownership/adoption

Here is a short description of what should be covered in each area.

Product Hypotheses: Product Features

The product features list is a one-page document consisting of one- or two-sentence summaries of the top 10 (or fewer) features of the product. (If there is some ambiguity in describing a particular feature, include a reference to a more detailed engineering document.) The features list is Product Development's written contract with the rest of the company. The biggest challenge will be deciding what features will ship in what order. We'll address how you prioritize first customer ship features a bit later.

Product Hypotheses: Product Benefits

The benefits list succinctly describes what benefits the product will deliver to customers. (Something new? Something better? Faster? Cheaper?) In large companies, it's normal for Marketing to describe the product benefits. The Customer Development model, however, recognizes that Marketing doesn't know anything about customers yet. In a startup Product Development has all kinds of customer "facts." Use this meeting to flush these out. At this point, the marketing people must bite their tongues and listen to the Product Development group's assumptions about how the features will benefit customers. These engineering-driven benefits represent hypotheses you will test against real customer opinions.

Product Hypotheses: Intellectual Property

In the next part of the brief, the product team provides a concise summary of assumptions and questions about intellectual property (IP). Are you inventing anything unique? Is any of your IP patentable? Do you have trade secrets to protect? Have you checked to see whether you infringe on others' IP? Do you need to license others' patents? Although most development groups tend to look at patents as a pain in the rear, and management believes the expense of securing patents is prohibitive, taking an active patent position is prudent. As your company gets larger, other companies may believe you infringe on their patents, so having intellectual property to horse-trade can come in handy. More importantly, if you own critical patents in a nascent industry, they can become a major financial asset of the company.

Product Hypotheses: Dependency Analysis

A dependency analysis is simpler than it sounds. The Product and Customer Development teams jointly prepare a one-page document that says, "For us to be successful (that is, to sell our product in volume), here's what has to happen that is out of our control." Things out of a company's control can include other technology infrastructure that needs to emerge (all cell phones become Web-enabled, fiber optics are in every home, electric cars are selling in volume), changes in consumers' lifestyles or buying behavior, new laws, changes in economic conditions, and so on. For each factor, the dependency analysis specifies what needs to happen (let's say the widespread adoption of telepathy), when it needs to happen (telepathy must be common among consumers under age 25 by 2010), and what it means for you if it doesn't happen (your product needs to use the Internet instead). Also write down how you can measure whether each external change is happening when you need it to (college kids can read minds by 2020).

Product Hypotheses: Product Delivery Schedule

In the product delivery schedule, you ask the product team to specify not only the date of the first release (the minimum feature set), but the delivery and feature schedule for follow-on products or multiple releases of the product as far out as the team can see (up to 18 months). In startups, this request usually elicits a response like, "How can I come up with a date for future releases when we barely know when our first release will be?" That's a good question, so you'll need to make clear to the product team why you need their cooperation and best estimates. These are important because the Customer Development team will be out trying to convince a small group of early customers to buy based on the product spec long before you can physically deliver the product. To do so they will have to paint a picture for customers of what the product will ultimately look like several releases into the future. It's because these customers are buying into your total vision that they will give you money for an incomplete, buggy, barely functional first product.

Asking for dates in this phase may result in an anxious Product Development team. Reassure them this first pass at a schedule is not set in stone. It will be used throughout Customer Discovery to test customer reaction but not to make customer commitments. At the beginning of the next step, Customer Validation, the teams will revisit the product delivery schedule and commit to firm dates that can be turned into contractual obligations.

Product Hypotheses: Total Cost Of Ownership/Adoption

The total cost of ownership (TCO) adoption analysis estimates the total cost to customers of buying and using your product. For business products, do customers need to buy a new computer to run your software? Do they need training to use the product? What other physical or organizational changes need to happen? What will be the cost of deployment across a whole company? For consumer products, it measures the cost of "adopting" the product to fit their needs. Do customers need to change their lifestyle? Do they need to change any part of their purchasing or usage behavior? Do they need to throw away or make obsolete something they use today? While the Customer Development team prepares this estimate, the Product Development team should provide feedback about whether the estimates are realistic.

When all of the six hypotheses about the product are written down, the company has a brief that describes the product in some detail. Paste your brief to the wall. Soon it will be joined by a few more. Soon after, you will be in front of customers testing these assumptions.

B. State Your Hypotheses: Customer Hypotheses

The process of assembling the customer briefs is the same as for the product brief, except this time the Customer Development team is writing down its initial assumptions. These assumptions cover two key areas: who the customers are (the customer hypothesis) and what problems they have (the problem hypothesis). In the course of Customer Discovery, you'll flesh out these assumptions with additional information:

- Types of customers
- Customer problems
- A day in the life of your customers
- Organizational map and customer influence map
- ROI (return on investment) justification
- Minimum feature set

Again, let's consider each part of the customer and problem briefs in turn.

Customer Hypotheses: Types of Customers

If you've ever sold a product, whether it's to a consumer buying a stick of gum or a company buying a million-dollar telecommunications system, you've probably discovered every sale has a set of decision-makers who get their fingers into the process. So the first question to ask is, "Are there different types of customers we should approach when we sell our product?" Whether you're selling process control software into a large corporation or a new type of home vacuuming device, chances are there are a number of people in a number of categories whose needs you must satisfy to sell the product. During Customer Discovery you will spend time understanding these needs. Later, when you are ready to develop your first "sales roadmap" in the Customer Validation step, knowing all the players in detail will be essential. Right now, it's sufficient to realize the word "customer" is more complicated than a single individual. Some of the customer types I have encountered include (see Figure 3.3):

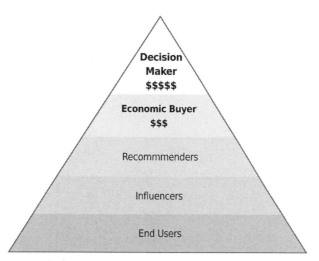

Customer Types *(Figure 3.3)*

End Users

These are the day-to-day users of the product, the ones who will push the buttons, touch the product, play with it, use it, love it and hate it. You need a deep understanding of the end users' needs, but it's important to realize in some cases the end user may have the least influence in the sales process. This is typically true in complex corporate sales where an entire food chain of decision-makers affects the purchasing decision. However, it's equally true in a consumer sale. For example, children are a large consumer market and the users of many products, but their parents are the buyers.

Influencers

Next up the sales chain are all the people who think they have a stake in a product coming into their company or home. This category could include the key techno-whiz in IT or the 10-year-old whose likes and dislikes influence the family's choices of consumer products.

Recommenders

These people influence product purchase decisions. They differ from the influencers in that they can make or break a sale. A recommender could be a department head saying any new PCs should come from Dell or the spouse who has a particularly strong brand preference.

Economic Buyer

Further up the decision chain is the economic buyer, the one who has the budget for the purchase and must approve the expenditure. (Don't you bet you are going to want to know who that is?) In a consumer purchase it can be a teen with a weekly music budget or a spouse with a vacation budget.

Decision-maker

The decision-maker could be the economic buyer, but it could be someone else even higher in the decision-making hierarchy. The decision-maker is the person who has the ultimate say about a product purchase regardless of the other users, influencers, recommenders and economic buyers. Depending on your product, the decision-maker could be a suburban soccer mom/dad or a Fortune 500 CEO. It is up to you to discover the ultimate purchase decision-maker and understand how all these other customer types influence his or her final decision.

Saboteurs

In addition to all these parties to the sale (and isn't it amazing with a process like this, anything gets sold?), one more group must be mentioned. You won't be looking for them, but they will see you coming. I call this group the saboteurs. In every large company, for example, there are individuals and organizations that are wedded to the status quo. If your product threatens a department's stability, headcount, or budget, don't expect this group to welcome you with open arms. Therefore you need to be able to predict who might be most threatened by your product, understand their influence in the organization, and ultimately put together a sales strategy that at worst neutralizes their influence and at best turns them into allies. Don't think saboteurs occur just in large corporations. For a consumer product, it may be a member of the family who has gotten comfortable with the old car and is uncomfortable about driving something new and different.

The first step in formulating your customer brief is to write down and diagram who you think will be your day-to-day users, influencers, recommenders, economic buyer, and decision-maker, including, in the case of sales to companies, their titles and where in the organization they are found. It's also worth noting if you think the economic buyer has a current budget for your product or one like it, or whether you will have to persuade the customer to get funds to buy your product.

Given you haven't been out talking to customers yet, you may have a lot of empty space in this part of your brief. That's fine. It just reminds you how much you need to find out.

Of course, not every product has so complicated a purchase hierarchy, but the sale of nearly every product involves multiple people. If it's a consumer product, these rules still apply. It's just that the influencers, recommenders, and so on are likely to have more familiar titles like "mom," "dad," and "kids."

Customer Hypotheses: Types of Customers for Consumer Products

Some consumer products (clothing, fashion, entertainment products, etc.) don't address a "problem," or need. In fact, U.S. consumers spend over 40 percent of their income on discretionary purchases, i.e. luxuries. How to sell to consumers starts with identifying customer types as described above. What's different is recognizing that since a real problem or need does not exist, for consumers to purchase a luxury, they must give themselves a justification for the purchase. In the Customer Creation step your marketing programs will promise consumers their unneeded spending will be worth it. It suffices in this phase to identify the consumer "customer types" and have a hypothesis about their emotional wants and desires. Describe how you can convince these customers that your product can deliver an emotional payoff.

Customer Hypotheses: Customer Problems

Next, you want to understand what problem the customer has. The reason is simple: It's much easier to sell when you can build the story about your product's features and benefits around a solution to a problem you know the customer already has. Then you look less like a crass entrepreneur and more like someone who cares coming in with a potentially valuable solution.

Understanding your customers' problems involves understanding their pain—that is, how customers experience the problem, and why (and how much) it matters to them. Let's go back to the problem of the long line of people trying to cash their paychecks at the bank. It's obvious there's a problem, but let's try to think about the problem from the bank's point of view (the bank being your customer). What is the biggest pain bank employees experience? The answer is different for different people in the bank. To the bank president, the pain might be the bank lost $500,000 last year in customer deposits when frustrated customers took their business elsewhere. To the branch manager, the biggest pain is her inability to cash customer paychecks efficiently. And to the bank tellers, the biggest pain is dealing with customers who are frustrated and angry by the time they get to the teller window.

Now imagine you asked the employees in this bank, "If you could wave a magic wand and change anything at all, what would it be?" You can guess the bank president would ask for a solution that could be put in place quickly and cost less than the bank is losing in customer deposits. The branch manager would want a way to process checks faster on paydays that would work with the software already in place and not force a change in the bank's day-to-day processes. The tellers would want customers who don't growl at them and please, no new buttons, terminals, and systems.

It's not much of a stretch to imagine running this same exercise for a consumer product. This time instead of a bank president and tellers, imagine the prototypical nuclear family discussing buying a car. Each family member likely has their own view of their transportation needs. You might naively assume the breadwinner with the largest paycheck makes the decision. But as with the different customer problems at the bank, 21st-century consumer purchases are never that simple.

These examples show that you need to summarize the customer's problem, and the organizational impact of the problem in terms of the different types of pain it causes at various levels of the company/family/consumer. Finally, writing down the answer to "If they could wave a magic wand and change anything at all, what would it be?" gives you a tremendous leg up on how to present your new product.

Earlier in this chapter, I discussed five levels of problem awareness customers might have. In this customer problem brief, you use a simple "problem recognition scale" for each type of customer (user, influencer, recommender, economic buyer, decision-maker). As you learn more you can begin to categorize your customers as having:

- A latent need (the customers have a problem or they have a problem and understand they have a problem)
- An active need (the customers recognize a problem—they are in pain—and are actively searching for a solution, but they haven't done any serious work to solve the problem)
- A vision (the customers have an idea what a solution to the problem would look like, may even have cobbled together a homegrown solution, and, in the best case, are prepared to pay for a better solution)

Now that you are firmly ensconced in thinking through your customers' problems, look at the problem from one other perspective: Are you solving a mission-critical company problem or satisfying a must-have consumer need? Is your product have-to-have? Is it nice-to-have? In our bank example, long lines on pay day costing the bank $500,000 a year might be a mission-critical issue if the bank's profits are only $5,000,000 a year, or if the problem is occurring at every branch in the country, so the number of customers lost is multiplied across hundreds of branches. But if you're talking about a problem at only one branch of a multinational banking organization, it's not mission-critical.

The same is true for our consumer example. Does the family already have two cars in fine operating condition? Or has one broken down and the other is on its last legs? While the former is an impulse purchase, the latter is a "must-have" need.

As I suggested earlier, one test of a have-to-have product is that the customers have built or have been trying to build a solution themselves. Bad news? No, it's the best news a startup could find. You have uncovered a mission-critical problem and customers with a vision of a solution. Wow. Now all you need to do is convince them that if they build it themselves they are in the software development and maintenance business, and that's what your company does for a living.

Customer Hypotheses: A Day in your Customer's Life

One of the most satisfying exercises for a true entrepreneur executing Customer Development is to discover how a customer "works." The next part of the customer problem brief expresses this understanding in the form of "a day in the life of a customer."

In the case of businesses, this step requires a deep understanding of a target company on many levels. Let's continue with our banking example. How a bank works is not something you will discover from cashing a check. You want to know how the world looks from a banker's perspective. How do the potential end users of the product (the tellers) spend their days? What products do they use? How much time do they spend using them? How would life change for these users after they had your product? Unless you've been a bank teller, these questions should leave you feeling somewhat at a loss. But how are you going to sell a product to a bank to solve tellers' problems if you don't know how they work?

Now run this exercise again, this time from the perspective of branch managers. How do they spend their day? How would your new product affect them? Run it again, this time thinking about the bank president. What on earth does the bank president do? How will your product affect her? And if you are installing a product that connects to other software the bank has, you are going to have to deal with the IT organization. How do the IT people spend their day? What other software do they run? How are their existing systems configured? Who are their preferred vendors? Are they standing at the door waiting to welcome yet another new company and product with confetti and champagne?

Finally, what do you know about trends in the banking industry? Is there a banking industry software consortium? Are there banking software trade shows? Industry analysts? Unless you have come from your target industry, this part of your customer problem brief may include little more than lots of question marks. That's OK. In Customer Development, the answers turn out to be easy; asking the right questions is difficult. You will go out and talk to customers with the goal of filling in all the blank spots on the customer/problem brief.

For a consumer product, the same exercise applies. How do consumers solve their problems today? How would they solve their problems having your product? Would they be happier? Smarter? Feel better? Do you understand how and what will motivate these customers to buy?

Your final exam doesn't happen until you come back to the company and, in meetings with the Product Development team and your peers, draw a vivid and specific picture of a day in the life of your customer.

Customer Hypotheses: Organizational Map and Customer Influence Map

Having now a deeper understanding of the day in the life of a customer, you realize that except in rare cases most customers do not work by themselves. They interact with other people. In enterprise sales it will be other people in their company, and in a sale to a consumer their interaction is with their friends and/or family. This part of the brief has you first listing all the people you can think of who could influence a customer's buying decisions. Your goal is to build a tentative organizational map showing all the potential influencers who surround the user of the product. If it's a large company the diagram may be complex and have lots of unknowns right now. If it's a sale to a consumer, the diagram might appear to be deceptively simple but with the same thought—it's clear consumers have a web of influencers as well. Over time this map will become the starting point for the sales roadmap described in detail in the next chapter.

Once you have the organizational map, the next step is to understand the relationships among the recommenders, influencers, economic buyers, and saboteurs. How do you think a sale will be made? Who must be convinced (and in what order) for you and your company to make a sale? This is the beginning of your customer influence map.

Customer Hypotheses: ROI (Return On Investment) Justification

Now that you know everything about how a customer works, you're done, right? Not yet. For purchases both corporate and consumer, customers need to feel the purchase was "worth it," that they got "a good deal." For a company this is called return on investment, or ROI. (For a consumer this can be "status" or some other justification of their wants and desires.) ROI represents customers' expectation from their investment measured against goals such as time, money, or resources as well as status for consumers.

In our banking example, the ROI justification is relatively easy. From listening to your customer, you figure the bank is losing $500,000 in gross customer revenue per year. The profit on every customer is 4 percent. Therefore, at every branch $20,000 in profit leaves with those lost customers. (When you first construct your brief, numbers like these are just your guesses. As you get customer feedback, you can plug in more accurate amounts.) Now suppose you've found out 100 other branches have the same problem. That's a $50 million problem and $2 million in profit gone. Your software to solve this problem costs $200,000, plus $50,000 per year in maintenance fees. Integration and installation will probably take 18 person-months—say, another $250,000 in customer costs. The customers will need to dedicate a full-time IT professional to maintain the system; you budget another $150,000 for this. Finally, training all the tellers in 100 branches will cost another $250,000.

Let's round up all the direct costs (money the bank will pay you) to $500,000 and the indirect costs (money the bank spends on its own staff) to $400,000. As you can see from Figure 3.4, the bank would spend $900,000 for your solution. That seems like a lot of money just to make customer lines shorter. But because you understand how the bank works, you know installing your product will save the bank over $2,000,000 a year. Your product will pay for itself in less than six months, and every year the bank will have an extra $1.85 million in profit. That's an amazing return on investment.

Our Software Costs		Bank Savings	
Software costs	$200,000	Revenue/branch	$500,000
Maintenance fees	$50,000	Gross profit @ 4%	$20,000
Integration	$250,000	Branches	100
Total software cost	*$500,000*	Gross revenue	$50,000,000
Indirect Costs			
One IT headcount	$150,000		
Teller training	U$250,000U		
Total ongoing costs	*$400,000*		
Total Year One Cost	**$900,000**	**Savings Per Year**	**$2,000,000**
Payback time is less than six months			

ROI Calculation for ABC Bank (Figure 3.4)

Imagine having a slide showing this type of calculation in your customer presentation!

Most startups are unprepared to deal with the customer's ROI. At best, they ignore it, and at worst, they confuse it with the price of the product. (ROI, as you'll see, involves a lot more than price.) Now, most customers never directly ask a startup about ROI because they assume no outside vendor would be familiar enough with their internal operations to develop valid ROI metrics. Suppose you were the exception. Imagine you were able to help customers justify the ROI for your product. That would be pretty powerful, wouldn't it? Yep. And that's why you include the customer's ROI as part of the customer problem brief. To do that you have to decide what to measure in calculating ROI. Increased revenues? Cost reduction, or cost containment? Displaced costs? Avoided costs? Intangibles?

Your earlyvangelists will end up using your ROI metrics to help sell your product inside their own company! It's with that end in mind that you include an ROI justification in the customer/problem brief. Early on, it's a placeholder for the powerful tool you'll develop as you learn more about your customers.

Customer Hypotheses: Minimum Feature Set

The last part of your customer/problem brief is one the Product Development team will be surprised to see. You want to understand the smallest feature set customers will pay for in the first release.

The minimum feature set is the inverse of what most sales and marketing groups ask of their development teams. Usually the cry is for more features, typically based on "here's what I heard from the last customer I visited." In the Customer Development model, however, the premise is that a very small group of early visionary customers will guide your follow-on features. So your mantra becomes, "Less is more, to get an earlier first release." Rather than asking customers explicitly about feature X, Y or Z, one approach to defining the minimum features set is to ask, "What is the smallest or least complicated problem the customer will pay us to solve?"

C. State Your Hypotheses: Channel and Pricing Hypotheses

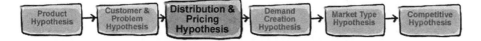

Your channel/pricing brief puts your first stake in the ground describing what distribution channel you intend to use to reach customers (direct, online, telemarketing, reps, retail, etc.), as well as your first guess at product pricing. As you'll see, decisions about pricing and distribution channels are interrelated.

Let's take distribution channels first. Distribution channels make up the route a product follows from its origin (your company) to the last consumer. If you are selling directly to customers, you may need additional partners to help you install or deliver a complete product (system integrators, third-party software.) If you are selling indirectly, through middlemen, you need channel partners to physically distribute the product. Figure 3.5 illustrates how this process works. At the far right are the customers who have a problem that can be solved by your company's product and/or services.

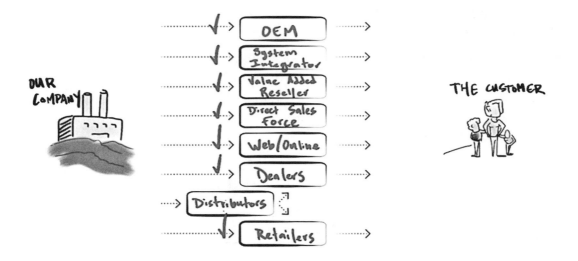

Distribution Channel Alternatives (Figure 3.5)

In the middle of the figure, original equipment manufacturers (OEMs) and system integrators derive a relatively small percentage of their total revenue from the sale of your product, and a greater percentage from their value-add in business process and unique solutions to customer problems. At the bottom of the diagram, retailers and mass merchants derive most of their revenue from the sale of your product. The primary value of retailers and mass merchants is providing products that are accessible and available off-the-shelf. Between these two extremes are a variety of sales channels that provide a combination of products and services. All but one are "indirect channels." That means someone other than your company owns the relationship with the customer. The exception is a direct sales channel, where you hire and staff the organization that sells directly to your customer.

A startup picks a sales channel with three criteria in mind: (1) Does the channel add value to the sales process? (2) What are the price and the complexity of the product? And (3) Are there established customer buying habits/practices? In a "value-added" channel the channel may provide one-on-one sales contacts, special services such as installation, repair or integration. In contrast, a "shrink-wrapped" product is often purchased directly from catalogs, online or from store floor displays. Typically, professional products are sold for higher prices than shrink-wrap products; hence channels servicing shrink-wrap products (such as retailers and mass merchants) can operate at lower margin points.

In your channel/pricing brief, you spell out your initial hypotheses about how your product will reach customers. In the example of the $200,000 banking software described earlier, the first question you must answer is, how will customers initially buy from you? Directly from your company? From a distributor? Through a partner? In a retail store? Via mail order? Via the Internet?

The answer depends on a number of factors, beginning with the product's projected price, its complexity and the established customer buying preferences.

There are a few questions you can ask yourself to help understand what pricing best fits your product. If there are products somewhat like yours, how much do customers spend for them today? If users need a product like yours, how much do they pay to do the same thing today? In the case of your new banking software, suppose you discovered banks were already buying products with fewer features for over $500,000. This would give you a solid data point that your $200,000 price would be well accepted. In the case where there is no product like yours, ask how customers would solve their problem using piece-part solutions from a variety of vendors. How much would the sum of those multiple products cost?

Two final thoughts about pricing. The first is the notion of "lifetime value" of a customer; how much can you sell to a customer not just from the first sale, but over the life of the sales relationship? For example, having decided to sell your banking software direct, your first thought might be to sell the bank a single product, then charge annual maintenance fees. However, once you thought about all the work it would take to sell a single bank, it might dawn on you that you could offer this bank a suite of products. This would mean you could go back and sell a new product year after year (or as long as the new products met the needs of the bank). By thinking dramatically about the lifetime value of your customers, you can affect your product strategy.

The second idea is one I use with customers all the time in this phase. I ask them, "If the product were free, how many would you actually deploy or use?" The goal is to take pricing away as an issue and see whether the product itself gets customers excited. If it does, I follow up with: "OK, it's not free. In fact, imagine I charged you $1 million. Would you buy it?" While this may sound like a facetious dialog, I use it all the time. Why? Because more than half the time customers will say something like, "Steve, you're out of your mind. This product isn't worth more than $250,000." I've just gotten customers to tell me how much they are willing to pay. Wow.

D. State Your Hypotheses: Demand Creation Hypotheses

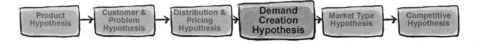

Some day you will have to "create demand" to reach these customers and "get" them into your sales channel. Use the opportunity of talking to them to find out how they learn about new companies and new products. This brief reflects your hypotheses about how customers will hear about your company and product once you are ready to sell.

In the course of Customer Discovery, you'll flesh out these assumptions with additional information on creating customer demand and identifying influencers.

Demand Creation Hypotheses: Creating Customer Demand

In a perfect world customers would know telepathically how wonderful your product is, drive, fly or walk to your company, and line up to give you money. Unfortunately it doesn't work that way. You need to create "demand" for your product. Once you create this demand you need to drive those customers into the sales channel that carries your product. In this brief you will start to answer the questions: How will you create demand to drive them into the channel you have chosen? Through advertising? Public relations? Retail store promotions? Spam? Website? Word of mouth? Seminars? Telemarketing? Partners? This is somewhat of a trick question, as each distribution channel has a natural cost of demand creation. That means the further away from a direct sales force your channel is, the more expensive your demand creation activities are. Why? By their very appearance on a customer's doorstep a direct sales force is not only selling your product, they are implicitly marketing and advertising it. At the other extreme, a retail channel (Wal-Mart, a grocery store shelf or a website) is nothing more than a shelf on which the product passively sits. The product is not going to leap off the shelf and explain itself to customers. They need to have been influenced via advertising or public relations or some other means, before they will come in to buy.

You also need to understand how your customers hear about new companies and products. Do they go to trade shows? Do others in their company go? What magazines do they read? Which ones do they trust? What do their bosses read? Who are the best salespeople they know? Who would they hire to call on them?

Demand Creation Hypotheses: Influencers

At times the most powerful pressure on a customer's buying decision may not be something your company did directly. It may be something someone who did not work for you said or did not say. In every market or industry there is a select group of individuals who pioneer the trends, style, and opinions. They may be paid pundits in market research firms. They may be kids who wear the latest fashions. In this brief you need to identify the influencers who can affect your customer's opinions. Your brief includes the list of outside influencers: analysts, bloggers, journalists, and so on. Who are the visionaries in social media or the blogger, press/analyst community customers read and listen to? That they respect? This list will also become your roadmap for assembling an advisory board as well as targeting key industry analysts and press contacts in the Customer Validation step.

E. State Your Hypotheses: Market Type Hypotheses

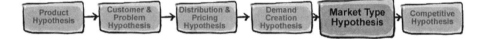

In Chapter 2, I introduced the concept of Market Type. Startup companies generally enter one of four Market Types and ultimately your company will need to choose one of these. However, unlike decisions about product features, the Market Type is a "late-binding-decision." This means you can defer this final decision until Customer Creation but you still need a working hypothesis. In the next two chapters, I'll come back to the Market Type your company is in and help you to refine and deepen your analysis after you have learned more about your customers and your market.

However, because the consequences of the wrong choice are severe, you would be wise to develop initial Market Type hypotheses you can test as you move through the Customer Development phase. To do this, the Customer Development team should record its initial Market Type and brainstorm with the Product Development team. In this brief, you will seek a provisional answer to a single question: Is your company entering an existing market, resegmenting an existing market or creating a new market?

For some startups the choice is pretty clear. If you are entering a market where you are in a "clone business," such as computers or PDAs, the choice is already made for you: you are in an existing market. If you have invented a radically new class of product no one has seen before, you are likely in a new market. However, most companies have the luxury to choose which Market Type to use. So how to choose? A few simple questions begin the process:

- Is there an established and well-defined market with large numbers of customers?
- Does your product have better "something" (performance, features, service) than the existing competitors? If so, you are in an existing market.
- Is there an established and well-defined market with large numbers of customers and your product costs less than the incumbents'? You are in a resegmented market.
- Is there an established and well-defined market with large numbers of customers where your product can be uniquely differentiated from the existing incumbents? You are also in a resegmented market.

If there is no established and well-defined market, with no existing competitors you are creating a new market. Don't worry if you waver among the four Market Type choices. As you start talking to customers, they will have lots of opinions about where you fit. For now, go through each of the market types and pick the one that best fits your vision today. Table 3.1, which you saw in Chapter 2, is a reminder of the trade-offs.

	Existing Market	Resegmented Market	New Market
Customers	Existing	Existing	New/New usage
Customer Needs	Performance	1. Cost 2. Perceived need	Simplicity & convenience
Performance	Better/faster	1. Good enough at the low end 2. Good enough for new niche	Low in "traditional attributes", improved by new customer metrics
Competition	Existing incumbents	Existing incumbents	Non-consumption / other startups
Risks	Existing incumbents	1. Existing incumbents 2. Niche strategy fails	Market adoption

Market Type (Table 3.1)

Market Type Hypotheses: Entering An Existing Market

If you believe your company and product fit in an existing market, you need to understand how your product outperforms those of your competitors. Positioning your product against the slew of existing competitors is accomplished by adroitly picking the correct product features where you are better. Summarize your thinking in a brief. If you believe you are entering an existing market, good questions to address in your brief include:

- Who are the competitors and who is driving the market?
- What is the market share of each of the competitors?
- What are the total marketing and sales dollars the market share leaders will be spending to compete with you?
- Do you understand the cost of entry against incumbent competitors? (See the Customer Creation step in Chapter 5)
- Since you are going to compete on performance, what performance attributes have customers told you are important? How do competitors define performance?
- What percentage of this market do you want to capture in years one through three?
- How do the competitors define the market?
- Are there existing standards? If so, whose agenda is driving the standards?
- Do you want your company to embrace these standards, extend them, or replace them? (If you want to extend or replace them, you may be trying to resegment a market. However, if you truly are entering an existing market, then you will want to ensure you also fill out the competitive brief discussed in Step F. It will help shape your positioning further.)

One way to capture your thinking on an existing Market Type is to construct a competitive diagram. Usually a company picks two or more key product attributes and attacks competitors along axes corresponding to these attributes, such as feature/technology axis, price/performance axis, and channel/margin axis. The competitive diagram used in an existing market typically looks like Figure 3.6, with each of the axes chosen to emphasize the best competitive advantage about the product.

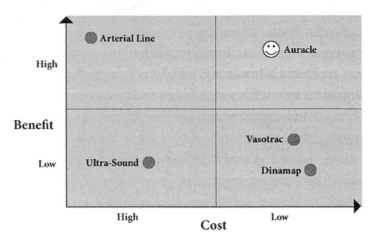

Example of a Competitive Diagram *(Figure 3.6)*

Picking the correct axes for the basis of competition is critical. The idea is that in entering an existing market, positioning is all about the product and specifically the value customers place on its new features.

Market Type Hypotheses: Resegmenting An Existing Market

An alternative to going head to head with the market leaders in an existing market may be to resegment an existing market. Here your positioning will rest on either a) the claim of being the "low-cost provider" or b) finding a niche via positioning (some feature of your product or service redefines the existing market so you have a unique competitive advantage).

If you believe you are resegmenting an existing market, good questions to address in this brief include:

- What existing markets are your customers coming from?
- What are the unique characteristics of those customers?
- What compelling needs of those customers are unmet by existing suppliers?
- What compelling features of your product will get customers of existing companies to abandon their current supplier?
- Why couldn't existing companies offer the same thing?
- How long will it take you to educate potential customers and grow a market of sufficient size? What size is that?
- How will you educate the market? How will you create demand?

- Given no customers yet exist in your new segment, what are realistic year one-through-three sales forecasts?

For this type of startup, you need to draw both the competitive diagram (because, unlike startups in a wholly new market, you have competitors) and the market map (because you are in effect creating a new market by resegmenting an existing one). Taken together, these two diagrams should clearly illustrate why thousands of new customers will believe in and move to this market.

I have always found it helpful in a resegmented or new market to draw a "market map" (a diagram of how this new market will look) as shown in Figure 3.7. The map shows at a glance why the company is unique. A standing joke is that every new market has its own descriptive TLA (three-letter acronym). Draw the market map with your company in the center.

A resegmented market assumes it is going to get customers from an existing market. Draw the existing markets from which you expect to get your customers (remember a market is a set of companies with common attributes.)

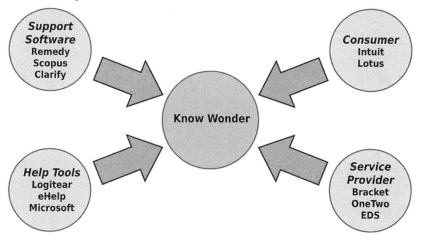

Example of a Market Map (Figure 3.7)

Market Type Hypotheses: Entering a New Market

At first glance, a new market has great appeal. What could be better than a market with no competitors? And no competition typically means pricing is not a competitive issue but one of what the market will bear. Wow, no competitors and high margins! Yet even without competitors the risks of market failure are great. Without sounding pedantic, creating a new market means a market does not currently exist—there are no customers. If you believe you are entering a new market, good questions to address in your brief include:

- What are the markets adjacent to the one you are creating?
- What markets will potential customers come from?
- What compelling need will make customers use/buy your product?
- What compelling feature will make them use/buy your product?
- How long will it take you to educate potential customers to grow a market of sufficient size? What size is that?
- How will you educate the market? How will you create demand?
- Given no customers yet exist, what are realistic year one-through-three sales forecasts?
- How much financing will it take to soldier on while you educate and grow the market?
- What will stop a well-heeled competitor from taking the market from you once you've developed it? (There is a reason the phrase "the pioneers are the ones with the arrows in their back" was coined.)
- Is it possible to define your product as either resegmenting a market or as entering an existing one?

As I noted in Chapter 2, you compete in a new market not by besting other companies with your product features, but by convincing a set of customers your vision is not a hallucination and solves a real problem they have or could be convinced they have. However, "who the users are" and the "definition of the market" itself are undefined and unknown. Here the key is to use your competitive brief to define a new market with your company in the center.

F. State Your Hypotheses: Competitive Hypotheses

Next, the Customer Development team assembles a competitive brief. Remember, if you are entering an existing market or resegmenting one, the basis of competition is all about some attribute(s) of your product. Therefore you need to know how and why your product is better than those of your competitors. This brief helps you focus on answering that question.

(If you are entering a new market, doing a competitive analysis is like dividing by zero; there are no direct competitors. Use the market map you developed in the last phase as a stand-in for a competitive hypothesis to answer the questions below as if each of the surrounding markets and companies will ultimately move into your new market.)

Take a look at the market you are going to enter and estimate how much market share the existing players have. Does any single entrant have 30 percent? Over 80 percent? These are magic numbers. When the share of the largest player in a market is around 30 percent or less, there is no single dominant company. You have a shot at entering this market. When one company owns over 80 percent share (think Microsoft), that player is the owner of the market and a monopolist. The only possible move you have is resegmenting this market. (See Chapter 5 for more details.)

- How have the existing competitors defined the basis of competition? Is it on product attributes? Service? What are their claims? Features? Why do you believe your company and product are different?
- Maybe your product allows customers to do something they could never do before. If you believe that, what makes you think customers will care? Is it because your product has better features? Better performance? A better channel? Better price?
- If this were a grocery store, which products would be shelved next to yours? These are your competitors. (Where would TiVo had been shelved, next to the VCRs or somewhere else?) Who are your closest competitors today? In features? In performance? In channel? In price? If there are no close competitors, who does the customer go to in order to get the equivalent of what you offer?
- What do you like most about each competitor's product? What do your customers like most about their products? If you could change one thing in a competitor's product, what would it be?
- In a company the questions might be: Who uses the competitors' products today, by title and by function? How do these competitive products get used? Describe the workflow/design flow for an end user. Describe how it affects the company. What percentage of their time is spent using the product? How mission critical is it? With a consumer product, the questions are similar but focus on an individual.
- Since your product may not yet exist, what do people do today without it? Do they simply not do something or do they do it badly?

A natural tendency of startups is to compare themselves to other startups around them. That's looking at the wrong problem. In the first few years, other startups do not put each other out of business. While it is true startups compete with each other for funding and technical resources, the difference between winning and losing startups is that winners understand why customers buy. The losers never do. Consequently, in the Customer Development model, a competitive analysis starts with why customers will buy your product. Then it expands into a broader look at the entire market, which includes competitors, both established companies and other startups.

This brief completes your first and last large-scale paperwork exercise. The action now moves outside the building, where you will start to understand what potential customers need and thereby qualify your initial assumptions.

Phase 2: Test And Qualify Your Hypotheses

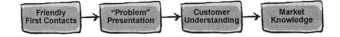

In this phase the Customer Development team begins to test and qualify the hypotheses assembled in Phase 1. I use the phrase "test and qualify assumptions," because very rarely do hypotheses survive customer feedback intact. You won't simply be validating your hypotheses—you'll be modifying them as a result of what you learn from customers. Since all you have inside the company are opinions—the facts are with your customers—the founding team leaves the building and comes back only when the hypotheses have turned into data. In doing so, you will acquire a deep understanding of how customers work and more importantly, how they buy. In this phase you will make or acquire:

- First customer contacts
- The customer problem presentation
- In-depth customer understanding
- Market knowledge

Since you have developed a complex series of hypotheses, trying to gather all the data on a first customer meeting would be ludicrous. Instead, your first set of customer meetings isn't to learn whether customers love your product. It's to learn whether your assumptions about the problems customers have are correct. If those assumptions are wrong, it doesn't matter how wonderful the product is; no one will buy it. Only after you gather sufficient data on your understanding of the customer do you return to customers to get feedback on the product itself, in Phase 3.

A. Test and Qualify Your Hypotheses: First Customer Contacts

The first step in qualifying assumptions is to leave the safe confines of your office and conference room and venture out to the real world where the people who will pay your bills live. Regardless of whether you are selling to large corporations or consumers at home, your friendly first contacts are the people who will start your education about customers and their problems. Better yet, they may become your customers.

Start by making a list of 50 potential customers you can test your ideas on. Fifty names sounds like a lot of leads, but as you'll soon see, you'll go through them quickly. Where do you get these names? From your social networks, friends, investors, founders, lawyers, recruiters, trade magazines, business reference books, accountants, and any other source you can think of. For these visits, even if you're selling to businesses your customers' titles and their level in their organization are irrelevant. And if you're selling to consumers, whether they currently have the slightest interest in your product is also inconsequential. What matters is what you want to learn from them. At this stage, you are less interested in big names and titles or the "exact right" consumers. You are interested in individuals who will give you some of their time and who you think even loosely fit the profile embedded in your customer hypotheses.

At the same time you're building a contact list, you begin to develop an innovators list. Innovators are the companies, departments in a company, or individuals in your field who are smart, well-respected and usually out in front of a subject. For consumer products, they may be the "gadget freak" everyone asks for advice or the group of people others look to spot a trend. You'll use this list two ways. First, you need to find and meet with the visionaries who are known to "get" new ideas. Some people view innovation as a dangerous virus that must be kept out of their companies. Others look forward to hearing about and understanding what's new. Those are the ones you'll talk to. Second, your innovators list will give you a great contact list for advisory board members and industry influencers.

Keep in mind the goal of this initial flurry of calling is not only to meet with people whose names you collect but also to use these customer contacts to network your way up "the food-chain of expertise." Always keep asking your contacts, "Who's the smartest person you know?" Remember, the ultimate goal in this Customer Discovery step is to make sure you understand the customers problem(s) and to ensure your product as spec'd solves that problem.

The first step in this phase is the hardest—contacting potential customers who don't know you and convincing them to give you some of their time. But this step gets a lot easier if you do two things: (1) get a referral and (2) carefully prepare a reference story that gets you in the door.

In a business, since secretaries exist to block your calls, you want to reference someone else, if possible: "Bob at BigBank Inc. said I should talk to you." Recall you got your list by asking everyone you know who they know. You reference the people who supply the leads. The best introduction to a prospect, when you can manage it, is through a peer within his or her company. A consumer product at times can be just as challenging—how do you get ahold of someone you don't know? Use the same technique—a reference from someone they know.

First, create an introductory email. Include a one-paragraph description of your company, a general description of what you are doing, and a statement of what's in it for your contact to spend time with you. No, you aren't going to send cold email; the people who gave you the leads are. Forward your email to them and ask them to send it on to the contact they gave you.

Then follow up with a phone call. Before you pick up the phone and talk to someone you don't know, it's a good idea to know what you want to say. What you don't want to say is, "Hi this is Bob at NewBankingProduct Inc., and I'd like to tell you about our new product." (Well, if you are a passionate founder that is exactly what you want to say, but restrain yourself.) Instead create a reference story that explains why you are calling. This story emphasizes the problems you are trying to solve, why it's important to solve them, and the solution you are building.

Start with an introduction: "Hi this is Bob at NewBankingProduct Inc., and as you remember I was referred to you by [insert helpful reference name here]." Now give them a reason to see you: "We are starting a company to solve the long teller line problem, and we are building our new Instanteller software, but I don't want to sell you anything. I just want twenty minutes of your time to understand how you and your company solve your own teller problem." What's in it for your contact? "I thought you might give me some insight about this problem, and in exchange I'll be happy to tell you where the technology in this industry is going." Exhale.

Obviously, you will need to vary and tweak the story, but the goal remains the same: Get meetings scheduled. This may sound easy on paper, but if you are not a professional salesperson, it can be very hard. I hated calling people I didn't know. I would stare at the phone, walk around it, pick it up, and put it down without calling. But eventually I placed the calls. And you know what? There is nothing more satisfying than a potential customer saying, "Why, yes, that's exactly the problem we have. I can spare twenty minutes to chat—why don't you come in Tuesday." Yes!

To make this work, you and your co-founders need to make 10 (yes, 10) phone calls a day. Keep calling until you have your schedule booked with three customer visits a day. Get used to being turned down, but always ask, "If you're too busy, who should I talk to?" It's helpful to keep hit-rate statistics (were any reference stories better than others, were any lead source better, were you more successful calling on managers, directors, vice presidents?) And by the way, while this works for calling on companies, the same holds true for consumer products.

As a rule of thumb, your 50 follow-up phone calls should yield five-10 scheduled visits. You will use these visits to test your customer/problem hypotheses—who your customers are and why they will use your product. These visits are a first step toward achieving a deep understanding of how customers work, their problems, their organization, and how they fit in their company. Before you go out to visit customers, though, carefully plan how you're going to break the ice and elicit the information you need. The place to start is with the development of what I call a "problem presentation."

B. Test and Qualify Your Hypotheses: The Customer Problem Presentation

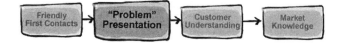

In Phase 1, you came up with hypotheses about what problems your customers have. In our corporate example for banking it was long teller lines. Now based on those hypotheses, develop a presentation about this problem and test it in an ongoing dialog with customers.

In contrast to a product presentation, a problem presentation isn't designed to convince customers. Instead, you develop it to elicit information from customers. The presentation summarizes your hypotheses about customers' problems, along with some potential solutions, so you can test whether your assumptions are correct. This presentation is your icebreaker when you meet customers.

Developing a problem presentation is easy. You have already done the hard work of articulating the customer problems and some solutions, including your own, in Phase 1. Now put these assumptions into slides. For a corporate presentation, consider a simple one-slide presentation. In this slide (see Figure 3.8) the list of the problems as you understand them go in column 1, today's solution to the problems in column 2, and your company's solution in column 3. (In meetings with consumers where slides are inappropriate, a simple flip chart presentation will do.)

List of Problems	Today's Solution	New Solution
1.	1.	1.
2.	2.	2.
3.	3.	3.

Customer Problem Presentation (Figure 3.8)

When you have the slide done, be prepared to present it using a whiteboard, or simply one-on-one across a table. Remember, though, "presenting" in this context really means inviting the customers' responses. So, after describing your assumed list of problems in column 1, pause and ask the customers what they think the problems are, whether you are missing any problems, and how they would rank-order the problems.

What if a customer tells you the issues you thought were important really aren't? Realize you've just obtained great data. While it may not be what you wanted to hear, it's wonderful to have that knowledge early on. Do not—I repeat, do not—try to "convince" customers they really have the problems you describe. They are the ones with the checkbooks, and you want them to convince you.

If they agree with you about the problems, get them to explain why they think it is important to solve them (there is nothing better than playing validated customer needs back to them). Casually ask, "How much does this problem cost you (in terms of lost revenue, lost customers, lost time, frustration, etc.) today? You'll use this number later in the Customer Validation step when you develop an ROI presentation.

With agreement on the problems and their cost, you can display column 2, the solutions available today. Again pause, ask the customers what they think the solutions to the problem are, whether you are missing any, and how they would rank-order the viability of the existing solutions. What you are looking for is an understanding of how customers solve this problem today, or how they think others solve it (for example, more tellers, faster software, bigger server). If the problem is painful or important enough, you will usually get a set of interesting answers. While you're at it, another critical piece of information is, who shares these problems? In our corporate banking example, is it other branch banks? Other consumers who do x or y? Other people in the same company? Others in an industry? Others with the same title? A set of people with common problems equals a common value proposition. This means you can describe the value of your product in a message understood across a broad audience.

When RoboVac, a consumer products company, was researching a robot vacuum for the home, the results of their problem presentations to customers surprised them. They initially thought their robot was going to be used as a simple replacement for vacuuming. As they talked with more and more potential customers, those who got most excited were not the ones who vacuumed their floors on a regular basis. In fact, they were the opposite—they were single men who barely knew where their vacuum was and would buy a robot vacuum for the novelty, the technology and the "leave and forget it" nature of its use. RoboVac's earlyvangelists wanted to leave their vacuum running, and come home and find a completely clean floor. For some earlyvangelists the connection was even stronger. Some treated the RoboVac like it was a family pet. Some scientists believe that robot pets trigger a hard-wired nurturing response in humans. It appears robot vacuums tap into the same instincts. The point is no discussion around the conference room table would have discovered these responses.

Finally, for both corporate and consumer products, display your company's solution (not a set of features, but only the big idea) in column 3. Pause and watch the customers' reactions. Do they understand what the words mean? Is the solution evident enough that they say, "Aha, if you could do that, all my problems would be solved?" Alternatively, do they say, "What do you mean?" Then do they have to listen to you explain for 20 minutes and still not understand? Ask how your solution compares to the current solutions you just discussed. Once again, the point is not to give a sales pitch. You want their reaction, and a discussion.

My favorite summary of this discussion is to ask two questions I alluded to earlier: "What is the biggest pain in how you work (or in RoboVac's case—how you clean)? If you could wave a magic wand and change anything in what you do, what would it be?" I call these the "IPO questions." Understand the answers to these questions and your startup is going public.

Of course, what you learn from these discussions depends on what sticks with you when you walk out the door. After you meet with a series of customers, their responses tend to blur together. Therefore, it's helpful to take your hypothesis briefs with you when you make these visits. Look at all the information you want to gather. Then, before each call, shorten the list to "What are the three things I need to learn before I leave?" Make sure you get at least those three questions covered. Over time, as you get confirmation on the key issues, begin to ask different questions.

The problem presentation facilitates the collection of the critical information you need early on—why customers buy and what they would buy. However, it's not the entire purpose of your first meetings with customers. You want to probe deeply in order to understand customers' needs.

C. Test and Qualify Your Hypotheses: In-Depth Customer Understanding

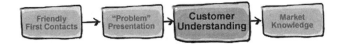

In addition to checking your assumptions about customer problems and your solution, you need to validate your hypotheses concerning how customers spend their day, spend their money and get their jobs done. Regardless of whether it's an esoteric product for corporate customers, or a new type of lifestyle product for consumers, you want to understand in detail how their life/job works and how the workflow/design flow happens. If they are in a company, is their job done in isolation? If not, how do they interact with other departments? What other products do they use? Is the problem they've identified limited to them, or do others in the company share it? Is it possible to quantify the impact (dollars, time, costs, etc.) across the entire organization? The same questions work for consumers. Will they use the product themselves? Does it depend on their friends and family using it?

You also want to check your assumptions about whether people will pay for your solution. What would make customers change the current way they do things? Price? Features? A new standard? In our banking example, would bank tellers change their behavior if they had a portable device they could use to walk up and down the line of waiting customers and service them before they got to the teller window?

If your customers' eyes haven't glazed over yet, dip your toe into the hypothetical product spec. "If you had a product like this [describe yours in conceptual terms], what percentage of your time could be spent using the product? How mission critical is it? Would it solve the pain you mentioned earlier? What would be the barriers to adopting a product like this?"

Since some day you are going to have to create demand to reach these customers, use this opportunity to find out how they learn about new products. Who are the visionaries in the press/analyst community they read? That they respect?

Finally, you never want to pass up an opportunity to spot talent. Can these customers be helpful in the future? For the next round of conversations? For an advisory board? As a paying customer? To refer you to others?

Your goal, after enough of these customer conversations, is to be able to stand up in front of your company and say, "Here were our hypotheses about our customers, their problems, and how they worked. Now here's what they are saying their issues really are, and this is how they really spend their day."

I've said that your goal is to understand the customer in depth. What do I mean by "in depth?" I don't mean you know their jobs as well as they do. How could you? I mean being so thoroughly conversant with what truly matters to them that you can discuss their issues convincingly.

Here's an example: I once worked in a startup building a new type of supercomputer. One of the markets we had picked was the arcane field of production geology. Since I knew nothing about the field, I realized before I could even hire a domain expert to manage this market, I needed to get educated in depth. I traveled to all the petroleum geology trade shows and conferences, I spoke to customer after customer to understand their needs. I spent days in the Houston petroleum engineering library. Just when I thought I knew enough to fake it as a technical expert in this area, I convinced Chevron's La Habra research center to allow me to offer their research group a two-hour course on the use of graphics supercomputers in petroleum applications. I promised it wouldn't be a sales pitch, just an update on what advances were occurring in computing that were relevant to petroleum geologists. In front of an audience of 30 or so, I spoke about the state of the art in computational reservoir simulation and what could be accomplished on the new class of machines that were coming from companies like ours.

During the question-and-answer session my heart was in my throat, since my depth of knowledge, like any good marketer, was no more than one level away from being a complete idiot. At the end of the talk, the head of the research facility approached me and said, "That was a great presentation. We're glad your company hired real petroleum engineers to come speak to us. We hate it when the sales and marketing types show up and try to get us to buy something." For one of the few times in my life I was at a loss for words, and I was completely unprepared for what came next. "Here's my card. If you ever want to consider a career in Chevron research, we'd be happy to talk to you." That's what I mean by understanding your potential customers and problems in sufficient depth.

D. Test and Qualify Your Hypotheses: Market Knowledge

Now that you have a good understanding of the customer and their problem you want to round out your understanding of the overall marketplace. You need to meet with companies in adjacent markets, industry analysts, people in the press, and other key influencers. Going to industry trade shows and conferences is also key to help you understand the shape and direction of the market you are in or about to create.

When I start a company, I buy a lot of lunches. I typically have some vague notion of what companies are in adjacent markets or are part of the infrastructure or ecosystem of my business. Through my own contacts, and through introductions, I take my peers out to lunch. In exchange, I want information—not competitive information, but answers to questions such as: What are the industry trends? What are key unresolved customer needs? Who are the key players in this market? What should I read? Who should I know? What should I ask? What customers should I call on?

Why will these people meet with you? Most won't out of the goodness of their hearts; they will meet because you will offer a trade. In exchange for information, you will share a little about the problem you are solving and the product that will solve it.

Just as you did with your problem presentation to potential customers, don't present, don't sell; just listen and learn. Spend the time to take a few of the friendliest customers to lunch and ask them who they see as potential competitors, both internally and externally. Who do they think has similar products? Who else is an innovator in this space? Has this solution been tried elsewhere in their company? Is anyone else inside their company trying to build this product? It's amazing how much you can learn from the people who eventually will buy your product.

Ask the same questions of peers in adjacent markets. After practicing on them, try to make contact with the key industry influencers and recommenders you listed in Phase 1. Ask them the same set of questions.

Next, start gathering quantitative data about your market. More than likely Wall Street analysts issue reports on your market or adjacent markets. Get copies of all these reports. More important, read them. You need to understand what the analysts believe are the trends, the players, business models, and key metrics.

Finally, industry conferences and trade shows are invaluable and essential. Never say, "I'm too busy to attend." Attend at least two key conferences or tradeshows (you picked the important ones in Phase 1). Not only will you get to take home some great trinkets for your kids, but conferences and trade shows are prime areas for talent-spotting and trend-spotting. Ask your usual questions about trends and players, but this time you want to accomplish a few things you can't anywhere else. You want to get demos of competitive and adjacent products. You want to get your hands on them, get competitors' literature, talk to their salespeople, and generally immerse yourself in the business you are entering. Attend as many conference sessions as you can, listening to others describe their products. What are their visions of the future, and how do they compare with yours?

Phase 3: Test And Qualify The Product Concept

The previous phase, Test and Qualify Assumptions, tested your hypothesis briefs about customer problems while making sure you had a complete understanding of their needs. In Phase 3 you move to testing the product hypotheses on potential customers in your potential market—once again, not to sell them, but to get their feedback. This phase has five parts:

- Meet with Product Development for a reality check
- Create the product presentation
- Make more customer visits
- Meet with Product Development for a second reality check
- Identify first advisory board members

A. Test and Qualify the Product Concept: First Company Reality Check

Now that you have a deeper understanding of customers and their problems, it's time to come back to the company for a reality check. To start this phase, gather as much of the company management as you can (not just the VPs but directors and managers) for your Product/Customer Development synchronization meeting. (You had the first of these meetings in Phase 1 when you put together your product hypotheses.) In the reality check the Customer Development team shares what was learned in the field and reviews customer feedback on the assumptions made in Phase 1. Then the Customer Development and Product teams jointly adjust their assumptions, product spec's, or both.

Before the meeting, the Customer Development team gathers all the customer data and builds a workflow map of the prototypical customer. At the meeting, the spokesperson for the team diagrams and describes how customers do their jobs and who they interact with. This is your reality check on your customer hypotheses. Keep diagramming and drawing until you can explain how customers' businesses and lives work today, including how they spend their time and money. Compare this description to your initial hypotheses. (While corporate customers may have a more formal organization to diagram, a consumer will have more external influencers to track.)

Once the customer workflow and interactions are fully described, you can get into the real news. What problems did customers say they have? How painful were these problems? Where on the "problem scale" were the customers you interviewed? How are they solving these problems today? Draw the customer workflow with and without your product. Was the difference dramatic? Did customers say they would pay for that difference? In general, what did you learn about customers' problems? What were the biggest surprises? What were the biggest disappointments?

Once the Customer Development team has presented its findings, the fun begins. You can now ask the most difficult question, "Do we have product/market fit?" Given all you have learned talking to customers, how well do your preliminary product specs solve their problems? Dead on? Somewhat? Not exactly? If the answer is somewhat or not exactly, this meeting becomes a painful, soul-searching, company-building exercise. Is it because you haven't talked to the right people? To enough people? Because you haven't asked the right questions? This assessment is critical because of a fundamental assumption of the Customer Development model: Before changing the product, you need to keep looking for a market where it might fit. If, and only if, you cannot find any market for the product do you discuss changing the feature list.

This rigor of no new features until you've exhausted the search of market space counters a natural tendency of people who talk to customers: You tend to collect a list of features that if added, will get one additional customer to buy. Soon you have a 10-page feature list just to sell 10 customers. The goal is to have a single paragraph feature list that can sell to thousands of customers.

What do you do if you believe you are talking to the right customers but their feedback tells you you're building the wrong product? Something has to change. Don't continue building the product and think miracles will happen. Either get back outside the building and find a different set of customers who will buy the product or consider changing the features or how the product is configured.

Assuming your product is at least a partial fit for customers' problems, continue examining your product assumptions and specs. Based on customer feedback, review the Phase 1 feature list. Prioritize the features in terms of importance to the customer. Can the Customer Development team match each feature to a customer problem? If not, why not? While figuring out what features to ship is important, knowing which features don't matter is equally important. Which features did customers not care about? Can any features on the product spec be deleted or deferred? Remember, in a startup the Customer Development team is not supposed to add features; it is supposed to find out the minimum feature set for the first release, based on input from visionary customers.

Next, review and get agreement on the delivery schedule, again revising your Phase 1 assumptions as necessary. As I noted earlier, visionary customers, particularly in corporations, will be buying into your entire vision, not just your first product release. They will need to hear what your company plans to deliver over the next 18 months. The agreement between the Product and Customer Development groups must be that:

- All features past the first version are up for grabs
- Features spec'd in the first release are subject to change/deletion to get the product out;
- Product Development will provide a one-page 18-month or 3-release product schedule
- Finally, as a group, review your other phase 1 hypotheses. (Now you can see why you took the trouble to write them down.) Given all the feedback from customers, which of the four Market Types are you in? Why are you different? What will be your basis for competing? Do your pricing and delivery channel assumptions hold up? What did you learn about influencers?

B. Test and Qualify the Product Concept: Product Presentation

Once your Product and Customer Development teams agree on your revised assumptions, the next step is to assemble your first product presentation. This product presentation is emphatically not the presentation the company used for fundraising or recruiting. Nor is it the problem presentation you used when you visited customers in

Phase 2. Toss those slides out and start over. The goal of this presentation is to test your revised assumptions about the product itself. This goal has two parts: To reconfirm your product will solve a serious customer problem and to validate your product and its features.

Along the way, you will further test your understanding of customers' pain, their workflow, and the organizational impact of your product. Accordingly, develop a solution-oriented presentation that describes the product in terms of solving the customer's problem. If it's too early for a real product demo, the product presentation should cover the five (no more!) key product features. Include a story about "life before your product" and "life after your product." Draw the customer' workflow or consumer's day with and without your product. Leave out all the marketing, positioning and fluff. Finally, detail the future of the product at least 18 months out, broken down into features by release.

As before, rehearse how you will give this presentation to customers. Keep in mind you are still not selling in this phase. Instead, you are trying to discover whether you have a salable product. You are gathering enough information so when you do try to sell something, you will be confident there is a group of customers who will buy.

C. Test and Qualify the Product Concept: Yet More Customer Visits

When your product presentation is ready, decide which customers you will visit. Ideally, you'll give this presentation to everyone who heard your first presentation on the "problem" (at least those who are willing to see you again). In addition, your earlier visits should have netted you more names to call on. Accordingly, expand your original set of customer contacts to include a second set with at least five new potential customers for enterprise software, (for consumer products this might mean 50 customers). These new contacts allow you to keep the momentum going and start laying the groundwork for actually selling something in Step 2.

Just as in Phase 1, to get enough visits, make a list of 50 potential customers. However, in this phase you want to test your assumptions about the titles of the people who will make the purchasing decision. In our banking example, they would include bank CIOs and vice presidents of branch operations. Try to target the appropriate titles and roles as if you were selling. Once you have your list, create an introductory email, reference story, and sales script as you did before.

Now get out of the building and talk to customers. You will get more information if you start by reminding your audience what problem your product is designed to solve. Describe why your company believes it is important to solve this problem. Pause here and see if you get agreement on the value of solving the problem. You should, since your presentation is based on what you've already learned from customers about their issues. With any luck, no surprises will pop up but if they do, go back to Phase 2.

With agreement on the problem and its significance, you finally get to describe the product (you've probably wanted to do this since day one, so you should be ready by now). Demonstrate the product if you can; even a prototype of a key concept can help a customer understand your solution. Pause here to gauge the customer's reaction.

Next, draw the customer workflow with and without your product. Pause again to see if you get agreement on the "before and after" workflow. Describe who else in the customer's organization you believe your solution might affect. Listen here and see if you get agreement.

The whole product presentation should take no more than 20 minutes. Now it's time to listen. What are the customers' first reactions? Does your product solve a painful problem for them? Would the customers buy a product to solve this problem? Do they believe others in their company feel the same? How about in other companies?

Ask about the features you've described. Do they match the customers' needs? What features must you have on day one? What features could wait until later? What features are simply missing? What is a "complete product" in the customer's mind? What other features are needed to move the product into the mainstream? Are third-party products or services needed to make your offering a mainstream product?

Since your company will be spending a ton of money and lots of time trying to figure out how to position your product, why not ask these customers what they think? After hearing your product description, how do they think your product is different? Do they think you are creating a new market? Or do they think the product is a better version of an existing product (and, if so, better in what way)? Or do they shrug and say, "It's somewhere in the middle, comparable to others, but it doesn't change the rules of the game"?

Check your other hypotheses. What do customers think about your pricing? What do they think are comparable prices for this kind of product?

When I found visionary customers who were truly interested in our products at E.piphany, an enterprise software company, I would ask several questions to test the pricing boundaries. They included the IPO questions I mentioned earlier, the first of which was, "Would you deploy our software enterprise-wide if it were free?" I used this question to test the seriousness of a potential customer. If the customer wasn't ready to deploy the software even if it was free, then I was talking to the wrong person. When I found customers who would go through visualizing the pain of actually rolling out our product, I would ask them how they would deploy it, how many users would use it, what groups would get if first, what criteria would they use to measure its success, and so on. By the end of this visualization exercise I had potential customers who had mentally installed and deployed our software. Then I asked, "Would you pay $1 million for our software?" The answer was usually instructive. Suppose customers said, "Steve, we couldn't see paying more than $250,000 for the first set of applications." In their minds they had already bought the product and now the bill just came due. The first number out of their mouths usually was what they had in their immediate budget and would be the first purchase price. Once I got a first number, I always asked, "How much more would you expect to pay for professional services (the customization and installation)?" Most of the time they would say that cost was included in their budget number, but every once in a while someone would add more dollars. If they were still interested in brainstorming, I would push and see whether they would spend those dollars every year on our software. Then I would ask, "What would we have to do to get you to spend twice that? Three times that?"

After a few of these customer exercises I understood the average selling price of E.piphany software could be $250,000 and the lifetime value of a customer could be close to a million dollars. (I arbitrarily set a customer "lifetime" as three years.)

OK, you've talked about pricing. Now, what about distribution? Test your assumptions by asking customers what channel they would most likely use to buy your product. Retail store? From the Web? Direct sales?

From there, ask customers how you would reach them via marketing: "If you were interested in a product like this, how would you find out about it? How do you find out about other new products like this? Do you ask others for their opinions before buying? If so, who? Do you or your staff go to trade shows? What industry-specific magazines or journals do you read? What business publications?" If it's a consumer product, what general interest publications, newspapers, and websites would best connect with them?

Next, probe the customer's product acquisition process. If a corporate product, try to understand how a purchase order is approved in their company: "Let's assume for a minute I built a product you really wanted to buy. How does your company buy products like this? Could you walk me through the approval cycle? Exactly who is involved?" If it's a consumer product, understand the buying process. Is this an impulse buy? Do they buy only known brands? Items advertised on TV?

Be sure to get to the "who has the money" question. There's nothing more frustrating than having a series of great customer meetings for months only to find out way late in the sales cycle that no department wants to cough up the dough for a product. Ask questions like "By the way, is there a current budget for a product like this? Which department or individual would have the budget for this product?" The information you get will be critical as you put together a sales roadmap.

On your way out the door, take another look at the customers you just met with. Are they candidates for a customer advisory board? Could you learn much more from them? Do they have great industry connections or insight? If so, ask them if you can follow up with some questions later on.

Of course, it's optimistic to expect your first customers to share all of this with you on your first product presentation. However, try to get answers to every one of these questions over the course of all your visits. Leaving this phase means you not only understand customers' problem in depth but have a solid grip on their level of interest in your product.

If you believe you will be using any form of indirect sales channel, there is one more group you need to present the product to before you get to go home: your channel partners. Earlier, in Phase 1, you hypothesized a distribution channel for your product. While it's too early to sign up channel partners with formal commitments, you want to meet them and understand what it would take to get an order. What do your channel partners need to hear or see from early customers? What do they have to have before they will give you access to their channel, and then volume orders? Is it articles in the business press, product reviews, and customers calling and asking for the product? Or is it financial inducements such as shelf-stocking fees or a guaranteed returns policy? Note that channel partners won't magically know how to position or price your products. For products in an existing market, it's easy to tell them, "It's like that other one you sell, but faster." For resegmented and new markets, indirect channels have a harder time understanding how to position your product. Make sure you spend the time helping them.

To make progress, you need to be sure you understand their business model. Why? There is no way you can understand how much product your channel partners should order or how much they should charge you and your customer unless you understand how the money flow works. A good way to understand how you might work with these partners is to see how other companies do. Are there other companies similar to yours? If so, it's time to have lunch again. Take other executives to lunch and ask about margins and discounts. The worst that could happen is that they won't tell you.

Keeping all this in mind, assemble a channel/service partner presentation with your business concept and what's in it for your partners. Then hit the street and present to them. Your goal is to start a dialog and learn about their business. How do companies like yours establish a relationship with them? How do they hear their customers asking for a product like yours? How does your potential partner make money? (By project? By hour? By reselling software? By profit on reselling?) How does their business model compare to others in their business? What is the minimum dollar size of a transaction interesting to them? The goal is to understand your channel partner's business model well enough to draw it on a whiteboard.

D. Test and Qualify the Product Concept: Second Company Reality Check

With your latest customer feedback in hand, it's time to come back to the company for another reality check, this time on the product. This is your third Product Development/ Customer Development synchronization meeting (the first occurred in Phase 1a, the second in Phase 2a.) You'll be discussing what Customer Development has learned about the product's features, pricing and distribution, once again testing your assumptions and revisiting your product spec.

Now that you have tested the product in front of customers, you can probably sort the reactions into four main categories:

- The customers unequivocally love our product; no changes are needed
- Customers like our product, but we've heard consistently they want this or that additional feature at first customer ship

- The customers can understand our product after a long explanation, but no one was jumping over the table to get us to sell it to them
- The customers don't see a need for our product

In this reality check meeting, the Customer and Product Development teams need to balance customer reactions with development time. The goal of Customer Discovery was to find a market for the product as spec'd. If most of the customers fall into category one, congratulations! You can move on to the next phase. However, that rarely happens the first time around in Customer Discovery.

The most dangerous customer responses are those in category two: "We need more features." As I have emphasized, knowing which features do not matter is just as important as knowing what features to ship the first time around. Why? Because the joke, "Normal people believe if it ain't broke, don't fix it. Engineers believe if it ain't broke, it doesn't have enough features yet," is true. The natural instinct of Engineering is to keep adding more.

Spend time "unpacking" the customer responses in this category. As a startup, your goal and battle cry should be "fast to market." Fast to market simply means getting your first release in the hands of paying customers as quickly as you can. The teams should constantly remind themselves the first release is not the ultimate product. A series of compromises is necessary to get the product in the hands of earlyvangelists. Accordingly, ask yourselves whether any of the requested features can be deferred (are they "nice to have" or "must-have" for your visionary customers only?). Once your first release ships, you are going to listen carefully to those visionary customers to find out what features and key pieces of functionality to add to your next release. If you keep listening to the right customers carefully, you will end up executing a successful product strategy.

This fast-to-market strategy is distinctly different from a first-to-market strategy. First-to-market emphasizes competing with other startups to win market share quickly by low price, discounting, and the liberal use of marketing dollars in establishing a brand. Its key theme, whether explicit or not, is "get customers at any price." In contrast, fast-to-market says if a new market is large, whoever wins the first few sales is not going to matter. What matters is learning how to make money from day one.

Answers in categories three and four—customers aren't jumping over the table, or don't see a need for your product—are typical during a first round of Customer Discovery. However for technology products, they can be indicative of a profound problem, sometimes referred to as positioning, but more accurately described as "technology packaging." Technology packaging is a pitfall most technology startups have to deal with at some point in their lives. A technology-driven startup's first product is usually determined by the founding Product Development team. There is not much research about how the features and functionality get put together. The thought, if any goes into it, usually is to hand the product to Sales and Marketing saying, "Hey, here's what we are building, go write the datasheets, price it, and go sell it." Sometimes this works. Sometimes the Product Development team has a perfect feel for what the customer needs are and how the customers want to buy the product. Most of the time they don't. Most of the time, the product as initially configured by Product Development needs further refinement by the Customer Development team. While the core technology might be spot-on, its match for customer needs and how customers want to buy can be off. Imagine the product as delivered to Customer Development was a single monolithic software package. It may be too expensive or too complex to sell that way. Technology repackaging would look at the problem and say, "Perhaps it can be sold as modules, or as a subscription service, or some other permutation, without requiring Product Development to completely reengineer the product." If this problem is not caught and dealt with in Customer Discovery, it will continue to grow until it affects your company's ability to survive as a viable enterprise.

Our story at the beginning of this chapter about Steve Powell at FastOffice illustrates this point. The core technology he had designed was a data communications chip and software that offered voiceover data communications lines. It was Steve's idea to wrap an entire office system around this unique invention. As Steve said later, "I thought it would be cool if I could have one of these systems for myself. So I thought I understood the customer's problem." Unfortunately, few other customers thought so. In hindsight, there were alternate ways the chip could have been used: sold to other office systems manufacturers' as part of their product, sold to data communications companies, etc. If Steve had spent the time thinking about those up front, or at least after he received customer feedback, FastOffice would still be in business.

E. Test and Qualify the Product Concept: First Advisory Board Members

As good as your founding team is, there are invaluable people outside your company you can't hire as full-time employees, but who will be willing to help in an advisory capacity. These advisors can help solve technical problems, introduce you to key customers, provide you with domain-specific knowledge, and share business expertise and wisdom. Early in Customer Discovery, as you began to meet customers and analysts, you began to think about who might fit on an advisory board. Your Product Development team should engage some advisors for specific help designing and building the product, and you may want to find a business mentor, someone who has been through the startup grind before. And as you begin to talk to customers, you'll realize that out of the morass of meetings you've been having, one or two voices stood out from the crowd. In this phase, you informally engage these people by asking them for advice, taking them to lunch and seeing if they are interested in helping you and your company. Later, in Customer Validation, you'll formalize the advisory board process.

Phase 4: Verify

After your second reality check, you have completed a substantial part of the Customer Discovery step. What you have been doing for the company is discovering whether your product and customer hypotheses were correct. What you have been doing for your investors is starting to validate your business model.

Now, in Phase 4, you summarize your findings by verifying what you've found about the problem and product, and spend time thinking about whether the business model still makes financial sense if you operate it under the conditions you have discovered thus far. So, in this phase, you do four things:

- Verify the problem
- Verify the product solution
- Verify the business model
- Assess whether to iterate or exit

A. Verify the Problem

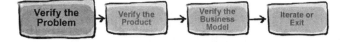

By now, you have talked to at least 10 or 20 customers, more if you have traveled the Customer Discovery loop more than once. "Verifying the problem" simply means summarizing everything you have learned and checking to see whether you have the problem nailed or need to go around the loop again.

Review the answers you've obtained on all the dimensions of your customer problem hypotheses. Capture them in a Problem Statement document. Make the statement clear, concise, and precise. Be sure to ask the hard question: Are you confident you've nailed a customer problem people will pay you to solve? If yes, proceed. If not, go around the loop again.

B. Verify the Product

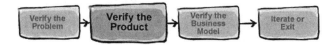

"Verifying the product solution" means summarizing everything you've learned about your product hypotheses. The short test for exiting Customer Discovery is to gather your executive team in a conference room. Raise your left hand and in a loud voice yell out the top three customer problems. Then raise your right hand and yell out the top three product features. Look at the faces of your team and see if the shock of the two hands not matching is evident. If so, and you lack product/market fit, and need to get back in front of customers; if not, go to the next step.

Of course, there's more to it than that. Review all the questions you have been asking customers about the product and the conclusions you have drawn about first-release features, subsequent features, pricing, distribution channel, and so on. Be sure to address questions like these: Given the customer feedback to date, do your current product plans meet the needs of the market? Do you want to emphasize different features? If you reconfigured or repackaged the product, do you think you would get a different customer reaction? Should you consider doing so? Capture what you've learned concisely in an Expanded Product Requirement document. This is your latest, greatest vision for your product (for now).

C. Verify the Business Model

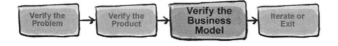

If you have gotten this far, you're probably feeling pretty cocky. You understand the customer's problem, you believe you've nailed the product features, and the resulting vision matches significant customer needs. However, there is the small matter of making money. When you originally put together your business plan, that wonderful multipage spreadsheet you gave your investors was your financial hypothesis. Now you get to rerun that financial model based on customer feedback and test how real your business model is.

The outcome of this testing process consists of two documents: an updated sales and revenue plan, and a sound business and product plan. Without trying to be exhaustive, here are some of the key issues to address as you prepare these documents:

- Is the projected selling price (taking into account what customers will pay) different from your initial business plan assumptions? Over the next three years, how many units will a customer buy? What do you believe the lifetime value of each customer will be?

- How will you sell the product to your customer? What will the cost of the distribution channel be? Are there new costs you had not originally planned on? What about your initial view of the sales cycle: Will a sale take more or less time than you originally planned?

- Does the product require any third-party installation, configuration, or technical support? How much will this cost you per customer? How much direct support will you need to provide? Was this service model accurately built into your business plan?

- Based on what you've learned from customers, what is the acquisition model? How will customers know about and ask for your product? How much will it cost to acquire each customer? How does that number compare to the original business plan?

- What is the market size? If you are creating a new market, what is the size of the closest adjacent markets? Can you be that large? Larger? If you are expanding an existing market, what is the size of the current market? Is the market still large enough for your revenue projections?

- Now that the Product Development team has a better understanding of customer needs, are the Product Development costs still the same? How much will it cost you to develop the first version? How much will it cost to implement the complete vision of the product?
- Is there any manufacturing involved in building the product? How much will the product cost to produce? How does the cost compare to your original plan? What manufacturing partners will you use?
- When you add up all the components of the business model, is it profitable enough for your needs?

D. Iterate or Exit

This is either the beginning of the end or, more likely, the end of the beginning. You have put a stake in the ground with a series of hypotheses, you've gone out and tested assumptions, potential customers have validated your product, and you have a base of potential visionary sales prospects. And you've captured all your learning in writing.

Now it's time to honestly assess if your modified hypotheses provide a sound foundation for moving forward.

- Have we identified a problem a customer wants solved?
- Does our product solve these customer needs?
- If so, do we have a viable and profitable business model?
- Can we draw a day in the life of our customer before and after purchase of our product?
- Can we create an organizational chart of users, buyers and channels?

Exhausting as the Customer Discovery process is, you may need to iterate it multiple times. Do you understand the market and have customers who cannot wait to buy? If not, take everything you learned in Phases 1 through 3, modify your presentations based on feedback, go back to Phase 1 and do it again. Try out several markets and users. Do you need to reconfigure or repackage the product offering? If so, modify your product presentations and go back to Phase 3 (product presentation) and do it again.

If you are ready to move to the next step, hold on to all the information you have collected from your customer interviews. You will find it is essential to help you move through the phases of Customer Validation, where you actually sell the product as the basis for developing a sales roadmap for the company.

I've spent quite a few pages on Customer Discovery because it is the foundation of everything you do in Customer Development. The summary chart on the next page recaps the phases of this step, the goals of each phase, and the deliverables that prove you've met the goals.

CUSTOMER DISCOVERY SUMMARY

Phase	Goals	Deliverables
0. Get Buy-in	Investors/founders agree on customer development, key hires and values.	Buy-in, Core Values
1. State Hypothesis	Set product specs, develop detailed hypotheses of product, first customers, channels and pricing, demand, market and competition.	Hypothesis Briefs
A. Product Hypothesis	Get agreement on product features, benefits, and release schedules.	Product Brief
B. Customer Hypotheses	Describe customers, their problems, and why they will use the product.	Customer Brief
C. Channel & Pricing Hypothesis	Develop a channel strategy and pricing model.	Channel & Brief Pricing
D. Demand Creation Hypothesis	Identify demand creation strategy, influencers, and trends.	Demand Creation Brief
E. Market Type Hypothesis	Describe what market you are in (new, existing, resegmented).	Market Type Brief
F. Competitive Hypothesis	Develop competitive analysis that fits your market type.	Competitive Brief
2. Treat & Qualify Hypotheses	Test hypotheses from phase 1. Understand customers' "day in the life"	Validate
A. First Customer Contacts	Create customer list and schedule the first customer contacts.	Customer List
B. Problem Presentation	Develop presentation of problems, current solutions, product solution.	Problem Presentation
C. In-Depth Customer Understanding	Understand how customers work, their problems and who else influences their decisions.	Customer Brief
D. Market Knowledge	Understand the market: meet with analysts and media, trade shows, research.	Positioning Brief
3. Test & Qualify Product Concept	Test product concept. Do customers' needs match the product?	Hypotheses
A. First Reality Check	Review customer/product feedback and test Phase 1 customer problem assumptions.	Revise Product Customer Briefs
B. Product Presentation	Create product presentation on how product solves customers' problems.	Product Presentation
C. More Customer Visits	Expand customer list to include five new potential customers.	Customer List
D. Second Reality Check	Review product feature feedback and test.	Updated Feature List
E. First Advisory Board Members	Spot and recruit first advisory board members.	Advisors on Board
4. Verify	Found the right market? Have a profitable business?	Validate
A. Problem Verification	Verify that you have identified a problem that a customer wants solved.	Problem Statement
B. Product Verification	Verify that the product solves customers' needs and its ROI.	Product Rqts Doc
C. Business Model Verification	Verify that you have a profitable business model.	Updated Revenue/Sales Plan
D. Iterate or Exit	Decide whether you have learned enough to go sell.	Business/Product Plan

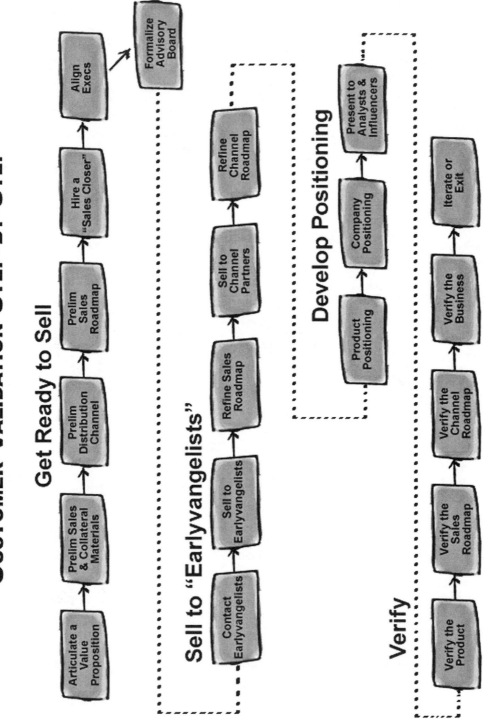

Customer Validation Step-by-Step

Get Ready to Sell

Articulate a Value Proposition → Prelim Sales & Collateral Materials → Prelim Distribution Channel → Prelim Sales Roadmap → Hire a "Sales Closer" → Align Execs → Formalize Advisory Board

Sell to "Earlyvangelists"

Contact Earlyvangelists → Sell to Earlyvangelists → Refine Sales Roadmap → Sell to Channel Partners → Refine Channel Roadmap

Develop Positioning

Product Positioning → Company Positioning → Present to Analysts & Influencers

Verify

Verify the Product → Verify the Sales Roadmap → Verify the Channel Roadmap → Verify the Business → Iterate or Exit

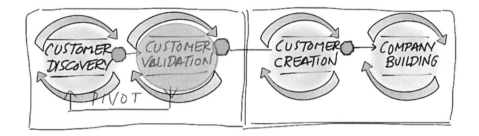

CHAPTER 4

Customer Validation

Along the journey we commonly forget its goal.
— Friedrich Nietzsche

WHEN I MET CHIP STEVENS IN 2002, he thought his startup, InLook, was on the road to success. Twenty months earlier, he had raised $8 million to build a new class of enterprise software for Fortune 1000 companies. Chip's product, Snapshot, would allow the chief financial officers of major corporations to manage profitability before the quarter closed. Snapshot measured every deal in a company's sales pipeline and compared the deals to top- and bottom-line corporate financial objectives. The software was able to forecast margin, revenue, and product mix, and allow a company to allocate resources before a deal closed. This meant sales cycles could be shorter, fewer deals needed to be escalated to senior management, and management could allocate resources to the best deals in the pipeline. While Snapshot could save a company substantial dollars in the long term, it was expensive, costing $250,000 or more.

Chip had raised his money in a tough economic climate, and while the economy still hadn't recovered, he was relatively happy with the state of his company. Product Development, after being seriously broken for the first year, was back on track. Chip had to personally take over engineering management for a while, but since his background included a stint as a VP and general manager, he felt he handled it well. Fifteen months after receiving funding, InLook shipped its first product.

About eight months before we met, Chip hired Bob Collins as his VP of Sales. Bob had never been the first VP of Sales in a startup, but he had a track record as a successful sales executive, and had built and scaled the sales force in his previous company. Bob joined InLook three months before the product shipped and helped the company find its beta customers. As is true at most startups, InLook's beta customers didn't pay for the product, but Bob had high hopes of turning them into the first paying customers. Following the traditional Product Development model, Bob hired five salespeople: two on the West Coast, one in Chicago, one in Dallas, and one in New York. The salespeople were supported by four sales engineers they could talk to about the technical aspects of the product. Backing up Bob's sales team was a two-person marketing department writing data sheets and sales presentations. In total, InLook had an 11-person team working on sales, and no revenue to date. Bob's budget called for doubling the sales team by the end of the year.

While Bob was busy interviewing, the board was getting nervous. While the venture capitalists on the board thought Chip was a seasoned executive competently managing the company, InLook had yet to close a major customer deal and was missing its revenue plan. It was at this point that I entered the picture. The venture capitalists that provided InLook with its first round of funding had seen one of my early Customer Development lectures. They asked me to take a peek at InLook and see whether there was anything glaringly broken. (I believe their exact words were, "Take a look and see if their positioning needs help.")

At our first meeting, Chip Stevens had the look of a busy startup CEO with much better things to do than take a meeting his venture capitalists had foisted on him. He listened politely as I described the Customer Development process and went through the milestones of Customer Discovery. Then it was Chip's turn, and he walked me through his company, his product, and his sales team. He ticked off the names of 40 or so customers he talked to during the company's first nine months and gave me a great dissertation on how his target customers worked and what their problems were. He went through his product feature by feature and matched them to the customer problems. He talked about how his business model would make money and how the prospects he talked to seem to agree with his assumptions. It certainly sounded like he had gotten Customer Discovery correct.

Next, Chip took me through his sales process. He told me that since he had been tied up getting the product out the door, he had stopped talking to customers, and his VP of Sales, Bob, had managed the sales process. In fact, the few times he had asked to go out in the field Bob said, "Not yet, I don't want to waste your time." For the first time I started squirming in my seat. Chip said, "We have a great sales pipeline. I insist on getting weekly status reports with forecasted deal size and probability of close." When I asked how close any of the deals on the forecast were to getting closed, he assured me the company's two beta customers—well-known companies that would be marquee accounts if they closed—were imminent orders.

"How do you know this?" I asked. "Have you heard it personally from the customers?"

Now it was Chip's turn to squirm a bit. "No, not exactly," he replied, "but Bob assures me we will have a purchase order in the next few weeks or so."

Now I really was nervous for Chip and his company. Very few large companies write big checks to unknown startups without at least meeting the CEO, if not talking to a few of the venture capitalists on the board. When I asked if Chip could draw the sales roadmap for these two accounts that were about to close, he admitted he didn't know any of the details, given it was all in Bob's head. Since we were running out of time, I said, "Chip, your sales pipeline sounds great. In fact, it sounds too good to be true. If you really close any of these imminent accounts, my hat is off to you and your sales team. If, as I suspect, they don't close, do me a favor."

"What's that?" Chip asked, looking irritated.

"You need to pick up the phone and call the top five accounts on your sales pipeline. Ask them this: If you give them your product today for free, are they prepared to install and use it across their department and company? If the answer is no, you have absolutely no customers on your forecast who will be prepared to buy from you in the next six months."

Chip smiled and politely walked me out of his office. I didn't expect to hear from him again.

Less than two weeks later, I picked up my voicemail and was surprised to hear the agitated voice of Chip Stevens. "Steve, we really have to talk again. Our brand-name account, the one we have been working on for the last eight months, told us they weren't going to buy the product this year. They just didn't see the urgency." Calling Chip back, I got the rest of the story.

"When my VP of Sales told me that," Chip said, "I got on the phone and spoke to the account personally. I asked them your question—would they deploy the product in their department or company if the price were zero? I'm still stunned by the answer. They said the product wasn't mission critical enough for their company to justify the disruption."

"Wow, that's not good," I said, trying to sound sympathetic.

"It only gets worse," he said. "Since I was hearing this from one of the accounts my VP of Sales thought was going to close, I insisted we jointly call our other 'imminent' account. It's the same story as the first. Then I called the next three down the list and got essentially the same story. They all think our product is 'interesting,' but no one is ready to put serious money down now. I'm beginning to suspect our entire forecast is not real. What am I going to tell my board?"

My not-so-difficult advice was that Chip would have to tell his board exactly what was going on. But before he did, he needed to understand the sales situation in its entirety, then come up with a plan for fixing it. Then he was going to present both the problem and suggested fix to his board. (You never want a board to have to tell you how to run your company. When that happens, it's time to update your resume.)

Chip had only begun to understand the implications of a phantom sales forecast, and he began to dig further. In talking to each of his five salespeople, he discovered the InLook sales team had no standardized sales process. Each salesperson was calling on different levels of an account and trying whatever seemed to work best. When he talked to his marketing people, he found they were trying to help sales by making up new corporate presentations almost weekly. The company's message and positioning were changing week by week. Bob, his VP of Sales, believed there was nothing really wrong. They just needed more time to "figure it out" and then they would close a few accounts.

With his company burning cash fast (11 people in sales and marketing), no real understanding of what was broken in sales, and no revenue in the pipeline, the Japanese Noh play was about to unfold again. Bob was about to become history. The "good" news was that as an agile and experienced business executive, Chip quickly understood what had gone wrong. He came to grips with the fact that after eight months InLook still did not have a clue about how to sell Snapshot. Worse, there was no process in place to learn how to sell, just a hope that smart salespeople would "find their way." Chip realized the company would have to start from scratch and develop a sales roadmap. He presented his plan to the board, fired the VP of Sales and seven of the sales and marketing staff, and dramatically slashed the company's burn rate. He kept his best salesperson and support engineer as well as the marketing VP. Then Chip went home, kissed his family goodbye, and went out to the field to discover what would make a customer buy. Chip's board agreed with his conclusion, wished him luck and started the clock ticking on his remaining tenure. He had six months to get and close customers.

Chip had discovered InLook lacked what every startup needs: a method that allows it to develop a predictable sales process and validate its business model. After Customer Discovery, startups must next ask and answer basic questions such as:

- Are we sure we have product/market fit?
- Do we understand the sales process?
- Is the sales process repeatable?
- Can we prove it's repeatable? (What's the proof? Full-price orders for a sale in sufficient quantity.)
- Can we get these orders with the current product and release spec?
- Have we correctly positioned the product and the company?
- Do we have a workable sales and distribution channel?
- Are we confident we can scale a profitable business?

Contrary to what happened at InLook (and what happens in countless startups), the Customer Development model insists these questions be asked and answered long before the sales organization begins to grow. Getting them answered is the basic goal of Customer Validation.

The Customer Validation Philosophy

Just as Customer Discovery was disorienting for experienced marketers, the Customer Validation process turns the world upside down for experienced salespeople, and in particular, Sales VPs. None of the rules sales executives learned in large companies apply to startups—in fact they are detrimental. In the Customer Validation step, you are not going to staff a sales team. You are not going to execute to a sales plan, and you are definitely not going to execute your "sales strategy." You simply do not know enough to do any of these things. You may have hypotheses about who will buy, why they will buy, and at what price they will buy, but until you validate them, they are merely educated guesses.

One of the major outcomes of Customer Validation is a proven and tested sales roadmap. You will create this map by learning how to sell to a small set of early visionary customers (earlyvangelists). They will pay for the product—sometimes months or even years before it is completed. However, the goal of this step is not to be confused with "selling." The reality is you care less about generating revenue at this point than you do about finding a scalable and repeatable sales process and business model. Building a roadmap to sales success, rather than building a sales organization, is the heart of Customer Validation. Given how critical this step is, a CEO's first instinct is to speed up the process by putting more salespeople in the field. This only slows the process.

In an existing market, Customer Validation may prove the VP of Sales' Rolodex is truly relevant and the metrics for product performance the company identified in Customer Discovery were correct. In a resegmented or new market, even a Rolodex of infinite size will not substitute for a tested sales roadmap.

For an experienced sales executive, these are heretical statements. They are disorienting and seem counterintuitive to what sales professionals have been trained to do. So let's look more closely at why the first sales in a startup are so different from later-stage sales or selling in a large company.

Validating the Sales Process

Ask startup Sales VPs what their top two or three goals are, and you'll get answers like, "To achieve our revenue plan," or "To hire and staff our sales organization, and then to achieve our revenue plan." Some might add, "To help engineering understand what additional features our customers need." In short, you'll get answers that are usually revenue- and head count-driven. While goals like these are rational for an established company, they are anything but rational for startups. Why? In established companies, someone has already blazed the trail through the swamp. New salespeople are handed a corporate presentation, price list, data sheets, and all the other accoutrements of a tested sales process. The sales organization has a sales pipeline with measured steps and a sales roadmap with detailed goals, all of which have been validated by experience with customers. A sales pipeline is the traditional sales funnel. Wide at the top with raw leads coming into it, it narrows at each stage as the leads get qualified and turn into suspects, then prospects, then probable closes, until finally an order comes out of the narrow end of the funnel. Nearly all companies with a mature sales force have their own version of this sales funnel. They use it to forecast revenue and the probability of success of each prospect. Most experienced Sales VPs hired into new startups will attempt to replicate the funnel by assembling a sales pipeline and filling it with customers. What they don't recognize is that it is impossible to build a sales pipeline without first having developed a sales roadmap.

A sales roadmap answers the basic questions involved in selling your product: Are we sure we have product/market fit? Who influences a sale? Who recommends a sale? Who is the decision-maker? Who is the economic buyer? Who is the saboteur? Where is the budget for purchasing the type of product you're selling? How many sales calls are needed per sale? How long does an average sale take from beginning to end? What is the selling strategy? Is this a solution sale? If so what are "key customer problems"? What is the profile of the optimal visionary buyer, the earlyvangelist every startup needs?

Unless a company has proven answers to these questions, few sales will happen, and those that occur will be the result of heroic, single-shot efforts. Of course, on some level most sales VPs realize they lack the knowledge they need to draw a detailed sales roadmap, but they believe they and their newly hired sales team can acquire this information while simultaneously selling and closing orders. This is a manifestation of one of the fundamental fallacies of the traditional Product Development methodology when applied to startups. You cannot learn and discover while you are executing. As we can see from the example of InLook, and from the rubble of any number of failed startups, attempting to execute before you have a sales roadmap in place is pure folly.

The Customer Validation Team

The InLook story illustrates one of the classic mistakes startup founders and CEOs typically make: delegating the Customer Validation process solely to the VP of Sales. In technology companies, a majority of founders are engineers and assume they need to hire a professional in a domain where they have no expertise. And in the case of a VP of Sales, they're probably hiring a professional who is proud of his or her skill and Rolodex. So the founders' natural tendency is to stay away and trust the abilities of their hires. This mistake is usually fatal for the VP of Sales and sometimes for the startup as well.

Sales execution is the responsibility of the VP of Sales. Sales staffing is the responsibility of the VP of Sales. Yet at this point in the life of a startup, you don't know enough to be executing or staffing anything. Your startup is still in learning mode, and your Customer Development team needs to continue to lead customer interaction through Customer Validation.

At a minimum, the company's founders and CEO need to be out in front of customers at least through the first iteration of the Customer Validation step. They are the people who, with help from the product team, can find their visionary peers, excite them about a product, and get them ready to buy. In enterprise or BtoB sales, if the founding team does not include someone with the skill to close an account, the company can hire a "sales closer," a salesperson with the skills to close a deal.

Early Sales Are to Earlyvangelists, Not Mainstream Customers

In Customer Validation, your startup is focused on finding the visionary customers and getting them to make a purchase.

Unlike "mainstream" customers who want to buy a finished, completed, and tested product, earlyvangelists are willing to make a leap of faith and buy from a startup. They may do so because they perceive a competitive advantage in the market, bragging rights with peers in their neighborhood or in an industry, or political advantage within their company. Earlyvangelists are the only customers able to buy a yet-to-be-delivered, unfinished product.

Recall who these visionary customers are. They not only understand they have a problem, but they have spent time actively looking for a solution, to the point of trying to build their own. In a company this may be because there is a broken mission-critical business process that needs to be fixed. Therefore, when you walk through the door, they immediately grasp the problem you are solving is one they have, and they can see the elegance and value of your solution. Little or no education is needed. In other cases their motivation might be that they are driven by competitive advantage and will take a risk on a new paradigm to get it.

Earlyvangelists "get it." However, they usually don't or won't get it from a "suit," a traditional salesperson. Earlyvangelists want to see and hear the founders and the technical team. In exchange, you will not only get an order and great feedback, but visionary customers will become earlyvangelists inside their companies and throughout their industry—or as consumers, to their friends and neighbors. Treated correctly they are the ultimate reference accounts. (Until you reach the Chasm in Chapter 6.)

There's one important caveat about earlyvangelists. Some startup founders think of earlyvangelists as only being found in the research and development labs, or the technical evaluation groups of large corporate customers—or for a consumer product, someone lucky enough to work in a new product test lab where their job is to evaluate products for potential use. These are emphatically not the earlyvangelists I'm referring to. At times, they may be critical influencers in a sale, but they have no day-to-day operational role, and no authority for ensuring widespread adoption and deployment. The earlyvangelists you need to talk to are the people I described in Customer Discovery—the ones who are in operating roles, have a problem, have been looking for a solution, have tried to solve the problem and have a budget.

Customer Validation has four phases, as depicted in Figure 4.1. Phase 1 consists of a series of "getting ready to sell" activities: articulating a value proposition; preparing sales materials and a preliminary collateral plan; developing a distribution channel plan and a sales roadmap; hiring a sales closer; ensuring that your Product and Customer Development teams agree about product features and dates; and formalizing your advisory board.

Overview of the Customer Validation Process

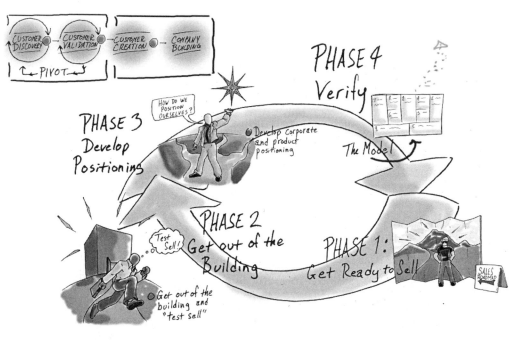

Customer Validation: Overview of the Process *(Figure 4.1)*

Next, in Phase 2, you leave the building and put your now well-honed product idea to the test: Will customers validate your concept by purchasing your product? You will attempt to sell customers an unfinished and unproven product, without a professional sales organization. Failures are as important as successes in this phase; the goal is to answer all the sales roadmap questions. At the end of this phase, you have preliminary meetings with channel or professional service partners.

With a couple of orders under your belt, you have enough customer information to move to Phase 3, in which you take your first cut at an initial positioning of the product and of the company. Here is where you articulate your profound belief about your product and its place in the market. You test this initial positioning by meeting with industry pundits and analysts for their feedback and approval.

Finally, in Phase 4, you verify whether the company is finished with Customer Validation. Do you have enough orders proving your product solves customer needs? Do you have a profitable sales and channel model? Do you have a profitable business model? Have you learned enough to scale the business? Only if you can answer yes to all these questions do you proceed to Customer Creation.

Phase 1: Get Ready to Sell

The initial phase of Customer Validation prepares the company for its first attempt at selling a product, which requires careful preparation, planning and concurrence. In particular, in this phase you will:

- Articulate a value proposition
- Prepare sales materials and a preliminary collateral plan
- Develop a preliminary distribution channel plan
- Develop a preliminary sales roadmap
- Hire a sales closer
- Align your executives
- Formalize your advisory board

A. Get Ready to Sell: Articulate a Value Proposition

From your customer's perspective, what does your company stand for, what does your product do, and why should I care? You probably had an idea when you started the company, but now you have some real experience interacting with customers, and it's time to revisit your vision in light of what you have learned. Can you reduce your business to a single, clear, compelling message that says why your company is different and your product is worth buying? That's the goal of a value proposition (sometimes called a unique selling proposition). A value proposition builds the bond between you and your customer, focuses marketing programs, and becomes the focal point for building the company. More relevant for this step, it gets the company's story down to an "elevator pitch," one powerful enough to raise a customer's heart rate. This value proposition will appear in all your sales materials from here on out. It is the sum of all you have learned about product/market fit in Customer Discovery. Don't worry about getting it perfect, because it will change, evolve, and mutate as you get feedback from customers, analysts, and investors. The idea of this phase is simply to acknowledge you need to craft and create one, and take your best shot at articulating it.

While a value proposition seems straightforward, it can be a challenge to execute. It takes serious work to get to a pithy statement that is both understandable and compelling. It's much easier to write (or think) long than to write (or think) short. The first step is to remember what you have learned in Customer Discovery about customers' problems, and what customers valued about your solution. What were the top three problems your customers said they had? Did a phrase keep coming up to describe this problem or the solution to the problem? Based on your understanding of how customers work, spend their time, or use other products, where does your product affect these customers most? How significant is the impact on how they work? If there are existing competitors or ways to solve the problem that use pieces of other solutions, what do you provide that your competitors can't or won't? What do you do better?

InLook's value proposition was, "Helping chief financial officers manage profitability." Short and to the point, it played right to the audience InLook was going after. A value proposition is (ideally) one sentence, and at most a few sentences. How did the founders know who their audience was? They went back to all they learned in Customer Discovery. The CFO was now their target audience (he wasn't when they first started Customer Discovery), "profitability" was an emotionally compelling word (they had a litany of words when they first started talking to customers), and managing profitability was a leverage point quantifiable in the minds of their customers (a point they were clueless about earlier).

One of the first tests of your value proposition should be, is it emotionally compelling? Do customers' heart rates go up after they hear it? Do they lean forward to hear more? Or do they give you a blank stare? Is the value proposition understandable in the users' language? Is it unique in their minds? In technology startups, one of the biggest challenges for engineers is to realize they want an oversimplified message, one that grabs customers' hearts and wallets, not their heads and calculators.

Second, does your value proposition make or reinforce an economic case? Does it have economic impact? Does it sound like your product gives a corporate customer a competitive advantage or improves some critical area in their company? If it's a consumer product, does it save a consumer time or money, or change their prestige or identity? The InLook example used the words "manage profitability." To a CFO these powerful words represent a quantifiable and measurable benefit.

Finally, does the value proposition pass the reality test? Claims like "lose 30 pounds as fat just melts away," "sales will increase 200 percent" or "cut costs by 50 percent" strain credibility. Moreover, the claim isn't the only thing that must pass this test. Is your company a credible supplier for the product you're describing? When selling to corporate customers, there are additional hurdles to think about. Are your capabilities congruent with your claims? Are your solutions attainable and compatible with customers' current operations? Do customers have complementary or supporting technologies in place?

One last thing to keep in mind is our continual question about Market Type. If you are offering a new product in an existing market, your value proposition is about incremental performance. Incremental value propositions describe improvements and metrics of individual attributes of the product or service (i.e., faster, better). If you are creating a new market, or trying to reframe an existing one, you will probably come up with a transformational value proposition. Transformational value propositions deal with how the solution will create a new level or class of activity—i.e. something people could not do before.

B. Get Ready to Sell: Prepare a Preliminary Collateral Plan

Once you have a value proposition, it's time to put it to work in sales and marketing collateral. This is the sum of the printed and electronic communications your sales team will hand or present to potential customers. To sell a product in the Customer Validation step, you need to prepare a complete set of sales materials, product data sheets, presentations (sometimes different ones for different groups inside a company), price lists, and so on. But unlike material you will produce later on in the company's life, this is all "preliminary," all subject to change, produced in low volume at low cost.

You just completed the first step in writing this material by coming up with your value proposition. You'll use it as the central theme in most of your sales materials.

Before any material is developed, figure out what sales material you need. Instead of randomly writing product specs and presentations, it's helpful to develop a "collateral plan," a list of all the literature you will put in front of a customer in different phases of the selling process (see Table 4.1 for an example of a business-to-business collateral plan).

	Awareness	Interest	Consideration	Sales
Early-vangelist Buyers	Corporate website Brochure	General sales presentation(s)	Tailor presentations to each customer	Contacts
	Solution data sheets	White paper on business issue	Analyst report on business problem	Price list
	Influential bloggers	Product Presskit		
	Tech websites	Product brochure	ROI demonstration	
	Direct mail pieces	Viral marketing/ e-mail tools	Follow-up e-mail	
		Product data sheets	Pricing quote form	Thank-you note/e-mail
Technology Gatekeeper	Influential Bloggers	Tech presentation	Tech presentation on specific customer issues	Thank-you note
	Tech websites	Tech white paper	Tech white paper	
		Analyst report on technical problem	Tech overview data sheets with architecture diagrams	

Example of a Business-to-Business, Direct Sales Collateral Plan _(Table 4.1)_

At my last company, E.piphany, I belatedly realized our positioning and strategy were a bit deficient; after presenting to the CIO we were thrown out of the fifth consecutive potential sale. In looking at our presentation I realized the slides were telling the CIO the same value proposition I had shared with his operating divisions: "You don't need your IT organization to give you information. Tell them to stuff it, and buy an E.piphany system." Needless to say, sales were going to be difficult when we needed the backing of the CIO. We came up with a value proposition and presentation tailored to the CIO, the IT organization and technology gatekeepers.

In this example the sale was to a large corporation. The product was software used by employees but had to be installed and maintained by the IT department. Here the company must recognize there are two targets for its collateral: the earlyvangelist buyers and technology gatekeepers. If the sale is to a consumer, the collateral plan will focus on communications materials the sales channel will use. It can include shelf talkers, retail packaging, coupons, and so on. Regardless of the distribution channel or whether the product is sold to businesses or consumers, the collateral plan distinguishes with whom each collateral piece will be used and when in the sales process it will be used.

Don't worry about whether the collateral plan is perfect. It will change as you talk to customers, then change again as your customer base moves from visionary to mainstream. Test-drive all the collateral you produce, because what you write in the confines of an office often has little relevance in the field. Keep your collateral plan handy, as you'll be adding to it and updating it at each step of the Customer Development process.

It's helpful to realize visionary customers require different materials than mainstream customers. Visionary customers are first buying the vision and then the product. Therefore, make sure your materials are clear and detailed enough on the vision and benefits so your earlyvangelists can use your literature to sell your idea themselves, i.e., inside their own companies or to their friends and family. The Customer Development team and the founders should articulate the vision. For the product-specific details, Product Development should write the first draft. This way you can see if there are any surprises in what features the technical team would emphasize.

Remember, don't spend money on flashy design or large print runs in this phase. The only worthwhile investment is a good PowerPoint template and the two or three diagrams illustrating your key ideas.

Here are guidelines on some of the principal items that go into the collateral roadmap:

Websites

Websites at this stage of a startup should have clear information on the vision and problem you are solving, with enough detailed product information for the customer to want to engage in a conversation or actually make a purchase. This is a fine balance; you do not want a customer to have enough information to make a decision not to buy without you. Later you will use the same philosophy on your data sheets and product specs.

Sales Presentations

Your sales presentation should be an updated and combined version of the problem and product presentations used in Customer Discovery, with your value proposition added. However, very rarely does one presentation fit multiple audiences in a company or work across multiple industries. In Customer Discovery, you may have found you needed different presentations depending on the types of people who played a role in purchase decisions inside a company or different consumer audiences. Did you need a separate presentation for a technical audience? How about for senior management versus lower-level employees? How about for different companies in different industries? For consumer products, was there a different presentation based on demographics? Income? Geography?

Keep in mind at this stage the core audience is earlyvangelists, not mainstream customers. The sales presentation to visionary customers should cover a brief outline of the problem, possible solutions to the problem, your solution to the problem, and product details. It should run no more than 30 minutes.

Demos

Many products are too hard to understand without a demo. If a picture is worth a thousand words, a demonstration is probably worth a million. A caveat, though: Product Development teams in startups sometimes confuse "demo" with a working product. All the Customer Development team needs is a slide-based "dummy-demo" to illustrate the key points. I rarely have sold to earlyvangelists successfully without having one.

Data Sheets

It's easy to confuse "product data sheets," which detail product features and benefits, with "solution data sheets," which address customer problems and big-picture solutions. If you are bringing a new product to an existing market, your focus will be on the product, so you should develop product data sheets. If you are creating a new market, the problem and solution data sheets are more appropriate. And if you are redefining a market, you need both.

In all cases you will likely need a technical overview with a distinctly deeper level of information for the other players in the sales cycle. As you begin to understand the sales process, issue-specific white papers may be necessary to address particular areas of interest or concern. Do these as you find they are necessary, but not before.

Listen and your customers will tell you what they need.

Especially in tight economic climates, one key piece of collateral customers ask for is a return on investment (ROI) white paper. This is a customer's fancy way of asking, "Show me how I can financially justify buying your product. Will it save me money in the long run?" Your earlyvangelist champions will usually have to make the case for your product before someone agrees to sign the check. For consumers the issue is the same. Just imagine kids trying to make the ROI issue for an Apple iPod. "I wont have to buy CDs and I'll pay for the songs out of my allowance."

Price Lists, Contracts and Billing System

Hopefully, as you go through the Customer Validation step, some farsighted customers will ask, "How much is your product?" Even though you can give them the answer off the top of your head, you will need a price list, quote form, and contracts. Having these documents makes your small startup look like a real company. They also force you to put in writing your assumptions about product pricing, configurations, discounts, and terms. For consumer products, you will need a way to take early orders. You will need a billing system with credit card verification, online store, etc.

C. Get Ready to Sell:
Develop a Preliminary Distribution Channel Plan

The Customer Development process helps you create a repeatable and scalable sales process and business model. The distribution channel plan and sales roadmap (developed in the next step) guide that effort.

Back in the Customer Discovery step, you refined your hypothesis about distribution channels using the information you learned in customer interviews. This phase assumes you have evaluated all the distribution channel alternatives and narrowed your distribution channel choices to one specific sales channel. Now you use that information to develop a preliminary channel plan.

A distribution channel plan comprises three elements. Initially, as you set up these elements, much of your thinking will be conjecture, based on the information you collected in Customer Discovery. However, as you move into the next phase of Customer

Validation and start interacting with your selected distribution channel, you will refine your initial theories with facts and cold reality.

The elements used to build your distribution channel plan are:
- Channel "food chain" and responsibility
- Channel discount and financials
- Channel management

Channel "Food Chain" and Responsibility

Remember the channel brief you created in Customer Discovery? (Look back at Figure 3.5 for an example.) In that brief you spelled out your initial hypotheses about how your product would reach customers. Now it is time to further refine your distribution channel plan.

Start by drawing the "food chain" or tiers of the distribution channel. What's a food chain? For a distribution channel it is made up of the organizations between your company and your customer. The "food chain" describes what these organizations are and their relationships to you and each other.

For example, imagine you are setting up a book-publishing company. You will need to understand how to get books from your company to the book-buying customer. If you were selling directly to consumers from your own Web site, the "food chain" diagram for your publishing distribution channel might look something like Figure 4.2.

Direct Book-Publishing Food Chain (Figure 4.2)

However, selling through the traditional publishing distribution channel "food chain" would look like Figure 4.3.

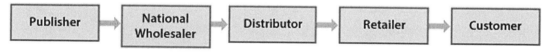

Indirect Book-Publishing Food Chain (Figure 4.3)

Regardless of the complexity of the diagram, your next step is to create a detailed description of each of the companies making up your channel's "food chain."

Continuing with our book-publishing example, the descriptions would look like this.

- National wholesalers: Stock, pick, pack, ship and collect, then pay the publisher on orders received. They fulfill orders but do not create customer demand
- Distributors: Use their own sales force to sell to bookstore chains and independents. The distributor makes the sale; the bookstore orders from the wholesaler
- Retailers: This is where the customer sees and can purchase books

It is useful to create a visual representation of all the information you have assembled on the distribution channel (see Figure 4.4).

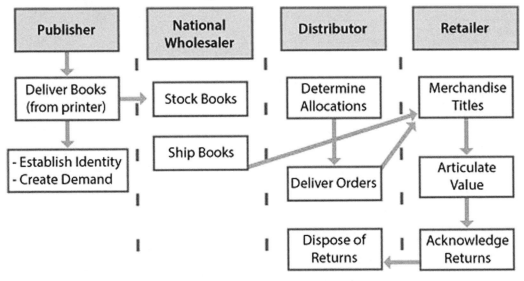

Channel Responsibility Map *(Figure 4.4)*

One mistake startups often make is assuming their channel partners invest in creating customer demand. For example, in Figure 4.4, it would be a mistake to think your book wholesaler does anything other than stock and ship books. The same is true for the distributor. They take orders from bookstores, and in some cases may promote your books to bookstores, but they do not bring customers into the store to buy your books.

A channel responsibility map allows you to diagram the relationships in a complex distribution channel. A written description of these responsibilities, much as you created for the "food chain," should accompany the diagram. It helps everyone on the team understand why you are using the channel and what to expect from it.

Channel Discounts and Financials

Each tier in the distribution "food chain" costs your company money since each tier will charge a fee for its services. In most channels, these fees are calculated as a percentage of the "list" or retail price a consumer will pay. The next exercise helps ensure you understand how the money flows from the customer to you. First, calculate the discounts each channel tier requires. Continuing with our book-publishing example, Figure 4.5 details these.

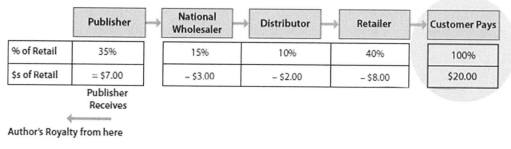

Channel Discounts (Figure 4.5)

As you can see, a book retailing for $20 would net our publishing company $7 after everyone in the channel took their cut. Out of this $7 the publisher must pay the author a royalty, market the book, pay for the printing and binding, contribute to overhead, and realize a profit.

Channel discounts are only the first step in examining how money flows in a complex distribution channel. Each tier or level of the channel has some unique financial relationship with the publisher. For example, most regular sales to a bookstore are on a consignment basis. This means unsold books can be heading back to you. Why is this a problem? A mistake companies frequently make when they use a tiered distribution channel is to record the sale to the tier closest to them (in this case the national wholesaler) as revenue. An order from a channel partner does not mean an end customer bought the product, just the channel partner hopes and believes they will. It's like a supermarket ordering a new product to put on the grocery shelf. It isn't really sold until someone pushing their cart down the aisle takes it off the shelf, pays for it and takes it home.

If you have a channel returns policy that allows for any kind of stock rotation, you must make allowances in your accounts for a proportion of that sale to be returned. Your channel financial plan should include a description of all the financial relationships among each of the channel tiers (see Figure 4.6).

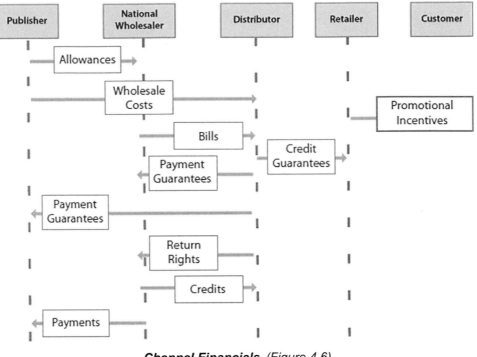

Channel Financials *(Figure 4.6)*

Channel Management

Your ability to manage your distribution channel will directly affect your ability to deliver on your revenue plan. Although every company's goal is a well-managed and carefully selected channel, failure to select the right channel or to control the channel often results in miserable sales revenue and unanticipated channel costs. You will need a plan to monitor and control your channel's distribution activities, particularly inventory levels. In a direct sales channel, it's straightforward: no goods leave the company until there is a customer order. However, in an indirect channel the biggest risk is not knowing how much end-user demand exists. Why? Looking at any of the channel "food chain" diagrams, you can see your company will have a direct relationship with only the tier of distribution closest to your company. You will be dependent on reports, often months out of date, to know how much of your product has "sold through" the channel—in other words, how much has been purchased by customers. Another risk is the temptation in an indirect channel to "stuff" the channel. Stuffing means getting a tier of the channel to accept more product on consignment than sales forecasts can reasonably have expected the channel to sell through. For companies that recognize revenue on sales into the channel, this can provide a temporary inflation of sales followed by a debacle later. All these potential issues need to be documented and discussed in the channel management plan to avoid costly future surprises.

D. Get Ready to Sell: Develop a Preliminary Sales Roadmap

Developing a sales roadmap is all about finding the right path through unknown and dangerous terrain. A fog of uncertainty hangs over the early steps of the sales journey. In Customer Validation, you pierce that fog by gathering sufficient information to illuminate how to proceed, one discrete step at a time, then assemble that information into a coherent picture of the right path to take.

Your goal is to determine who your true customers are and how they will purchase your product. You're ready to begin building a sales team only when you completely understand the process that transforms a prospect into a purchaser and know you can sell the product at a price that supports your business model. With the sales roadmap in their hands, your sales force will be able to focus on actual sales instead of the hit-and-miss experimentation you will experience as you move through Customer Validation.

The complexity of your company's sales roadmap will depend on a number of things: the size of your customer base, budget, the price of your product, the industry in which you are selling, and the distribution channel you've selected. Sales to Intel or Toys R Us, for example, will require a more involved process than sales to local florists or pet stores. Creating a roadmap and validating it may seem like an enormous investment of time and energy, and a huge distraction from the challenges of building a business. But it could make the difference between success and failure. Better to know how to sell your product while your company is lean and small than try to figure it out as you are burning through cash sending your sales and marketing departments out.

The sales roadmap comprises four elements. As with the distribution channel plan, much of your initial thinking here will be conjecture based on the information you collected in Customer Discovery. However, as you move into the next phase where you actually sell your product, you will refine your initial theories with facts.

The elements used to build your sales roadmap are:

- Organization and influence maps
- Customer access map
- Sales strategy
- Implementation plan

Organization and Influence Maps

Remember the organization and influence map briefs you created in Customer Discovery? Pull them off the wall and study your findings. By now your early hypotheses have been modified to reflect the reality you encountered as you spoke with potential customers. Use this information to develop a working model of the purchase process for your target customer. Take a closer look at your notes from your encounters with possible earlyvangelists. You might also want to bring in customer information from other sources such as a company's annual report, Hoovers, Dun & Bradstreet or press articles.

The E.piphany sales cycle is a good example of how an influence map is derived. Given E.piphany's software cost hundreds of thousands of dollars, an executive must have had a significant pain, recognized it was a pain, and have been committed to making the pain go away if E.piphany was to get a deal. Second, selling our product required "top-down selling." Working your way up from low levels is not only more difficult but much less likely to end in success. Third, E.piphany changed the status quo: Our products impacted many people and many organizations. Typically, those who oppose change or who have a large stake in the status quo will oppose software others regard as progress.

The bad news: Multiple "Yes" votes were required to get an E.piphany order. Other enterprise software like sales automation or customer support just needed support from a single key executive or from a single user community to drive a sale to closure. With those packages IT personnel generally had input in the selection of a software package, but the users enjoyed substantial power in the decision-making process. An E.piphany sale was different. IT, though not the driver, was an active participant in the decision-making process and often enjoyed veto power. Likewise, our experience showed we needed to sell "high" and "wide" on both the user and technical sides of an account. After getting thrown out of multiple accounts we built a simple two-by-two matrix to show where we needed to get support and approval from in each of our prospect accounts:

	Operational	Technical
High	Executive	CIO or Division IT Executive
Low	End Users	Corp. IT Staff or Division IT Staff

Support and Approval Matrix _(Figure 4.7)_

This matrix basically said even with a visionary supporting the purchase of the E.piphany product, we had to sell to four constituencies before we could close an order.

Without support on the operational side and "approval" by the IT technical team, we couldn't get a deal. If the IT organization became determined to derail an E.piphany deal, it would probably succeed. This insight was a big deal. It was one of the many "aha's" that made E.piphany successful. And it happened because we had failed, and a founder was part of that failure and spent time understanding the solution.

Our early sales efforts fell short largely because we ignored the fact that selling E.piphany into the enterprise was different from the sale of other enterprise products. The most glaring oversight was our failure to enlist the support of the IT organization. In our sales calls we had found it was easier to get people on the operational side excited about our products and win their support than it was to get IT professionals to buy into a packaged data warehouse and a suite of applications to serve the needs of marketing. In some cases we had taken prospects on the operational side at their word when they indicated they could make IT "fall into line" should they need to. In other cases, we skipped some needed steps and assumed several enthusiastic users could do our deal. Rarely did this prove to be true.

We took that sales failure and success data and put it together into an Influence Map. Remember by this time we had established that 1) we needed to win the support of four groups to get a deal done; 2) IT would probably be harder to win over than the users; and 3) low-level IT personnel would oppose us. So how should we proceed? The Influence Map in Figure 4.7a illustrates the execution strategy for E.piphany sales. It diagrams the players, and maps the order in which they need to be convinced and sold. Each step leveraged strengths from the step before, using momentum from groups that liked our company and products to overcome objections from groups that did not. The corollary was if we tried to shortcut the process and skip a sales stage, more often that not we would lose the sale.

Once understood, the Influence Map set the execution strategy for sales. Call on: 1) high-level operational executives (VPs, divisional GMs, etc.) first. Use that relationship as an introduction to 2) high-level technical executive (CIO or divisional IT executive), then 3) meet the operational organizations end users (the people who will use our product), and finally, 4) use that groundswell of support to present to, educate and eliminate objections from the Corporate or Division IT staff.

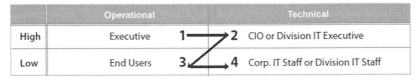

	Operational		Technical
High	Executive	1 → 2	CIO or Division IT Executive
Low	End Users	3 → 4	Corp. IT Staff or Division IT Staff

Example of an Influence Map *(Figure 4.7a)*

Customer Access Map

Now turn your attention to answering the proverbial sales question: How do you get your foot in the door? For a corporation, depending on the size of the organization you are approaching you may need to move through different layers or departments before you can set up meetings with the people you identified in the organization and influence maps. As you begin to develop an access map for the companies you are targeting, you may draw a lot of blanks. But once you begin to call on actual customers, you will be able to add information and perceive patterns. Figure 4.8 illustrates an access map in a corporate account.

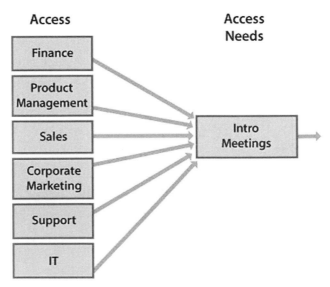

Example of an Access Map *(Figure 4.8)*

For consumer sales, finding the right entry to early customers can be equally difficult. Rather than making random calls, think of organizations and special-interest groups you can get to inexpensively. Can you reach customers through organizations they belong to, such as the PTA, book clubs, antique car clubs? Are there Web-based groups that may be interested?

Sales Strategy

Lay your corporate/consumer organization map and influence map side by side. For a corporate sale, your challenge is to move beyond the names and titles of the people you will call on to develop a strategy of how you will approach them. For example, imagine you are developing a sales strategy for InLook, which has created a software product for CFOs. In this phase, as you begin to develop a sales strategy, here are some questions to consider:

- At what level do you enter the account? Do you sell high to executives? Or low to the operational staff?
- How many people on the organizational map need to say yes for a sale?
- Does each department perceive the customer problem in the same way?
- In what order do you need to call on these people? What is the script for each?
- What step can derail the entire sale?

Similarly, if you were trying to reach twenty-somethings with a new consumer product the questions might be:

- Do you need access to a specific demographic segment? Do you sell to college students? Parents of children? Families?
- How many people need to say yes for a sale? Is this an individual sale or family decision?
- If this sale requires multiple members of a family or group to agree, in what order do you need to call on these people? What is the script for each?
- What step can derail the entire sale?

Again, as you move out into the marketplace to sell your product, you will learn what works or not. As predictable patterns emerge, your strategy will become clear.

Implementation Plan

You've made the sale, the visionary customer has said thumbs up. Don't open the champagne quite yet. Much can happen between when the decision-maker agrees to make a purchase and you receive the check. The goal of the implementation plan is to write down all the things left to happen before the sale is finalized and the product delivered, and to determine who will follow up to manage them. For example:

- Does the CFO and or CEO need to approve the sale?
- Does the board need to approve the sale?
- Does Mom or Dad need to approve the sale?
- Does the customer need to get a loan to finance the sale?
- Do other systems/components from other vendors need to be working first?

E. Get Ready to Sell: Hire a Sales Closer

In most startups it's likely the founding team is product-oriented and does not include a sales professional. While the founders can get quite far in finding visionary customers, they usually have no skill or experience turning that relationship into the first order. Now that you are about to sell, a key question is, does someone on the founding team have experience closing deals? Does the team have a word-class set of customer contacts? Would you bet the company on the founders' ability to close the first sales? If not, hire a sales closer.

A sales closer is not a VP of Sales who wants to immediately build and manage a large sales organization. A sales closer is someone with a great Rolodex in the market you are selling into. Good sales closers are aggressive, want a great compensation package for success, and have no interest in building a sales organization. Typically, they are experienced startup salespeople who love closing deals and aren't yet ready to retire behind a desk.

The founding team and sales closer make up the core of the Customer Development team. It becomes their job to learn and discover enough information to build the sales and channel roadmaps. You may want to go once around the Customer Validation loop without a sales closer. Then when you understand where the lack of sales skills is stunting progress, hire the closer. But while the sales closer will be an integral part of

Customer Validation, the founders and CEO still need to lead the process. Sales closers are invaluable in setting up meetings, pushing for follow-up meetings, and closing the deal. However, having a sales closer is not a substitute for getting founders to personally gather customer feedback.

F. Get Ready to Sell: Align Your Executives

Selling a product implies a contractual commitment between the company and a customer on product features and delivery dates. Before you leave the building to sell, the Customer Development and Product Development teams need to be in violent agreement about all deliverables and commitments the company will make. So it's essential executives review and agree on the following:

- Engineering schedule, product deliverables and philosophy
- Sales collateral
- Engineering's role in selling, installation, and post-sales support

Engineering Schedule, Product Deliverables, and Philosophy

In order to sell to visionary customers as part of Customer Validation, the Customer Development team is about to commit to "ship dates" to these customers. Now is the time to verify that your Product Development team is absolutely sure you can deliver a functional product for your early visionary sales. Missing your ship dates for these first customers means more than simply missing a delivery date would mean for a large, established company. If your dates slip badly, or if you have continual slippages, your earlyvangelists' positions in their companies (or in the case of a consumer product, with their friends and families) will weaken, and ultimately you will lose their support. Your product can acquire a taint of vaporware, an always announced but never shipping product. Avoid surprises. Look at the scheduled dates for key Product Development milestones, compare them to the actual delivery dates, and take the ratio to compute a "slip factor." Then apply that number to any dates Customer Development receives from Product Development to derive the dates that will be promised to customers.

Even harder than guaranteeing the ship date of the first product is getting a Product Development team struggling with first product release to understand the value of articulating what will be in the next three releases. As a group you came up with the first pass of this forecast in Customer Discovery Phase 1. Now your Customer Development team needs to know whether the engineering release schedule you tentatively proposed then is still valid. Both the Product and Customer Development teams need to ensure all changes from Customer Discovery Phases 3 and 4 have been integrated into the product spec and then agree on the committed features by release.

In exchange for this look into the future, both teams agree on a "good enough" philosophy for deliverables and schedule. The goal is to get earlyvangelists an incomplete, barely good enough product in the first release. The visionary customers can help you understand the minimum features needed to make the first release a functional product. This means Product Development should not strive for architectural purity or perfection in the first release. Instead, the goal for Product Development should be to build the product incrementally and iteratively—getting it out the door and quickly revising it in response to customer feedback. The purpose is not "first mover advantage" (there is none), or a non-paying alpha or beta test, but to get customer input on a product that's been paid for.

There are two reasons for this "good enough" minimum feature set philosophy. First, regardless of what the users say, it's very hard to be 100 percent certain what's important to them until they have a first release in their hands. You may have talked to everyone in Customer Discovery and interviewed earlyvangelists but they may not know what's important until they use the product. Later, you may find when the product is used this important feature only gets exercised every six months. The minor feature you ignored? They use it six times a day. The second reason for this "good enough" philosophy is this first product is for earlyvangelists, not mainstream users who often have different expectations of what features are important.

This "ship it before it's elegant and pristine" concept is hard for some Product Development teams to grasp. Its implementation is even harder. There is a fine line between shipping a "good enough" product with a minimum feature set and an unusable product customers call junk.

Sales Collateral

There is no greater source of acrimony in a startup than finding out the company has sold something Product Development says it never committed to build. Therefore, it's essential for both teams to review and agree on the facts in all the sales collateral. To this end, Product Development reads and signs off on all Web pages, presentations, data sheets, white papers, and so on. This doesn't mean Product Development gets to approve or reject the collateral. It means they get to fact-check it and point out any discrepancies with reality.

Engineering's Role in Sales, Installation, and Post-Sales Support

In a company with products already shipping, the demarcation between Product Development and sales, installation, and customer support is clear. In a startup, these lines need to blur. Remember, you have agreed to make Product Development's life easier in two substantive areas. First, Customer Development's job is to find a market for the product as spec'd and to ask for more features *only* if a market cannot be found. Second, Customer Development has agreed the first release of the product will be incomplete, and the early visionary customers will help everyone understand the next release. In exchange, a critical feature of the Customer Development model is the agreement that Product Development will actively help with sales, installation, and support. This means the technical visionary and head of technical execution commit to sales calls and key engineers commit to helping answer detailed questions from customers. There is no substitute for direct, hands-on experience in "becoming the customer" for Engineering to make a better product. In the Customer Development model, 10 percent of Product Development's time is spent out in the field selling, installing, and providing post-sales support.

Keep in mind this notion of an "incomplete first release" with a minimum feature set is a walk on the knife of adroit execution, particularly in consumer markets. The goal is to get the product to market as early as possible to receive customer feedback, but not to distribute the product so widely that its limited feature set becomes etched in the customer's mind as the finished product.

G. Get Ready to Sell: Formalize Your Advisory Boards

In some cases you may have asked for advisors' help on an informal basis in Customer Discovery. In this phase, you formally engage them. There are no hard-and-fast rules for how large the advisory board should be. There can be as many people on the board as you want. Think strategically, not tactically, about the sphere of influence and reach of advisors. Recruit only the advisors you need now, but make exceptions for "brand names" and "influencers" you want to cultivate. Don't believe you need a formal advisory board meeting. All you want right now is time and access.

Begin by assembling an advisory board roadmap, much like the collateral roadmap you developed earlier. As shown in Table 4.2, this roadmap is an organized list of all the key advisors needed.

In this example the roadmap differentiates how each advisor will be used (technical, business, customer, industry and marketing). Product Development may need technical advisors on the "Technical Advisory Board" as early as Phase 1 of Customer Discovery. The technical advisory board is staffed for technical advice and points to technical talent. These advisors may be from academia or industry. As the company begins to sell product, these advisors are used as technical references for customers.

	Technical	Business	Customer	Industry	Sales/Marketing
Why	Product Development advice, validation, recruiting help.	Business strategy & Company Building advice.	Product advice & as potential customers. Later as customer conscience & as references.	Bringing credibility to your specific market or technology through domain expertise.	Counsel to help sort out sales, PR, press, and demand creation issues.
Who	Brand name technical luminaries for show, plus others with insight into the problems you are solving and are OK with getting their hands dirty.	Grizzled veterans who have built startups before. Key criteria: you trust their judgment and will listen to them.	People who will make great customers, who have good product instincts, and/or who are part of a customer network.	Visible name brands with customer and press credibility. May also be customers.	Experienced startup marketers who know how to create a market, not just a brand.
When	Day one of company founding and continuing through first customer ship.	Day one of company founding & ongoing.	In Customer Discovery. Identify in phase 1, begin inviting in phases 2 & 3.	In Customer Validation. Identify in phase 1, begin to invite in phase 3.	In Customer Creation. Need diminishes after Company Building.
Where	One-on-one meetings with Product Development staff at company.	Late-night phone calls, panicked visits to their home or office.	Phone calls for insight & 1-on-1 meetings with business and Customer Development staff at company.	Phone calls for insight & 1-on-1 meetings with business and Customer Development staff at company.	One-on-one meetings and phone calls with marketing and sales staff.
How Many	As many as needed.	No more than two or three at a time.	As many as needed.	No more than two per industry.	One for sales, one for marketing.

Advisory Board Roles (Table 4.2)

Ensure key potential customers are on the "Customer Advisory Board." These are people you met in Customer Discovery who can advise you about product/market fit from the customer's perspective. I always tell these advisors, "I want you on my advisory board so I can learn how to build a product you will buy. We both fail if I can't." They will serve as a customer conscience for the product, and later some of them will be great references for other customers. Use them for insight and one-on-

one meetings with the business and Customer Development staff at your company.

Distinct from customer advisors is an industry advisory board. These domain experts are visible name brands who bring credibility to your specific market or technology. They may also be customers, but they are typically used to create customer and press credibility.

Finally, you may want to have some general business advice from a "been there, done that" CEO. Executives who can give you practical advice are more than likely those who have run their own startups. Sales and marketing advisors are the perfect foils for testing what you've learned in Customer Discovery, Validation and Creation.

The number of advisors for each domain will vary with circumstances, but there are some rules of thumb. Both sales and marketing advisors tend to have large egos. I found I could only manage one of those at a time. Industry advisors like to think of themselves as "the" pundit for a particular industry. Have two give you opinions (but don't have them show up on the same day). Business advisors are much like marketing advisors but usually have some expertise in different stages of the company. I always kept a few on hand to get me smarter. Finally, our Product Development team could never get enough technical advisors. They would come in and get us smarter about specific technical issues. The same was true for the customer advisors. We made sure we learned something new every time they came by.

Phase 2: Sell to Visionary Customers

In Customer Discovery you contacted customers twice, first to understand how they work and the problems they have, and then to present the product and get their reaction to it. Now, in Phase 2 of Customer Validation, the rubber meets the road. Your task is to see whether you truly have product/market fit and can sell early visionary customers before your product is shipping. Why? Your ability to sell your startup's product will validate whether all your assumptions about your customers and your business model are correct. Do you understand customers and their needs? Do customers value your product features? Are you missing any critical ones? Do you understand your sales channel? Do you understand the purchasing and approval processes inside a customer's company?

Is your pricing right? Do you have a valid sales roadmap you can use to scale the sales team? You want the answers as early as possible, before change is costly. Waiting until the product is completely developed and your sales and marketing departments are staffed is a fatal flaw of the Product Development model.

OK, so you want customer feedback early. But why try to sell the product now? Why not simply give it away to early brand-name customers to get them on the bandwagon? Why aren't you giving away product so Engineering can have alpha and beta sites? This question has bedeviled startups since time immemorial. The answer is: Giveaways do not prove customers will buy your product. The only valid way to test your assumptions is to sell the product.

Some readers may wonder what the role of the Customer Development team is in alpha and beta testing. The answer is a little bewildering to those who have done startups before: There is none. Alpha and beta tests are legitimate activities of the Product Development organization and part of the Product Development process. When the product is in an intermediate stage of development, good Product Development teams want to find real customers to test the product's features, functionality, and stability. For an alpha or beta test to succeed, the customer must be willing to live with an unstable and unfinished product, and to cheerfully document its problems. Good alpha and beta customers are likely found in advanced development, engineering, or non-mainstream parts of a company or market. Therefore, alpha and beta testing are Product Development functions that belong to engineering. They are about validating the product technically, not the market.

Since alpha and beta testing marks the first times a product leaves the company, salespeople have treated alpha and beta sites as opportunities to consummate the first sale of the product. This is a mistake, because it results in a sales process that focuses on Product Development as its model (bad) rather than on a Customer Development model (good). The reality is that testing an unfinished product for Engineering and testing a customer's willingness to buy an unfinished product are separate, unrelated functions. Customer Validation is not about having customers pay for products that are engineering tests. It's about validating the entire market and business model. While the Customer Development team may assist in finding customers for the Product Development organization to use in alpha and beta testing, the testing itself is not part of Customer Development. Companies that understand this can give away alpha and beta products for engineering test without compromising or confusing it with Customer Development.

Alpha and beta testers can be influential as recommenders in the sales process. Just don't confuse them with customers. It's important to inculcate a cultural norm in your company that you use the word "customers" only for people who pay money for your product.

Again: The way you validate your business model and whether you truly have product/market fit is by selling it to customers. Accordingly, in this phase you will:

- Contact visionary customers
- Refine and validate your sales roadmap as you persuade three to five customers to purchase the product
- Refine and validate the distribution channel plan by getting orders from channel and service partners

A. Sell to Visionary Customers: Contact Visionary Customers

The biggest challenge in this phase of Customer Validation is to spend your time with true visionary customers, not mainstream customers. Remember visionary customers not only recognize they have a problem, they're so motivated to do something about it that they have tried homegrown solutions and have budgeted money for a solution. Were there any key characteristics of visionary customers you saw in Customer Discovery? Would any of those help you identify where you can find more prospects? Use the same techniques you used in Customer Discovery: Generate a customer list, an introductory email, and a reference story/script. Even with all your preparation, assume one out of 20 prospects you call on will engage in the sales process. In other words, be prepared for 95 percent to say no. That's OK; you only need the other 5 percent. Of those, depending on the economic climate, 1 out of 3 to 1 out of 5 will actually close when you get around to selling. That's a lot of sales calls. (That's why your company is a startup.) The good news is by this phase you have a sales closer on board to handle the tedium of making contact and arranging meetings.

It is helpful at this point to distinguish earlyvangelists from other major categories of customers: early evaluators, scalable customers, and mainstream customers. Table 4.3 describes the differences among these groups in terms of their motivation, pricing, and decision power; the competition you face in selling to them; and the risks in selling to them.

	Early Evaluators	Earlyvangelists	Scalable Customers	Mainstream Customers
Motivation	Technology evaluation	Vision-match. Understand they have a problem and have visualized a solution you have matched.	Practicality. Interested in a product that can solve an understood problem now.	Want to buy the standard, need the "whole product" delivered.
Pricing	Free	Using their pain threshold, you get to make up the list price and then give them a hefty discount.	Published list price and hard negotiating.	Published list price and harder negotiating.
Decision Power	Can OK a free purchase	May be able to OK a unilateral purchase. Usually can expedite a purchase. Internal cheerleader for a sale.	Buy-in needed from all levels. Standard sales process. May be able to avoid competitive bake-off.	Buy-in needed from all levels. Standard sales process. Competitive bake-off and/or RFP.

Four Types of Customers (Table 4.3)

Think of early evaluators as a group of tire kickers you want to avoid. Every major corporation has these groups. When they show interest in a product, startups tend to confuse them with paying customers.

Earlyvangelists have already visualized a solution -- something like the one you are offering. They are your partners in this sales process. They will do their own rationalization of missing features for you as long as you don't embarrass or abandon them.

Scalable customers may be earlyvangelists as well, but they tend follow visionaries. Instead of buying on a vision, they buy for practical reasons. These will be your target customers in six months. They are still more aggressive purchasers of new products than mainstream customers.

Finally, mainstream customers are looking for the whole product and essentially need an off-the-shelf, no-risk solution. They will be your customers in one to two years.

B. Sell to Visionary Customers:
Refine and Validate the Sales Roadmap

Can you sell three to five early visionary customers before your product is shipping? The key to selling a product on just a spec is finding earlyvangelists who are high-level executives, decision-makers and risk-takers. The earlyvangelists you are looking for now are those who could deploy and use the product. You don't need many of them at this point. Why? Because the goal is not to generate a whole lot of revenue (even though you will be asking for near list price); the goal is to validate your sales roadmap.

Let's return for a minute to Chip Stevens, the InLook CEO who left his office to develop a sales roadmap. Figure 4.9 illustrates the organizational map Chip developed for InLook's Snapshot product.

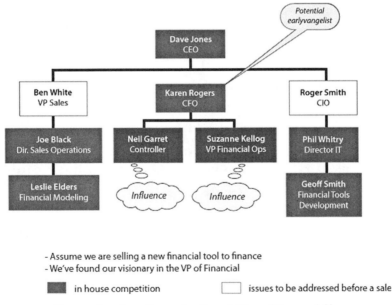

Example of an Organizational Map (Figure 4.9)

InLook's customer is the CFO, while the key influencers are the controller and the VP of financial operations. But in a series of companies, InLook discovered internal competition from IT, which championed its own homegrown financial tools. Additionally, InLook has learned many managers in the sales department believe financial modeling is their "turf" and have built a sales analyst group to provide this function. To be successful, InLook needs to eliminate opposition from sales and IT by educating the VP of Sales and the CIO.

Chip developed a sales strategy recognizing these competing internal interests and built on the interplay between purchasers and influencers in large corporate accounts (see Figure 4.10).

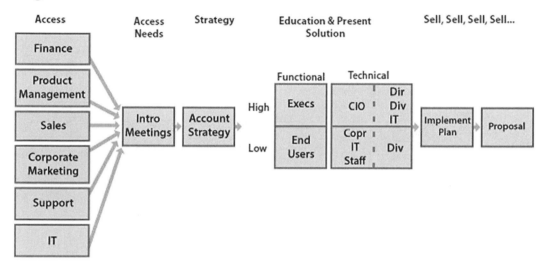

Example of a Selling Strategy *(Figure 4.10)*

Chip found he could gain access by meeting with and acquiring an executive sponsor—either the CFO, controller or VP of finance if the executive felt an acute need for InLook's software solution and had the vision and budget for the project. In addition, the executive sponsor would greatly influence the end users who generally want something their boss wants. Finally, the executive sponsor could represent the production solution to the CIO and help eliminate objections from and gain the support of the IT organization. Although a company's IT organization would not initiate a project to solve the CFO's problem, IT was a critical influencer in the sales process. So next InLook needed to meet with a company's IT executive and win his approval. Chip had also learned IT's attitude was a useful way to qualify accounts. If InLook could not win the IT support early in the sales cycle, it needed to think long and hard about investing more sales time and resources in that account.

The third move in InLook's strategy focused on finance managers who would use the product. They were generally enthusiastic about the software since it made their lives easier. Finally, InLook needed to engage the IT technical staff. If InLook executed properly on steps 1 through 3, the chances of getting approval from the technical staff were greatly enhanced, and not by accident: InLook has them surrounded. The users want the product, the finance executive wants it, and the head of IT has granted approval. (See the sales roadmap in Figure 4.11.)

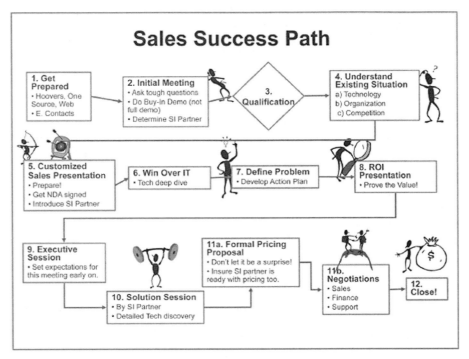

Example of a Sales Roadmap *(Figure 4.11)*

So far Chip had managed to avoid falling into the trap of early sales: the pressure to customize the product for each of your visionary customers. Your challenge is to sell the product your company will deliver at first customer ship. This means the standard product you have spec'd, not one with lots of special features. The distinction is important. One of the insidious traps of a startup is promising different customers a set of unique extensions or modifications. While it is sometimes essential to make such promises to get an order or two, the trap is you are building custom products. Building custom products is not a scalable business unless you explicitly revise your business plan. It's dangerous to proceed until Customer and Product Development get in sync on the product strategy.

Of course, sometimes these custom feature requests are good news. If enough customers have asked for the same set of "custom" features, then they are not custom at all. The customers have been trying to tell you what the product requirements really are. This is the time to pivot and incorporate those requests into your spec and declare them features.

While you're out selling to customers, keep in mind a few pricing goals. Anyone can give a product away to get an order, but your goal is to sell an unfinished, undelivered product for as near to list price as you can. Does this sound unrealistic? Only if you believe it is. Remember, you are looking for customers who will leap across the table and grab you by the collar to get early access to your product. They need what you are selling. The line from a first customer is usually, "We need a big discount because we are your first customer." You should turn this around and say, "You need to pay list price because you are going to be the first ones to use it." If that doesn't sound rational to the customer, you haven't found a visionary. Feel free to be flexible on the terms (no payment until delivery, no payment until it works as spec'd, etc.). But be tougher on discounts.

Why bother with getting near full price for your product? Part of testing the sales roadmap is testing the customer sales and approval process. You want to see whether your organizational map and selling strategy are correct. Hopefully as you work through this process you will close some orders. Your goal is to secure some orders from customers before you move on to the next step.

You can't know how well you're doing unless you keep win/loss statistics on sales calls and share them with the entire Customer Development team. Understanding why a customer said "no" is more important in this step than understanding why a customer said "yes." The goal is to understand where in the sales process you get turned down (introduction, product presentation, organizational issues, not-invented-here issues, technical issues, pricing) so you can refine your sales roadmap.

C. Sell to Visionary Customers: Refine and Validate the Channel Plan

In Customer Discovery and again in the first phase of Customer Validation, you guessed at how your product might reach customers, and you articulated a channel strategy. Now it's time to validate it in front of your channel partners by seeing if you can get a preliminary order or at least a firm commitment. Trying to get orders from these partners earlier, before you had enthusiastic customer response, would have been counterproductive. The partner response would have been predictable: "That sounds really interesting, but will there be any demand for this product? What do your customers think?" What your potential channel partner would really have been saying is, "Can I make money from your product? If so, how much?" Now that you have directly sold to customers and begun to understand why they would buy, you can answer these questions. So you're ready to go out to the channel and bring home an order.

There's one caveat in getting an order from a channel partner. One of the traps entrepreneurs fall into is confusing the role of channel partners with the role of a customer. This means convincing a channel partner to carry your product, or a big system integrator to work with your company, is emphatically not the same as getting a customer to buy your product. While channel partners may place orders for your product, they only do so if there is customer demand pulling the product out of their channel. End users pay the bills; channel partners take you seriously only when you can add to their revenue. While you may think this is blindingly obvious, lots of startups fall into the trap of thinking their sales problems are over once they have a channel partner signed up, and pop the champagne corks when they get their first "stocking" order from an indirect sales channel. Wrong. While you are a startup there is no demand for your product. No one is banging on the door of your partners asking for your product. Channel partners do not create this demand; only your startup can. This is an easy concept to grasp if you think of indirect channels as nothing more than shelves in a grocery store. Until customers become familiar with the brand, they will never look for the product.

Keeping all this in mind, update your channel/service partner presentation with information about early customer orders. Then hit the street and present to them. Your goal is to come back with a committed relationship (usually evidenced by an order).

Phase 3: Develop Positioning for the Company and Its Product

Positioning is the attempt to control the public's perception of a product or service as it relates to competitive products. In Customer Discovery, you began to think about the

Market Type you were entering and how your product competed in, redefined or created that market. You could have attempted to formally position the product early, before you made a sale, but you would have been guessing. Now you have real facts about why customers buy, and real customers with whom to test your positioning. In Phase 3 of Customer Validation, you take everything you have learned about customers and their reactions to your product and your initial value proposition, and develop two positioning statements: one for the company and one for the product. In this phase you will:

- Develop product positioning based on Market Type
- Develop your company positioning
- Make presentations to analysts and industry influencers

A. Develop Positioning: Product Positioning

Most technology-driven startups believe they need to have the professional "marketing people" from a public relations agency execute this "positioning" phase. In reality, the first pass is best done by the Customer Development team with feedback from Product Development. Right now, no one is closer to the customer. No one better understands what problems customers have said the product solves. No one else has struggled to get an order and find the repeatable sales roadmap. Your Customer Development team is more qualified than anyone to come up with a first pass of what makes the product and company unique. It's only later, in Customer Creation, that you need to bring in the "experts."

While you have been getting feedback from customers and channel partners in Customer Discovery and Customer Validation, you've continually asked yourself whether you were selling into an existing market, resegmenting a current market, or creating a new market. You wrote your first version of a positioning statement when you created the sales presentation, answering why an early customer should buy the product. Think about your customers' reaction to how you described your product. Did it generate excitement? Was it credible?

Now it is time to put a stake in the ground and formalize your product positioning based on Market Type (see Table 4.4). Your positioning doesn't have to be perfect, since you will refine it further in Customer Creation.

	Existing Market	**New Market**	**Resegmented Market**
Product Positioning Statement	Compare your product to your competitors. Describe how some feature or attribute of the product is better, faster - an *incremental improvement*.	It's too early for customers to understand what your product's features will do for them. Instead, describe the problem you product will solve and the benefits that the customer will get from solving it - a *transformational improvment*.	Compare your products to your competitors. If its low cost, describe price and feature set. If a niche, describe how some feature or attribute of the product solves the problem your customer has in a way comparable products do not. Describe the benefits that the customers will get from solving their problem this new way.

Product Positioning by Market Type (Table 4.4)

When InLook came up with new product positioning for Snapshot, they realized they had something innovative and unique, with no direct competitors. However, they were defining a new market. And in a new market focusing attention on detailed product features before customers understood what problem their product solved would be a distraction. The claims of a better, faster, cheaper product would simply be lost as customers tried to figure out what the product did and why they should care. Therefore InLook decided to position their product as providing "profitability visibility" for CFOs. The phrase resonated with their potential customers, who thought it sounded like something they might need. Time and again, the InLook sales team got invited in to explain what and how profitability visibility worked.

The end result of this product positioning exercise should be a "product positioning brief." Similar to the briefs you developed in Customer Discovery, this one-page document should cover the product positioning and its rationale. As you develop sales literature (data sheets, sales presentations, website), this brief will be used to keep all the messages "on point."

B. Develop Positioning: Company Positioning

Now that you've decided how to position your product in one of the three Market Types, you need to articulate a company positioning the same way. What's the difference between positioning the product and positioning the company? Product positioning focuses on the attributes of your specific product in a Market Type. Company positioning answers, "What does your company do for me?" and "Why does your company exist and how is it different?"

I like to write the first version of a company positioning statement as simply as possible, keeping the customer always in mind. I describe why I started this company in a way every one of my potential customers would say, "Tell me more; it sounds like you're solving a problem I have." The founders of InLook decided since they were in a new market, one they were creating, they could name this new market. They decided their company positioning was that they were creating the profitability management market. They described this market by viscerally grabbing CFOs who understood on a gut level that early visibility of profitability was a significant need for CFOs and the lack of these tools put companies at financial risk.

Table 4.5 illustrates company positioning by Market Type. Like product positioning, your company positioning doesn't have to be perfect, since you will refine it further in Customer Creation.

As a consistency check for company positioning, revisit the mission statement you wrote in Customer Discovery. Does it explain why your company is different or special? In addition, compare your company description and mission statement to those of your competitors. What is their company positioning? Are you missing something?

	Existing Market	New Market	Resegmented Market	Clone Market
Company Positioning Statements	Compare the product to its competitors. Describe how some feature or attribute of the product is better, faster – *an incremental improvement.*	It's too early for customers to understand what the product's features will do for them. Instead, describe the problem the product will solve and the benefits the customers will get from solving it – *a transformational improvement.*	Compare the product to its competitors. If it's low cost, describe price and feature set. If a niche, describe how some feature or attribute of the product solves the problem customers have in a way comparable products do not. Describe the benefits the customers will get from solving their problem this new way.	If users are familiar with foreign sites, compare to them. If not, treat as a new market.

Company Positioning by Market Type (Table 4.5)

As with product positioning, the end result of this company positioning exercise should be a "company positioning brief." As you develop marketing literature (press backgrounder, sales presentations, website), this brief will be used in conjunction with the product brief to keep all the messages consistent.

C. Develop Positioning:
Make Presentations to Analysts and Influencers

Industry analysts and industry influencers are part of the foundation of credibility a startup needs. What is an industry analyst? In the technology arena there are firms that charge customers to provide an "independent" and dispassionate analysis of markets, trends, or specific products. These firms vary in size and influence. In some technical markets (for example, enterprise software) a sale to a large company is very difficult until one of the large analyst firms (Gartner, Meta, Yankee) has blessed you. If you are in the entertainment business the analyst might be Kagan. If you are looking at consumer product sales it might be the NPD group. Industry influencers are a less formal category. In each industry a handful of people influence what gets talked about. They may be bloggers on Hacker News or they may write for Techcrunch or PandoDaily. They may be individuals in companies but speak at lots of conferences; they may be the writers at trade publications who have the most unique ideas; or they may be university professors.

You started identifying analysts and industry influencers in Customer Discovery. The goal in this phase is to meet with them, and get their insights and feedback on the initial positioning (market, product, and company) you have just created and their thoughts about your product features. You also want to see if you can get them to sing your song (and if not, you want to understand why). Even though early adopters will be evangelizing your product inside their company or to their friends and family, it helps to have other "outsiders" who will say, "Yes, we've heard of them, and while it's too early to say how good their product is, we think their idea is quite valuable." You also need to line up industry analysts and influencers as references for the press you will be getting in the Customer Creation step.

All this would have been difficult before you had real customer contacts, feedback, and orders, but now you have something to say and an idea of how to say it. First, contact the analysts and influencers you've been tracking since early in Customer Discovery. Hopefully, you've kept a database of who they are and have met them at conferences, seminars, and trade shows. You've also spent time understanding what opinions they hold on your market and product space (if not, don't use the meetings in this phase to get up to speed; do your homework first).

Before contacting analysts, make sure you understand what companies and industries their firms cover, and what particular area or companies the analysts you are calling cover. (There's nothing worse than going to see someone who is simply the wrong person or even in the wrong company. It reflects badly on you and your company. It tells everyone you didn't invest the minimal amount of time to do your homework.) Develop a short script explaining why they should meet with you. If you understand what they cover and why your company is going to shake up their market, and can explain why your company is important, the "what's in it for them" is obvious; they won't want to miss an influential and important company. Make sure you reference your early customers, and the problem/pain points you solve. When they agree to meet with you, ask how much time you will have, what presentation format they like (formal slides, demo, whiteboard talk, etc.), and whether the presentation should focus on technology, markets, customers, problems, or all of the above.

Next assemble the analyst presentation, remembering this is not a sales presentation. The focus will be on market and product positioning as well as details of product features. You want to influence analysts' thinking, not sell them a product. Each analyst organization has a view of the market you are in—make sure you have and understand that slide (you should know it well enough to draw it on the board). If you are creating a new market, get the slides describing their view of the adjacent markets you will affect.

Preparing to meet an industry influencer may require the same formal preparation as meeting an industry analyst, or it may be lunch at a nearby pub. Do your homework, and understand how the influencers acquire their information and how they disseminate it before you meet with them. Adjust your meeting style accordingly.

When you meet with the influencers and analysts, remember the goal is to gather feedback (and wild enthusiasm). You also want to use the interaction to gather intelligence about the marketplace. Make a mental checklist of what is critical for you to learn from them. For example, what other companies are doing anything like what you're doing? How does your vision fit with market needs? With customer needs? How should you position your product, market, and company? How should you price the product? How do others price theirs? Who in a company should you sell to? What obstacles will you face inside a company? What obstacles will you face as you try to build your company? Getting funded? Hiring? Competition? What do they think you should do next?

Once you have feedback from analysts and influencers, as well several real customers, you can move to the final phase of Customer Validation.

Phase 4: Verify

After meeting with analysts and influencers, you have gone all the way around the Customer Validation step. What you have done for the company is discover whether your customer, sales, and channel hypotheses were correct. What you have done for your investors is start to validate your business model. In the final phase, you summarize your findings and check whether you have learned enough to move on to Customer Creation. So, in this phase, you do five things:

- Verify the product solution
- Verify the sales roadmap
- Verify the channel plan
- Verify you have a profitable business model
- Iterate, return, or exit

A. Verify: The Product Solution

At the end of Customer Discovery, you verified that the product as spec'd met hypothetical customer needs, but you hadn't at that stage asked for an order. Now, at the end of Customer Validation, "verifying the product solution" means showing you have product/market fit with a product customers will buy. Of course, there's more to product verification than that. Review all the objections and feedback you have received from customers about the product and the conclusions you have come to about first-release features, subsequent features, and so on.

Be sure to address questions like these:

- Given the customer orders to date, does the product you are first shipping meet the needs of the market? How closely did your product match customers' pain? Did you lose deals because of missing features? What features stood out as clear "home runs"? Did you lose because your product wasn't important enough to buy until it was a "whole product"? Do you want to emphasize different features? Has the VP of Product Development heard customer issues firsthand? Did you oversell? Are customers happy?

- Did you lose deals over delivery schedule issues? Does your plan for future releases have the right features in the right order?
- Did you lose any deals over pricing? Was there any objection to your pricing? (If not, your product may be priced too low—you should always get a modicum of grumbling.) Besides the absolute price of the product, do you have the right pricing model?

The most important exit criterion is whether the sales closer believes other salespeople can sell the product as spec'd in a repeatable manner.

B. Verify: The Sales Roadmap

You have assembled your sales materials, found visionary prospects, combined an organizational map and selling strategy into a sales roadmap, and tried to sell and close customers. In this phase, verifying the sales roadmap means summarizing everything you have learned and checking to see whether you have the selling process nailed or need to go around the loop again. Review the answers you've obtained as you developed your sales roadmap:

- Did you get the organizational or consumer map right? Did you identify the right decision-makers? Did you understand the other key players? Did you lose deals because other influencers objected? Do you have a repeatable process identifying the key players consistently?
- Did you get the selling strategy right? Do you have a repeatable process taking you from person to person and group to group? Can you forecast the probability of an order based on this strategy?
- Did the organizational map and sales strategy result in a sales roadmap with a step- by-step sales forecasting process and sales pipeline?
- Most importantly, did you get orders? Whether the orders came by following a process or the process came by understanding how you got orders is irrelevant. Do the orders prove that a sales organization can scale and grow by simply following the sales roadmap? Can they sell it without the founding team calling on customers?

If you are confident you've nailed the sales roadmap, you can proceed. If not, go around the loop again.

C. Verify: The Channel Plan

Now that you have sold to customers either through an indirect channel or with a direct sales force, you understand how your distribution channel will work. Are your assumptions about the distribution channel correct? For example:

- What will the cost of the distribution channel be? Is this cost factored into your business plan?
- Are there other channel costs you didn't expect? Regardless of the channel there are almost always surprises (stocking costs, store advertising costs, extra pre-sales support, etc.).
- Can you articulate all the variables involved in using this sales and distribution model?

For example, how long is the sales cycle? Will a sale take more or less time than you originally planned? What is the average selling price? What will the revenue be per salesperson or store per year? If you anticipate building a direct sales force, how many people need to be in a sales team (salesperson, technical presales, post-sales integration, technical support, etc.)? How many teams will you need?

- If this is an indirect channel, can the channel scale? How will you train and educate the sales channel?
- What kind of demand-creation activities (advertising, PR, trade shows, etc.) will be needed to drive customers into the channel? How much will it cost to acquire each customer? Have you accounted for these costs in your business model? (While it may seem obvious, customer acquisition costs need to be less than customer lifetime value. Dollars spent in branding cannot scale a flawed or unprofitable business model.) If this is an indirect channel, are there hidden channel costs (channel incentives) or demand creation costs such as in-store displays and promotions?
- Were your assumptions about service/system integration correct? How much will this cost you per customer? Regardless of the channel, how much direct support will you need to provide?

D. Verify: The Business Model

Having orders in hand, you're probably feeling like the end is in sight. Your product solves real customer problems, and you believe you have a repeatable and scalable sales and distribution process. However, just as at the end of Customer Discovery, there is the small matter of making money. Now you have real numbers on the most critical variables of your business—how much customers will pay for your product, and how much it will cost you to sell it. It is imperative you rerun your financial model based on these facts and test how profitable your business model is.

The outcome of this testing process consists of two documents: (1) an updated sales and revenue plan and (2) an operations plan to scale the company. Without trying to be exhaustive, here are some key issues to address as you prepare these documents:

- How much additional funding do you need to reach profitability? How much funding do you need to get to positive cash flow? Is this amount realistic given your expansion plans?
- Now that the Product Development team is delivering a product, are the Product Development costs still the same? Are the costs to develop the first version still the same? How much will it cost to implement the complete vision of the product?
- Is any manufacturing involved in building the product? How much will the product cost to produce? How does that cost compare to your original plan? What manufacturing partners will you use?
- Is the projected selling price (taking into account what customers will pay) different from your initial business plan assumptions? Over the next three years, how many units will a customer buy? What do you believe the lifetime value of each customer will be?
- When you add up all the components of the business model, is it profitable enough for your needs?

E. Iterate, Return, or Exit

As grueling as Customer Validation is, you may need to iterate it again or even return all the way to Customer Discovery. This is the time to stop what you are doing and be reflective, think seriously about how you are doing. Did you really meet the Customer Validation objectives or are you just moving the goal posts so you can get to the next step? When you go to the next step, you are about to seriously crank up the burn rate of your company.

Were you able to sell the product? If not, the problem may be a lack of understanding of the sales process. Take everything you learned in Phases 1 through 3 of Customer Validation, modify your sales roadmap based on customer feedback, and return to Phase 1 of this step (Get Ready to Sell) and try it again.

However, in some cases there may be nothing wrong with the sales roadmap. The problem may be in the product itself. If you have exhausted all options in selling and positioning, you might need to reconfigure or repackage the product offering. This requires a loop all the way back to the first step, Customer Discovery. Once there, use the core technology and come up with another product configuration, then modify your product presentations and go back to Phase 3 (Product Presentation) and do it again.

Even if you have been successful selling, check your product delivery timing with your Product Development team. Schedules inevitably change, never for the better. Can you still deliver what you just sold when you said you would, or did you just sell vaporware? If you sold vaporware, at best your company secured a few pilot projects. Continuing to sell as if nothing has changed is a bad idea. As your schedules slip, the position of your earlyvangelists in their companies or with their friends and family weakens, and you will have no usable references. The good news is if this happens (and it happens more often than you think), you're in a recoverable situation. You don't have to fire a large sales staff, and your burn rate is relatively low. (You always want to have enough cash to get this phase wrong at least once.) The solution is to shut down any additional selling for a while, admit mistakes, and turn pilot projects into something useful -- first for the customer and then as a marketable product.

But if everything checks out, the end of Customer Validation is a major milestone. You have proven you have understood customer problems, found a set of earlyvangelists and delivered a product customers want to buy, developed a repeatable and scalable sales process, and demonstrated you have a profitable business model. And you've captured all of your learning in writing. You're ready for Customer Creation.

CUSTOMER VALIDATION SUMMARY

Phase	Goals	Deliverables
1. Get Ready to Sell	Produce preliminary version of sales materials and sales roadmap. Ensure all your executives are in agreement.	**Action**
A. Articulate Value Proposition	Develop value proposition.	Value Proposition
B. Prepare Sales Materials and a Prelim Collateral Plan	Develop sales materials and a preliminary collateral plan.	Collateral Sales Material & Prelim Sales Roadmap
C. Develop a Preliminary Channel Plan	Develop a preliminary distribution channel plan.	Channel Plan
D. Develop a Preliminary Sales Roadmap	Develop a preliminary sales roadmap.	Sales Roadmap
E. Hire a Sales Closer	Hire a sales closer.	Sales Closer
F. Align Your Executives	Agreement across company on schedule, deliverables, support, and collateral before you commit to product deliverables.	Product, Support, & Collateral Review
G. Formalize Your Advisory Board	Enlist needed advisors.	Advisory Board Roadmap
2. Sell to Visionary Customers	Test product and roadmap with earlyvangelists who can buy an unfinished and unproven product.	**Validation**
A. Contact Visionary Customers	Find visionary customers.	Visionary Meetings
B. Refine and Validate Sales Roadmap	Get 3 to 5 visionary customers to buy the product.	3 to 5 Purchase Orders & Repeatable Sales Process
C. Refine & Validate Channel Plan	Get early orders from channel and service partners.	Order from Potential Partners
3. Develop Positioning	Articulate belief about your product and your place in the market.	**Action**
A. Develop Product Positioning	Define what market you are in: Existing? New? Resegmented?	Product Positioning & Brief
B. Develop Company Positioning	Define what is unique about your company.	Company Positioning & Mission Statement
C. Present to Analysis and Industry Influencers	Get analysts/influencer buy-in for your vision.	Analyst Feedback & Approval
4. Verify	Have customers bought product and vision? Will it scale?	**Validation**
A. Verify Production Solution	Verify through orders that product solves customers' needs.	Product and Release Spec
B. Verify the Sales Roadmap	Verify a repeatable sales roadmap.	Final Sales Roadmap
C. Verify the Channel Plan	Verify a scalable sales and channel plan.	Final Channel Sales Roadmap
D. Verify the Business Model	Verify that you have a profitable business model.	Final Revenue Plan
E. Iterate, Return, or Exit	Have you learned enough to scale the business?	Confidence to Scale Business

Customer Creation Step-by-Step

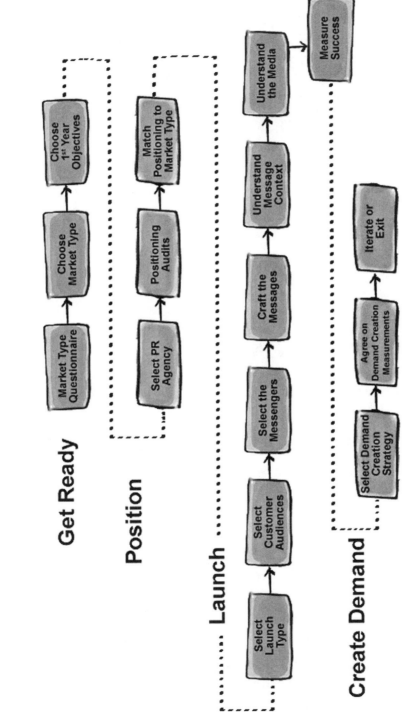

Get Ready

Market Type Questionnaire → Choose Market Type → Choose 1st Year Objectives

Position

Select PR Agency → Positioning Audits → Match Positioning to Market Type

Launch

Select Launch Type → Select Customer Audiences → Select the Messengers → Craft the Messages → Understand Message Context → Understand the Media → Measure Success

Create Demand

Select Demand Creation Strategy → Agree on Demand Creation Measurements → Iterate or Exit

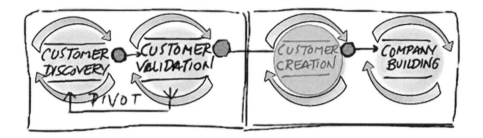

CHAPTER 5

Customer Creation

To every thing there is a season, and a time to every purpose under
the heaven.
— Ecclesiastes 3:1

PHOTOSTOYOU WAS A PRESCIENT IDEA. Way before others saw the opportunity in the late 1990s, Ernie, Chen, and Dave, the founders of PhotosToYou, realized that sales of digital cameras were starting to take off. Back then, the only way to see digital pictures was to print them out at home. It dawned on Ernie, Chen, and Dave there was an opportunity for a service to provide photo printing for digital pictures via the Internet. Not just the type of prints one would get from a low-end ink jet printer at home, but 35 mm-quality prints from high-quality photofinishing equipment. PhotosToYou would then mail the prints directly to customers.

When PhotosToYou was founded, the photography market was in rapid transition from film-based to digital. At the time, 82 billion photos were being taken annually with traditional cameras, and more than $37 billion was being spent to develop those photos. At the same time, sales of digital cameras were starting to skyrocket. Growing at a rate of over 50% annually, the installed base of digital cameras was projected to be 25% of the consumer camera market by 2004. In fact, as PhotosToYou got started, digital cameras were projected to be one of the top two consumer electronics sellers over the next three holiday seasons. To the founders, digital photography without an easy "finishing" solution seemed like computers without printers. They were convinced convenient online printing was the "killer application" for digital cameras.

I met Ernie, Chen, and Dave when PhotosToYou was just the three of them and they were still working out of the small offices of their lead investor. I was giving them a hand trying to understand the digital photography market. In talking to digital camera owners, we found they loved digital cameras for the convenience and immediate gratification, but regretted giving up quality prints. They used the digital camera when they wanted to take photos they could view immediately (or share online), but they still carried their 35 mm camera to capture photos they could turn into lasting memories. If they could get 35 mm prints from their digital camera, it would be the only camera they would use. Until then, it was a two-camera world.

Fast-forward a year. PhotosToYou hired a talented team of imaging experts from the photo industry as well as leading universities. The company had developed color correction and image enhancement technology that optimized prints for specific digital camera models. It had built the first all-digital print process using digital printers and an entire digital production facility. And it had created an incredibly easy Web application to upload and order photos. Supporting all of that were customer service, order tracking, and email and phone support. PhotosToYou was in the process of creating long-term strategic partnerships. And like any good startup it was worried about the 800-pound gorilla—in this case, Kodak—as well as the swarm of competitors that had emerged. But PhotosToYou was in good shape. Digital cameras were selling well, the company had raised a pile of money, and beta customers liked the product and were starting to tell their friends about the service. The founders were on the brink of launching the company and its online photofinishing service.

So what could go wrong? For PhotosToYou the trouble started when the company hired a new CEO and VP of Marketing, both passionate believers in "branding."

PhotosToYou's new executive team believed the difference between winning and losing on the Internet was "brand," and they wanted PhotosToYou to be the first company to develop a brand associated with digital photo printing. They believed a strong brand would allow them to drive end-user demand to their website and grab market share early on that they would never relinquish. The marketing department quickly translated this theory into practice by executing branding on multiple levels. The goal was to hit customers with the PhotosToYou brand at stores when they bought the camera, again through the company's digital camera and photofinisher partners, and yet again in their mailboxes. To make this happen PhotosToYou would have to get deals with retailers, digital camera manufacturers, Internet community sites and photo portals. The branding strategy also included a national, broad-based advertising campaign as well as targeted advertising. A large and expensive corporate identity program began.

Then reality set in. The PhotosToYou partnership strategy, which sounded great in the conference room, didn't happen. Digital camera manufacturers were reluctant to partner with just one digital photofinisher. The large Internet portals like AOL and Yahoo were more than happy to do a deal, but PhotosToYou would have to pay them a ton of money up front. The same was true for the deals with the PC manufacturers and retailers. Sure, some of them would be happy to bundle the PhotosToYou software with their PCs, but it was going to cost PhotosToYou a bundle. This left advertising and promotions as the one sure thing the company could control. So PhotosToYou embarked on a national advertising campaign.

What do you think of the company's strategy at this point? Does it make sense? Was PhotosToYou on the narrow path to success or the broad road to disaster? Was "branding" the answer to the challenge the company faced in introducing its product? What would an alternative strategy look like?

If you've followed the line of reasoning of this book to this point, you might guess the answers to these questions. PhotosToYou's strategy might have made sense in an existing market, but not for a startup in a new market. Not understanding Market Type almost sank PhotosToYou. In fact, once you understand how Market Type affects Customer Creation activities, you'll understand why the mistakes PhotosToYou made are taught as a case study in my business school class. PhotosToYou did not need a branding strategy. It needed a set of rules to identify its Market Type, and apply the appropriate Customer Creation strategies and tactics. Those strategies are the focus of the Customer Creation step. In the rest of this chapter, you'll find out what went wrong at PhotosToYou and how to avoid making the same mistakes.

The Customer Creation Philosophy

As part of the marketing advisory board at PhotosToYou, I listened to the company's launch, rollout, and branding strategies emerge. It seemed to me the company was making several mistakes.

First, in being so exclusively focused on branding tactics and launch, the company ignored the fundamental discussion of which kind of market PhotosToYou was in. No one had stopped to consider whether the company was entering an existing market, resegmenting an existing market or creating a new market. (Remember our Market Type definitions from Chapter 2; you're in a new market when you enable customers to do something they couldn't do before.)

The only people who could be PhotosToYou customers were digital camera customers. Therefore, the company's revenue was bounded by the size and growth of the new digital camera market. I argued even if they acquired 100% of all the digital camera customers with high-speed Internet access it wouldn't matter, because there were so few of them (remember this was in 1999). Since we were creating a new market, I suggested that the PhotosToYou business would take three to five years to develop. For the next two years, their market growth would be limited by outside factors (digital camera and broadband Internet adoption rate) and this was going to be a long-term war, not a short-term grab for nonexistent market share. The relevance of this argument to their marketing and branding strategy was that in a new market, spending money early to grab market share was a very bad idea. A consumer choice in this area wasn't permanent (as early customers were likely to experiment with multiple photo printing sites), and next year, when there would be eight times as many available customers, PhotosToYou wouldn't have the marketing dollars to reach them. I suggested that, rather than start expensive demand-creation activities now, PhotosToYou preserve its huge pile of cash and hunker down for the long term. Instead of a huge formal onslaught launch, they should implement an early adopter launch.

I also offered that in a new market the first year's marketing communication goals should be focused on fostering market adoption, not market share, and the company's demand-creation activities should be low-cost attempts to educate customers about the new online photofinishing market, not hugely expensive customer acquisition programs for the few customers who existed at that time. My belief was in a new market, only the early adopters—the earlyvangelists—will find the product and spread the word.

The PhotosToYou executives didn't get it. "Why are you telling us about this different

Market Type stuff? It has nothing to do with how we launch and promote our products. We've always done it this way in big companies and startups."

Trust me, this is not the advice you want to give to young, high-testosterone marketers—particularly ones being encouraged by even higher testosterone board members whose mantra was "get big fast." The board and the marketing executives thought I just didn't get it. So, my recommendations notwithstanding, the PhotosToYou marketing spending machine started like it was in an existing market and, like a steamroller going downhill, there was no stopping it.

The result was predictable. As the outside advertising and PR service providers pocketed the company's money, PhotosToYou burned through its large pile of venture money in the first two years. While the company had customer growth that would have been impressive by most metrics, it was nowhere near its optimistic revenue projections, and customer-acquisition costs were sky-high. In addition, customers proved to be fickle as they tested each online photofinishing service. Customer churn and retention turned out to be equally as important as customer acquisition. Consequently, PhotosToYou was forced to go back to the market for more money during one of the worst downturns in the technology business.

Luckily, the company's solid (but small) customer base saved it. PhotosToYou found new investors, albeit after a "cram-down" financing round – one in which the investors valued the company at one-tenth of its previous value, thereby dramatically diminishing the percentage ownership of earlier investors. In addition, the new investors insisted it replace the entire executive staff (including Ernie, Chen, and Dave), banish the nebulous term "branding" from its lexicon, and focus on the basic blocking, tackling, and execution of a more mature digital camera photofinishing business.

The story of PhotosToYou is a cautionary tale of what can go wrong in customer creation. Now let's take a look at the thinking behind this key step.

Customer Creation Versus Marketing Communications Execution

In the Customer Development model, the phrase "customer creation" represents the essential marketing activities necessary to help customers learn about a product and create a desire to buy it. In most startups this job falls under the general rubric of marketing communication. I call these activities Customer Creation rather than marketing communication to make the points that (1) in a startup these events are occurring for the first time; (2) they are not about the marketing department, they are about customers; (3) they are creation events, not follow-on execution activities;

and (4) the types of appropriate marketing programs differ widely, depending on Market Type.

Why is this distinction important? Traditional marketing communications strategy has six elements: (1) an internal and external PR audit to understand customer perceptions, (2) development of a unique company and product positioning, (3) enlistment of key industry influencers and recommenders, (4) recruitment of enthusiastic beta customers ready to sing the praises of the product, (5) product launch at first customer ship, and (6) ramped-up demand creation spending (advertising, public relations, trade shows, etc.). However, the implicit assumption is that all startups are in existing markets. And these six steps work in every existing market. However, in at least two of the four types of startups these traditional rules don't work. Unfortunately, in lieu of developing a strategy that fits their own particular circumstances, most startup marketers tend to fall back on timeworn marketing phrases and programs, typically those they used at their last company. This is a mistake. Launching a new product and company should not be confused with executing a laundry list of marketing tactics. What every startup needs is a thoughtful Customer Creation strategy and plan tailored to their Market Type. My emphasis on Customer Creation rather than marketing communications execution is meant to make clear the people involved need to be strategists rather than tacticians.

To develop a successful Customer Creation strategy, you must answer two questions: (1) What type of startup are you? (2) What are your positioning messages (based on your deep understanding of who the customers are and what they want)?

In Customer Discovery and Validation you identified who will buy your product and acquired extensive information about those customers. In Customer Creation you will use that information to forge a strategy—not disconnected tactics—to reach customers.

Market Typing: The Four Types of Startups

In Customer Discovery and Validation you began to consider what Market Type your startup is entering. (Existing, Resegmented Low End, Resegmented Niche, or New Market.) Now in Customer Creation, you need to definitively answer that question. Market Type determines how you shape your Customer Creation strategy. It is the source of all the company's positioning activities. (Keep in mind that Market Type is not immutable – you may have lots of leeway in positioning. For example, almost every product that fits as a product in an existing market could be positioned as a niche in a resegmented market. And every product that first looks like it's in a new market has to be positioned there.)

	Existing Market	Resegmented Market	New Market
Customers	Existing	Existing	New/New usage
Customer Needs	Performance	1. Cost 2. Perceived need	Simplicity & convenience
Performance	Better/faster	1. Good enough at the low end 2. Good enough for new niche	Low in "traditional attributes", improved by new customer metrics
Competition	Existing incumbents	Existing incumbents	Non-consumption / other startups
Risks	Existing incumbents	1. Existing incumbents 2. Niche strategy fails	Market adoption

Types of Markets *(Table 5.1)*

Choosing your Market Type starts with a review of everything you have learned about your potential customers in the Customer Discovery and Validation steps. By now, you should have a pretty good handle on customer needs. In talking to and selling to early customers, you have also discovered who else is trying to satisfy those same needs. Now you consider all your qualitative analyses and quantitative research about the market and your competitors. With these data in hand, take a look at Table 5.1, the four types of markets, and see where your product fits best.

New Lanchester Strategy

One of the best tools I've found for sorting out Market Type choices is derived from a military operations research theory called the New Lanchester Strategy. (These ideas have been put to use in marketing strategy in Japan, but they have always lost something in the translation by the time they have arrived in the United States. I don't swear I can derive the New Lanchester formulas and prove the theorems, but the results when applied to markets come out looking uncannily like the real world.) The New Lanchester Strategy suggests a few simple rules companies can use to analyze an existing market:

- If a single company has 74% of the market, the market has become an effective monopoly. For a startup, that's an unassailable position for a head-on assault. (Think Microsoft.)
- If the combined market share for the market leader and second-ranking company

is greater than 74% and the first company is within 1.7 times the share of the second, it means the market is held by a duopoly. This is also an unassailable position for a startup to attack. (In the telecom sector, Cisco and Juniper's share of the core router market fits this description.)

- If a company has 41% market share and at least 1.7 times the market share of the next largest company, it is the market leader. For a startup, this, too, is a very difficult market to enter. Markets with a clear market leader are, for a startup, an opportunity for resegmentation.

- If the biggest player in a market has at least a 26% market share, the market is unstable, with a strong possibility of abrupt shifts in the company rankings. Here there may be some entry opportunities.

- If the biggest player has less than 26% market share, it has no real impact in influencing the market. Startups that want to enter an existing market find these the easiest to penetrate.

One more rule in the New Lanchester Strategy is relevant for a startup. If you decide to attack a market that has just one dominant player, be prepared to spend three times the combined sales and marketing budget of that dominant player. (Ouch, so much for going head-on with Microsoft.) In a market that has multiple participants, the cost of entry is lower, but you still need to spend 1.7 times the combined sales and marketing budget of the company you plan to attack. (To enter an existing market you must steal market share from an incumbent, hence the analogy to war.) Table 5.2 summarizes the market cost of entry.

	Market Share	Cost of Entry (vs. Leader's Sales/ Marketing Budget)	Entry Strategy
Monopoly	>75%	3x	Resegment/New
Duopoly	>75%	3x	Resegment/New
Market Leader	>41%	3x	Resegment/New
Unstable Market	>26%	1.7x	Existing/Resegment
Open Market	>26%	1.7x	Existing/Resegment

Market Cost of Entry (Table 5.2)

Thinking about this strategy, many of the rules marketers learn painfully in the field now make a lot more sense. In looking at any existing market, your startup is the weakest player with the least resources. Therefore, attacking the strongest players head-on is foolish. You want to choose strategies that acknowledge your weaknesses and play to your agility. (Both Bill Davidow in his seminal work *High Technology Marketing* and Geoff Moore in *Crossing the Chasm* articulated the same type of rules for startups and new products based on observation and experience. Now we can derive them directly.)

Now that you know the rules, what do they mean for choosing Market Type? Let's say you are going after a well-defined existing market. If there is a dominant player with more than 74% market share, do not attack that market head-on. Why? Because of the rule that says you need three times the resources of the market leader, you'll be out of business shortly. Instead, target your attack at the point where your limited resources can make a difference. You will segment the existing market to create a submarket where your product can be unique or substantially different. Or if you can create an entirely new market; you can define a space the market leader does not address.

Your goal is to become No. 1 in something important to your customer. It could be product attribute, territory, distribution chain/retailer, or customer base. Keep segmenting the market (by age, income, region, etc.) and focusing on the competitors' weak points until you have a battle you can win. You know your segmentation is correct when you have created a niche where you can be No. 1. Remember, any company can take customers away from any other company—if it can define the battle.

If the dominant player has between 26% and 74% market share, pick your battles carefully. Remember the cost of a head-on attack: Three times the budget of a single competitor or 1.7 times a competitor in a crowded market. Most startups don't have access to those financial resources. Therefore, resegmenting the market or creating a new market is almost always the default when faced with a dominant incumbent. All the marketing tricks for nipping at the heels of an entrenched competitor can be used here: Most of them were invented 2,500 years ago by Sun Tzu' and described in his book, *The Art of War*: "All warfare is based on deception. If your enemy is superior evade him. If angry irritate him. If equally matched, fight and if not split and re-evaluate."

If there is no single company with more than 26% market share in an existing market, then the startup gods have smiled on you. You can still choose to resegment the market, but the cost of entry is low and the market is ripe for innovation. It is yours to lose.

What if there are no competitors? What if after talking to all your early customers you continue to hear, "There's nothing else like what your company is offering?" What if after looking at all the quantitative data you can't find other companies with comparable products? Congratulations: You are creating an entirely new market. A company creating a new market is radically different from one entering or reframing an existing market. While there are no market-share battles with competitors, there are also no existing customers. This means even an infinite demand-creation budget at the point of product launch will not garner market share. Creating a new market is about long-term customer education and adoption.

Given the long-term and deep-pocket commitment necessary in a new market, why not just position the company as one resegementing an existing market? That can be a viable option, but the one piece of great news about creating an entirely new market is once the market is established, as the market leader you are guaranteed at least 41% market share. You can certainly lose that share, and your success will attract other competitors, but the market is yours to start. (The notion of a new market is also tantalizing because of the misunderstood and much-abused phrase "first mover advantage." We'll talk about that later in this chapter.)

With the tantalizing goal of dominance of a new market in mind (dominant players set the standards, pricing and positioning), I'll add one final rule: Startups creating new markets will not create a market of substantial size to generate a profit until three to seven years from product launch. This sobering piece of data is derived from looking at the results of hundreds of high-tech startups in the last 20 years. While you may be convinced your startup is the exception, the odds say unless you are in a "bubble economy" it takes time for new ideas and products to diffuse and catch on. (A bubble economy is defined as a time of irrational exuberance in a market when all normal rules are repealed. Examples include the biotech boom in the early 1980s and the dot-com and telecom boom in the late 1990s.) With the rules governing the four types of markets for startups in hand, let's examine how fundamental the choice of Market Type is to this Customer Creation step.

Customer Creation Strategies to Match Market Type

Now that we understand a bit about Market Type, it's hard to believe that with monotonous regularity startups with no revenue still announce new products using the same positioning and product launch strategy as a billion-dollar, 75-year-old company announcing its 43rd follow-on product. This disconnect contributes to the high-burn rate and less-than-dazzling market penetration of more than a few startups. In a forgiving economy, heaps of funding will hide these problems, but when money is scarce, getting it right the first time matters. And that means matching your positioning, launch, and demand-creation strategies to the type of startup you are.

The big idea is since there are existing, resegmented and new Market Types, there must be Customer Creation strategies to match. More specifically, each building block of customer creation—company and product positioning, company and product launch, demand-creation activities, and first-year goals—differs depending on the type of startup. These are radical new ideas, and their consequences are a bit sobering. There isn't just one type of product launch for a startup; there are three. There isn't just one type of positioning; there are three. There isn't just one type of demand-creation activity; there are three. And there isn't just one appropriate first-year goal; there are three. (Table 5.3 summarizes the Customer Creation building blocks for the three types of startups; the rest of this chapter elaborates on the details.)

	Company Positioning	Product Positioning	Company Launch	Product Launch	Demand Creation Activities	Year One Objectives
Existing Market	Differentiate and credibility	Product differentiation	Credibility and delivery	Existing basis of competition	Create, drive demand into the sales channel	Market share
New Market	Vision and Innovation in the new market	Defining new the market, the need, and the solution	Credibility and Innovation	Market education, standards setting, and early adapters	Customer education, drive early adopters into sales channel	Market adoption
Resegmented Market	Innovation	differentiation	Innovation	competition	sales channel	share

Customer Creation Activities for the Three Types of Startups *(Table 5.3)*

In hindsight, it's obvious that PhotosToYou did not understand Market Types. If the founders had understood they had a new product entering a new market, their choices for Customer Creation would have been a lot clearer.

The Four Building Blocks of Customer Creation

Common to all startups are four building blocks for Customer Creation. Being able to articulate them is the first step in assembling a coherent Customer Creation plan. The four building blocks are:

- Year one objectives
- Positioning: both company and product
- Launch: both company and product
- Demand creation (advertising, public relations, trade shows, etc.)

Some of these building blocks, such as company launch, are one-time events. Others happen infrequently (company and product positioning), and still others occur continually (demand-creation activities). Still, every company that launches a new product—whether the company is a startup or a venerable firm with a 100-year track record—must organize and execute with these four building blocks. Most startups execute these building blocks haphazardly and without thought of how they interconnect to build the company.

One of PhotosToYou's problems in setting out its marketing priorities was a lack of clarity in terminology. The company used the word "branding" in lieu of a more precise description of the three types of Customer Creation activities.

Customer Creation Timing

Although Customer Creation as a set of specific activities is one step in the Customer Development model, implicit in the entire model is the idea that Customer Creation does not happen in one day, one week, or even one month. Rather, it is a continuous, ongoing process that starts the day the company is founded. The whole premise of this book is that a startup needs to learn and discover as early as possible. That having been said, one of the most egregious mistakes a startup can make is beginning some of the expensive Customer Creation activities (advertising, heavy PR, etc.) too early. A key tenet of the Customer Development philosophy is there should be no serious spending in marketing until the company has a proven and repeatable sales roadmap. It's in this sense that Customer Creation is a discrete step that follows Customer Discovery and Customer Validation.

As shown in Table 5.4, however, all four building blocks of Customer Creation require intensive preparation in the prior Customer Discovery and Customer Validation steps.

If you have followed the Customer Development process up to now, you are well prepared for Customer Creation. And as you notice, one of the persistent themes from the earliest stages of Customer Development was asking, "What Market Type is our company in?"

In Customer Discovery, the company articulates the customer problem and product concept, and tests it with potential customers. During this process the company gains an understanding of how customers perceive other vendors who can solve the same problem. As it continues to talk to customers the company starts asking, "What type of startup are we?" As it understands how customers work it also acquires information about how customers buy, what they read, what trade shows they attend, and so on. The founders attend trade shows and conferences, listening to the presentations, watching demos, and noting the positioning of the others in their space. The company begins to develop lists of key press contacts, analysts, and influencers. By this point the Customer Development team should be able to describe how customers do their jobs without, and then with, the company's new product or service. If the team can do this, they're in shape to launch the product. If they can't, then the company's ability to create meaningful positioning that connects with customers is suspect.

When the company moves to Customer Validation, the level of information gathering intensifies. By now the company has built a first pass of a sales roadmap and has an understanding of the early customer path to purchase. The company tests its initial company and product positioning with earlyvangelists and other early customers by using it to sell.

Finally in Customer Creation, the company finalizes its positioning and launches the company and product. All the standard marketing communications activities begin to ramp up. However, the next surprise about this step is that the type of launch is dependent upon the type of startup. There is no "one-size fits all" company or product launch.

	Customer Discovery	Customer Validation	Customer Creation
Year One Objectives	• Estimate of year one sales • Market Type?	• Refine year one sales numbers • Preliminary customer creation thoughts • Market Type?	• Commit to year one sales numbers • Execute appropriate customer creation strategy • Market Type?
Positioning *Company* *Product*	• Market Type? • Understand customer perception of competitors • Articulate problem and product concept	• Market Type? • Create initial company positioning. Test with early adopters • Create initial product positioning. Test with early adopters	• Market Type? • Agency positioning with audit • Agency positioning with audit
Launch *Product* *Company*	• How do customers do their job? • What type of startup is the company? Attend trade shows. Estimate market size	• Test product launch strategy with early adopters • Test corporate launch strategy with early adopters	• Launch now. Type of launch depends on type of startup • Introduce company now. Type of launch depends on size of startup
Demand Creation	• Market Type? • Discover press contacts, analysts, influencers • How do customers make buying decisions?	• Market Type? • How do customers purchase products? Understand analysts' and influencers' viewpoints • Establish target press, analyst, and influencer lists and relationships	• Market Type? • Implement demand creation • Type of demand creation depends on market type

Four Building Blocks of Customer Creation (Table 5.4)

Customer Creation and the Customer Development Team

One last point about Customer Creation: Most startups know only too well the frustration of finally bringing an innovative new product to market and then getting disappointing early sales. Not only frustrating, it's usually the beginning of internecine warfare between Sales and Marketing as they engage in a rising chorus of finger-pointing exercises. Marketing accuses Sales of poor salesmanship. Sales counters with claims of poor positioning, inadequate pricing models, or inaccurate market analysis. Engineering believes both groups are made up of bozos who don't understand the product's technical attributes and benefits.

One key insight of the Customer Creation strategy is that there is no "pass the buck" hand-off of a product from Engineering to Marketing, and then to Sales. The entire Customer Development model is predicated on the notion of a Customer Development team that understands the customer's problem, validates a sales roadmap, and works together to select, then execute the correct Customer Creation strategy. This is the antithesis of departmental-level buck passing.

Also note the absence of a marketing communications department at this phase of a startup's life. In fact, there is no marketing department, or sales department. And therefore there is no marketing budget, or sales budget. There is only a Customer Development team and budget. Sure, there are people who write the marketing literature and others who specialize in closing a sale, but they are all working for Customer Development. Only after the company has identified its customers; validated the sales roadmap; and entered, created, or resegmented the market will the organizations within the company begin to differentiate into their traditional roles in Step 4, Company Building.

Overview of the Customer Creation Process

Customer Creation has four phases, as shown in Figure 5.1. Phase 1 begins with a series of "getting ready to launch" activities: choosing a Market Type (and therefore the type of Customer Creation strategy) and setting year one Customer Creation and sales goals. As part of this process the company makes a serious effort to understand market size, total available market, and available customer budgets. Finally, the company writes down its strategy, goals, objectives, and milestones, and puts together the Customer Creation budget.

Customer Creation: Overview of the Process *(Figure 5.1)*

Next, in Phase 2 the company develops the company and product positioning messages. In Phase 3 the company launches its product; defines the audience, messengers, and messages; and establishes metrics for gauging success. Finally, in Phase 4 the company matches demand-creation activities (advertising, adwords, public relations, trade shows, etc.) to the sales roadmap.

Note this step does not cover traditional marketing communications demand-creation tactics such as adwords, advertising and public relations. Rather, it covers new ideas for Customer Creation strategy. With that understanding, let's look at each phase in detail.

Phase 1: Get Ready to Launch

This phase of Customer Creation sets the "big-picture" strategy for all the company's Customer Creation activities. Historically, marketing communication in startups has acted as an "execution" function. While a startup will need execution later, Customer Creation strategy should come first. In this phase you do the following:

- Construct a Market-Type questionnaire
- Choose the Market Type
- Agree on the company's first-year customer creation and sales objectives

A. Get Ready to Launch:
Construct a Market-Type Customer Questionnaire

Now that you have collected qualitative and quantitative data about customers and your market, you are ready to choose your Market Type. In gathering this data you have an enviable advantage you did not have before: your early customers. Unlike startups that are trying to figure their Market Type before they have talked to customers, you have had months, if not years, in front of customers in the Customer Discovery and Validation steps. In fact, you have passionate earlyvangelists as customers who typically have opinions about everything. In addition, you've spoken to hundreds of suspects and prospects. Why not start by asking your existing customers and prospects what they think?

Do this by first assembling a Market-Type Questionnaire. An example is shown in Figure 5.2 (in this example, the startup is marketing to businesses). In an actual questionnaire, substitute your company name where "the startup" appears.

Customer Market-Type Questionnaire

Customer Focus

☐ Does the startup understand the business you are in?

☐ Does the startup understand what you do at this company?

☐ Does the startup understand the top three problems you have?

☐ Do you believe that the startup's product will sove these prolems? How?

Market Focus

☐ Are there other products in the market that are similar to the startup's?

☐ If so, how are the startup's products different?

☐ Which products do you like the best? Why?

☐ If not, how would you describe the space the startup is in?

☐ Are the startup and its product unique? If so, why?

Competition

☐ Who do you think the startup will compete with within its first year?

☐ Who do you think are the startup's ultimate competitors?

☐ What does the startup need to do to win against these competitors?

Positioning

☐ Have you heard the startup describe its positioning? Do you believe it? Is it right? Would you change it?

☐ Have you heard the startup's mission statement? Do you believe it? Is it right?

Trends

☐ What technology/product trends should the startup worry about?

☐ Who are the key opinion leaders in this technology? Whom do you respect?

☐ What business trends should the startup worry about?

☐ Who are the key opinions leaders in these business trends? Whom do you respect?

Example of a Customer Market-Type Questionnaire (Figure 5.2)

B. Get Ready to Launch: Choose the Market Type

Understanding your Market Type can help your company avoid the sort of expensive errors PhotosToYou encountered. If PhotosToYou had understood it was in a new market, it would have known no amount of spending to develop branding would create enough customers. Equally important, it would have known its revenue projections were unrealistic. (The effect of Market Type on sales revenue will be discussed in Step 4, Company Building.)

With the results from the Market-Type Questionnaire, combined with the Market Type analysis outlined in Figure 5.2, you now have sufficient information to pick your Market Type. Picking Market Type is more than just semantics. As we saw earlier in this chapter, all Customer Creation activities need to match the Market Type and startup. Assessing the risks and tradeoffs between each Market Type is first a matter of data collection, then a matter of data analysis, but in the end it is one of judgment. In some startups the choice between positioning as a company resegmenting an existing market or as entering an existing market is a matter of risk, reward, and instinct.

In Customer Discovery, Phase 1, I noted that for each type of startup there are four variables: knowledge of the customers, knowledge of the market, how important the product features are at first to the market, and the depth and breadth of competition. Now as part of your final selection of what type of company you are, add "risk" as one more item to think about, as shown in Table 5.5.

	Customers	Market	Product Features	Competitors	Risk
Existing Market	Known	Known	Critical	Many	Cost of entry: product development; sales/distribution
New Market	Unknown	Unknown, definition critical	Irrelevant at first	None at first (other startups)	Long evangelism and education cycle
Resegment New Market	Possibly known	Unknown, definition critical	Critical, tied to existing market	Many if wrong, few if right	market redefinition: product redefinition

Types of Positioning, with Risk Added *(Table 5.5)*

The major risk in entering an existing market is the dominance of the competitors and the consequent cost of entry. Startups should not underestimate the cost of sales and marketing in taking on entrenched competitors. Even the world's best products need distribution channels and heavy demand-creation spending to become known by potential purchasers. Since sales/distribution channels are "owned" by the incumbents, the cost of establishing your own or a parallel channel is another risk. Remember the rule of thumb: Attacking a competitor with a monopoly in an existing market requires three times the competitor's spending. Attacking a market with multiple competitors requires 1.7 times the spending of the weakest player. For a startup these can be huge sums.

In addition, in an existing market the incumbents have set measures of performance. A startup can attempt to respond by picking the bases of competition (features, price, performance, etc.). Typically these are product features, so the ability of the new company to provide differentiated products is critical. For example, Transmeta, a new microprocessor company, attempted to challenge Intel head-on with an Intel-compatible chip that consumed drastically lower power. They had hoped better performance would allow them to target markets (i.e., hand-held devices) existing Intel chips could not satisfy. Unfortunately, the early Transmeta chips did not live up to the hype. Hence one risk of success in entering an existing market is predicated on Product Development.

The risks in a new market are different. You must define the new market in a way that aligns with users' perceptions of their problem and your solution. Just as important for management and investors, a new market is a long-term investment. New market creation is not about quick returns and instant gratification. For example, Tivo positioned its Digital Video Recorder (DVR) as a new market category. Instead of comparing themselves to a VCR, they decided to create a new category, the DVR, where their products could be priced and differentiated from commodity VCRs. This new market creation takes deep pockets and a long-term vision.

The risks in resegmenting an existing market are a combination of those associated with creating a new market and entering an existing one. The segmentation of the existing market has to be spot-on, and the company must convince existing users their current vendors' products don't solve their problems. In addition, the product has to be different enough so existing customers of competitive products can clearly see its unique attributes and benefits. Ikea is a great example of a regsementation strategy that was both low-cost and targeted a niche. They offer low-cost furniture to customers who want a sense of style. Ikea lowers its costs by eliminating in-store assistance, having a limited variety of furniture (four styles), no delivery, and low-end quality. On the other hand, they delight low-cost buyers with on-site daycare, a great café, innovative housewares and toys, and airy and ultra-modern stores.

A Note on "First Mover Advantage"

This is probably as good a place as any to talk about the fallacy of "first mover advantage," which was first popularized in a 1988 paper by Stanford Business School professor David Montgomery and his co-author, Marvin Lieberman.[4] This phrase was the theoretical underpinning of the out-of-control spending by startups during the dot-com bubble. Some Silicon Valley VCs used it to justify the wanton and reckless "get big fast" strategies of the era. Over time it gained mythical status until the idea that market-share leaders have been the first (not just early) entrants into their categories became unchallenged conventional wisdom in Silicon Valley. The only problem? It's simply not true. The irony is that in a retrospective paper 10 years later (1998), the authors backed off from their claims. By then it was too late.

In fact, a 1993 paper by Peter N. Golder and Gerard J. Tellis had a much more accurate description of what happens to startup companies entering new markets.[5] In their analysis Golder and Tellis found almost half of the market pioneers in their sample of 500 brands in 50 product categories failed. Even worse, the survivors' mean market share was lower than that found in other studies. Further, their study shows early market leaders (as distinct from first entrants) have much greater long-term success; those in their sample entered the market an average of 13 years later than the pioneers. What's directly relevant from their work is a hierarchy showing what being first actually means for startups entering new markets:

- Innovator — First to develop or patent an idea
- Product Pioneer — First to have a working model
- Market Pioneer — First to sell the product — 47% failure rate
- Early market leader — Entered early but not first — 8% failure rate

---

4 TD. Montgomery, M. Lieberman.1988 "First Mover Advantage." T*Strategic Management Journal*, 9(T9):41–58.T

5 P. N. Golder and G. J. Tellis. 1993. "Pioneer Advantage: Marketing Logic or Marketing Legend?" *Journal of Marketing Research*, 30(2):158–170.

First mover advantage (in the sense of trying to be the first one on a shelf or with a press release) is not real, and the race to be the first company into a new market can be destructive. Therefore, startups whose mantra is "we have to be first to market" usually lose. There are very few cases where a second, third, or even 10th entrant cannot become a profitable or even dominant player. For example, Ford was the first successfully mass-produced car in the United States. In 1921, Ford sold 900,000 Model Ts for 60 percent market share compared to General Motors' 61,000 Chevys, a 6 percent market share. Over the next 10 years, while Ford focused on cost reductions, General Motors built a diverse and differentiated product line. By 1931 GM had 31% of the market to Ford's 28%, a lead it has never relinquished. Just to make the point that markets are never static, Toyota, a company that sold its first car designed for the U.S. market in 1964, is poised to become the dominant American car company. The issue is not being first to market, but understanding the type of market your company is going to enter.

C. Get Ready to Launch:
First-Year Customer Creation and Sales Objectives

Once Market Type is selected, the year-one revenue, spending, and market-share objectives for both Customer Creation and sales can be set. While this book can't do justice to the complex interplay among initial sales forecasts, sales budgets, spending for customer awareness, demand creation, and customer acquisition, they are all intimately linked as part of a Customer Creation strategy. This section attempts to simplify this ball of twine by noting there are radically different first-year goals depending on Market Type.

For an Existing Market

If entering an existing market, the year-one objective is to take as much market share as possible from incumbents. Consequently, all Customer Creation activities must single-mindedly focus on demand creation and customer acquisition. To determine how big the opportunity is, use market research data to estimate the size of the total available market. However, a more meaningful number for planning is the size of the serviceable available market. This subset of the total available market is the target market for first-year sales. To calculate the serviceable available market, subtract all the customers who are unreachable in the first year. They may be unreachable because they have already bought a competitive product, because they have product needs broader than your startup's initial offerings, or because they need a "whole product" (your product plus service, support, and other infrastructure only a mature company can deliver).

Next, put together a sales forecast. Since you've been out selling to earlyvangelists, this should be more than a guess. By now you have a pretty good feel for who to sell to, how long the sales cycle is, and what your pricing should be. Start with an exercise that says, "If we had no competition and the product were free, how many customers could we get in year one?" Follow that with, "OK, the product is still free, but now we have competitors. How many customers would use our product in year one?" You'd be surprised how many times an answer greater than the total number of available customers comes back from overenthusiastic salespeople. Keep refining the questions: "Given our actual pricing, how many customers could afford our product in year one?" "Given how fast we could hire and train salespeople (or bring on a distribution channel), how many could we sell?" Then take these numbers and compare them to the industry norm of dollars per salesperson or per channel. Since you are in an existing market, these numbers exist, some published, some not. Take all of this to derive the upper bound of potential first-year revenue. Very few startups ever exceed their first-year forecast.

Using this revenue number, calculate the number of customers your sales organization will need in order to achieve the first-year revenue goal. From there, start working the sales forecast model backwards. How many qualified prospects will you need to close an order? How many raw leads will that number require? If Sales had everything it wanted, where would the most qualified leads come from? For example, for a Web-based product, this exercise should result in understanding how to optimize a search engine strategy and Google ads to drive customers to your site. For a direct-sales organization this should result in understanding how many leads the traditional demand creation activities need to pour into the sales pipeline for sales to make its first-year revenue plan. With that number as a goal you can start thinking about how much to spend on customer acquisition activities.

The first year of a startup includes one-time costs not found in an existing company: product and company launch, as well as distribution channel one-time costs (headcount, training, channel stocking costs, etc.). Add these one-time costs to the ongoing demand-creation and customer acquisition costs to come up with the Customer Creation budget for year one. More often than not, a first pass through these numbers exceeds the gross national product of small countries. It usually takes several iterations to get numbers a startup can afford. As you redo the budget, it's easy to forget the goal. Remember, the objective is market share, which in an existing market is achieved by product differentiation. The Customer Creation goal is to create and drive end-user demand into the sales channel.

Finally, test your budget number against the New Lanchester Strategy: If a single company has a monopoly on the market, your first-year spending should be three times your competitor's sales and marketing budget. If there are multiple competitors in the market, then you can enter with 1.7 times the sales and marketing budget of the smallest player.

For a New Market

If entering a new market, the year-one objective has nothing to do with market share. This idea alone is worth the price of this book. There is no way a new company can get meaningful orders from a market that doesn't exist. Therefore, spending money on a massive launch to garner customers and market share is ludicrous.

PhotosToYou is a good example of how smart startups fall into this trap because they believe the hyperbole of first mover advantage. The momentum of the marketing communications execution team inexorably pushes a startup down a spending path from which there is often no recovery. A Customer Creation strategy can eliminate these types of errors.

The year-one objective for a company in a new market is to drive or grow adoption of this market. The limited demand-creation activities the company engages in are focused on (1) customer education about the new market and (2) turning earlyvangelists into "reference customers" for the emerging market to emulate. The success criterion for year one is that the number of potential customers has gone from zero to meaningful.

For Resegmenting a Market

If resegmenting an existing market, the year-one objective is doubly difficult. Not only do you have to garner as much market share as possible, but you must educate customers about the new issues in the market. The Customer Creation activities must create demand and acquire customers while segmenting the market in a way that is meaningful to customers.

In entering a market you are resegmenting, the budget process is the same as for entering an existing market. As in an existing market, test your budget number against the New Lanchester Strategy; while the rules are the same, if you've segmented the market correctly, the number of your competitors should be significantly reduced.

Phase 2: Position the Company and Product

Phase 2 of Customer Creation aggregates all the company's positioning efforts to date. By this time you have a lot of data to help develop effective positioning. In Customer Discovery, you gained an understanding of customer perceptions of other competitors that might solve their problem. In Customer Validation, you acquired earlyvangelists as paying customers and heard their feedback on your proposed corporate and product positioning. You also articulated a value proposition for the product. Based on feedback from early customers, this value proposition became the initial positioning for the company and product. Now, in this phase, you will further refine the corporate and product positioning by gathering customer, press, and analyst feedback.

Remember, the goal of positioning is to control the public's perception of a product or service as it relates to competitors' alternatives. The company and product positioning you develop in this phase becomes the touchstone for communications, marketing, and relationships. All company and product messages are derived from this positioning.

In this phase you should:
- Select a public relations agency
- Conduct internal and external positioning audits
- Match positioning to Market Type

A. Position the Company and Product: Select a Public Relations Agency

Because Customer Creation begins with thinking and planning (strategy) rather than just spending money on marketing communications (execution), the company may need to bring in specialized help. What the company needs at this stage is help in strategic communications. This expertise is typically found in some public relations agencies. Good PR agencies are adroit at helping a company (1) position itself and its products, (2) articulate its message and refine its audience, and (3) get industry influencers and messengers to communicate the company's message.

Hiring an agency does not mean the Customer Development team abdicates its role in the process. Your company is not along for the ride. It's your responsibility to set your organization's goals and to understand the wants and needs of your target customers. The agency's job is to understand what the company's goal is, provide additional customer insights from their other projects, and develop positioning and craft messages that effectively communicate how your product uniquely meets customer needs.

In hiring an agency for the Customer Creation step, make sure you are evaluating the agency's ability to think about positioning and communication strategy, not just its skill with "how to get press" tactics. Are they knowledgeable about your market or adjacent markets? Do they have any customer-specific knowledge? That is, does their research extend past the press to actual target customers? Are they creative? Will they come up with better insights than your own team? Is strategy a core strength of their agency? Have they shown you examples that made you smarter? Do they have metrics in place to measure success for each client? Does talk of measurement make them nervous? Once you've satisfied yourself with the answers to these questions, get a written agreement that the individuals who impressed and convinced you their firm could do the job will actually spend time on your account.

Finally, make sure your agency understands and buys into the notion of Market Type. If the people at the agency resolutely believe that all startups are launched the same way, hiring them will be an expensive mistake. The good news is that most sophisticated agencies know there are different Market Types—they just have never used the terminology before.

B. Position the Company and Product: Conduct Internal and External Audits

Before the company spends a dime on positioning, it's a good idea to air out the conference room and get some facts. The best way to do so is with a market tool called an audit. An audit is an unbiased way to learn how others perceive your company and products. In an external audit the PR firm calls customers and messengers (industry analysts and influencers, members of the press, and others we'll define later in this chapter) and asks them a series of questions, similar to the kinds of questions you asked in your market-type about how they perceive your company. Think of the results as a baseline of the perceptions others have about your company.

External Audit Questionnaire

Recognition
- ❏ Have you heard of the company? Do you know what they do?

Market Focus
- ❏ Are there other products in the market similar to the company's?
- ❏ If so, how are the company's products different?
- ❏ Which do you like the best? Why?
- ❏ If not, how would you describe the space the company is in?

Customer Focus
- ❏ Are you familiar with the types of customers the company is calling on?
- ❏ Are you familiar with the kinds of problems these customers have?
- ❏ Do you believe company's product will solve these problems? How?

Product Focus
- ❏ Do you know what the top three features of the company's product are?
- ❏ Are these "must have" features?
- ❏ What features must the company get to market in the next release? The next release?
- ❏ What do you think of the company's core technology? Is it unique? Defensible? How does it compare to others coming into the market?

Positioning
- ❏ Have you heard the company describe its positioning? Do you believe it? Is it credible?
- ❏ Have you heard the company describe its mission? Do you believe it?

Competition
- ❏ Who do you think the company will compete with in its first year?
- ❏ Who do you think are the company's ultimate competitors?
- ❏ What does the company need to do to win against these competitors?

Sales/Distribution
- ❏ Is the company's distribution strategy the right way to reach customers?
- ❏ Is the company's sales strategy effective?
- ❏ Does the company have the right pricing? Is it charging too much? Too little?

Strengths/ Weaknesses
- ❏ What are the strengths of the company? (Product, distribution, positioning, partners, etc.)
- ❏ What are its weaknesses? (Lack of "whole product," sales, product features, etc.)

Trends
- ❏ What technology/product trends should the company worry about?
- ❏ Who are the key opinion leaders in this technology? Who do you respect?
- ❏ What business trends should the company worry about?
- ❏ Who are the key opinion leaders in these business trends? Who do you respect?

Acquisition Information
- ❏ What do they think is the best way for the company to get product information to its customers? What do you think influences customers' opinions?
- ❏ What is the best way for the company to get you to be interested in its products? Can the company call you?

Example of an External Audit Questionnaire (Figure 5.3)

Once you understand what others think (usually a surprise to most startups breathing the rarified air of their own conference rooms), the company can work to change and shape those opinions. An example of an external audit is shown in Figure 5.3.

While conducting an audit is the kind of activity PR agencies excel at, handing this function off completely is a serious mistake in a startup. Just as your early sales calls were too important to be handled by salespeople, your early audits are too important to be handed off to a PR agency. The founding team should make the first five or so calls.

Listening to external voices share their perceptions about the company is one half of this audit step. Listening inside the company is the other half. An internal audit directs the same questions to the founding team and executive staff. Most startups assume they have internal unanimity on all the issues in the external audit. An internal audit will probably reveal you have a cacophony of voices. The goal of the internal audit is to hear those differences and extract new ideas. When the company has agreed on a final positioning at the end of this phase, you then communicate those ideas back to the entire organization so it speaks with one voice.

C. Position the Company and Product: Match Positioning to Market Type

Company positioning answers, "What does your company do for me?" A great company positioning begins and ends with the customer in mind. If potential customers heard your company positioning statement, would they care? Would they get excited and want to feel connected with the company? For example Apple Computer positions itself as a manufacturer of "cool computers," appealing to trend-setting customers. The positioning leaves you with a sense of whether you want to investigate the company's product offerings further by what you believe Apple stands for and excludes some people who are turned off by the positioning.

As suggested earlier, the messages the company wants to send about itself and its products differ by Market Type. So now it's time to match the positioning to the Market Type you have selected. An experienced PR agency or consultant can help you brainstorm, but you must make the Market Type choice by the end of this phase.

For an Existing Market

If you are entering an existing market, then company positioning is about creating the notion that your company is both different and credible. When Handspring entered the personal digital assistant market, people understood that the company was a manufacturer of Palm-like devices but they were going to be expandable, faster, cheaper, and somehow better. Handspring also had immediate credibility since the founders were the creators of the Palm and the entire PDA market.

Once the positioning for the company is chosen, product positioning follows. Since in an existing market comparable products exist, product positioning typically describes how and why your product is different along an existing axis/basis of competition. Differentiation in an existing market can take one of three forms. You can describe differences in product attributes (faster, cheaper, less filling, 30% more), in distribution channel (pizza in 30 minutes, home delivery, see your nearest dealer, build it yourself on the Web), or in service (five-year, 50,000-mile warranty; 90-day money-back guarantee; lifetime warranty). For example, Handspring differentiated on product attributes. It said that all Handspring PDAs were different and better because they were "expandable with a Springboard expansion module, and had 16 versus 8 megabytes of memory."

Because the market already existed, and customers understood the basis of competition, existing PDA customers understood what Handspring was talking about. The result was 30% of the Palm-compatible market in 15 months.

For a New Market

If you are creating a new market, company positioning cannot be about how different your company is, since there are no other companies to compare it to. Positioning here is about communicating a vision and passion of what could be. It answers the questions, "What is wrong with the world that you want to make right? What is it that your company is trying to change?" When Palm created the first personal digital assistant, the company positioning was about communicating a vision of how having a PDA was going to make life easier for consumers. As another example, PhotosToYou's passionate positioning should have been "allowing consumers to make hassle-free photo prints from your digital camera." That was a vision a digital camera customer could understand and connect with. Instead, PhotosToYou described itself as "the best online photofinisher." While technically correct, that message assumed potential customers understood what an online photofinisher was. When the market does not yet exist, customers need to first understand what problem your company is solving.

After positioning the company, positioning the product in a new market becomes pretty simple. Touting a new product's features is unproductive, since there is no context to understand the features—no comparable products exist. For example, if Palm had positioned its first PDA product as having 16 megabytes of memory and being expandable, no one would have had a clue what it was talking about. Instead Palm's product positioning talked about the problem the product solved ("Now executives can keep in sync with their computers") and how the product solved it ("A PDA allows you to put all those functions in your pocket").

For Resegmenting a Market

If you are resegmenting an existing market, then company positioning depends on segmentation of the market, not differentiation. Segmentation means you've picked a clear and distinct spot in customers' minds that is unique, understandable, and, most importantly, concerns something they value, and want and need now. Company positioning for this Market Type communicates the value of the market segment you've chosen and the innovation your company brings to it.

There are two types of market resegmentation: as a segmented niche or as a low-cost provider. Jet Blue is an example of low-cost resegmentation. Unlike Southwest Airlines, an example of low-cost resegmentation which offered cheap fares, matched by minimal frills, Jet Blue entered the airline business as a low-cost passenger airline that provides high-quality customer service on point-to-point routes. To contain costs, Jet Blue focused on underserved markets and large metropolitan areas that have high average fares.

The rise of Wal-Mart was an example of an entrepreneur recognizing an existing market was ripe for a niche resegmentation. In the 1960s and '70s, Sears and Kmart dominated big box discount retailing, opening large stores where they thought there was sufficient population to sustain them. Smaller communities either got catalog stores (Sears) or were simply ignored (Kmart). Sam Walton realized towns being dismissed as "too small" were an opportunity for a large discount retailer. "Small towns first" was the unique niche resegmentation Wal-Mart initially took. Once established, it proudly positioned itself as a "discounter"—a sobriquet the large retailers avoided like the plague. Wal-Mart sold name-brand health and beauty aids at cost. This strategy, supported by heavy advertising, pulled in customers who then purchased other products that, while priced low, carried high gross margins. Equally important, Wal-Mart's adoption of cutting-edge technology to track how people shop, and to buy and deliver goods more efficiently and cheaply than any rival, allowed it to reduce its cost of sales to a fraction of its competitors'. By 2002 Kmart was bankrupt and Wal-Mart was the largest company in the world.

When resegmenting a market, product positioning is a hybrid of positioning for a new market and positioning for an existing one. Since your segmentation has moved your product into a space adjacent to your competitors, product positioning describes how and why your new market segment is different and important to your customers.

Phase 3: Launch the Company and Product

Once the heavy lifting of positioning is complete, the company is ready to get to the tactics of launch. The launch phase of Customer Creation is the culmination of all your strategy efforts. A company launch is when your company communicates to an audience for the first time what it is, what it stands for, and what it's selling. A product launch describes why customers should want to buy your specific product. In a startup, these two launches often occur simultaneously. The process for launching is similar. You prepare communications materials, pick the audience you want to reach, craft the message, choose the messengers and context, and get ready to create demand. Then you check yourself by measuring how well you did so course correction can take place. Step-by-step you do the following:

- Select a launch by Market Type
- Select the customer audiences
- Select the messengers
- Craft the messages
- Understand the message context
- Understand the media for the message
- Measure success

A. Launch: Select a Launch by Market Type

Launching a company or a product is akin to launching an ICBM: what you hurl into the stratosphere is impossible to call back, and its impact can have immense consequences. Much like an ICBM launch, company launches should never be accidental, and they should require much forethought. The company needs to select and commit to a launch strategy matching its Market Type.

In the last phase you've said your company falls into one of the three Market Types. Now it is time to select the type of company and product launch to match that Market Type. There are three types of launches: onslaught, niche, and early adopter. Let's look at what is unique about each type.

For an Existing Market: Onslaught Launch

An onslaught launch is a full-frontal assault on a market using every available demand-creation tool. Most startups select this launch approach. However, it is the correct launch model for only one type of strategy: capturing market share in an existing market. Onslaught is an expensive, high-commitment move characterized by maximum exposure at a single point in time. This type of launch is heavily weighted to up-front expenditures on advertising, public relations, trade shows, direct mail, and so on.

The New Lanchester Strategy rules to determine the cost of market entry apply to this type of launch, but ironically, the bigger and more diverse your competitor, the better your odds. Why? Because in facing a diversified company, you are not facing the full brunt of your competitor's sales and marketing might. Its spending is spread over multiple divisions, multiple products, and multiple distribution channels. For example, suppose you decided to enter the computer mouse business. Microsoft is the dominant player, and according to our rules, you would need at least 1.7 times Microsoft's sales and marketing budget to enter this market (refer to Table 5.2). How on earth could you ever get that? At first glance, this looks hopeless. But on closer inspection, it may be doable. Competing with a company with multiple divisions and product lines means you can focus all your resources (read: every dollar you have) to compete with the division or product line that directly opposes your product, not the entire company. Therefore, again using Microsoft as the example, your cost of entering this market is now 1.7 times the spending of the Microsoft peripheral division. While still a formidable number (and perhaps still enough to scare you away), it allows you to calculate the true cost of entry.

Obviously we're only talking about market entry, not long-term competition. Kick a large company in the shins long and hard enough, and you will get its attention. (Ask Netscape what happened when it belittled Microsoft one too many times in the business press. Sometimes big, sleeping giants can awaken.) By the time your competitor turns its full marketing and sales prowess on to your company, you'd better have turned your early market advantage into defensible market share by using the chasm-crossing strategies in the Company Building step.

For a New Market: Early Adopter Launch

In contrast to onslaught and niche launches, the early adopter launch is a targeted, low-cost approach. The goal here is to prepare a new market for the day it will become a mass market. Since the target market does not support enough customers to justify spending to gain market share, the aim is to gain maximum mind share. The good news is by their very nature, early adopters tend to ignore expensive mass-market advertising and PR events. Instead, they rely on other media such as the Internet, focus groups, and word of mouth. An early adopter launch is the beginning of a long, drawn-out education campaign initially targeted to earlyvangelists. It uses the passion and enthusiasm of these earlyvangelists to diffuse a new idea into the collective consciousness of potential customers and thereby to create a market. Put another way, the goal is to create a "tipping point" in customer demand. (The best description of these "tipping point" strategies is in Malcolm Gladwell's book, *The Tipping Point: How Little Things Can Make a Big Difference*.[6]) This is the antithesis of the onslaught launch. New markets are not created overnight; it can take three to seven years from product launch for a new market to reach sufficient size for most startups to become profitable.

During the dot-com bubble, venture capitalists and PR agencies advocated the onslaught launch for companies entering new markets. They preached startups were all about first-mover advantage. An onslaught launch would persuade competitors to withdraw, or allow the startup to consolidate a fragmented industry, or at least

---

[6] M. Gladwell. 2000 (February). *The Tipping Point: How Little Things Can Make a Big Difference*. Boston: Little Brown & Company.

deter competitors from expanding their presence. The reality was much different. At PhotosToYou, for example, a cascading series of wrong assumptions had the company executing an onslaught launch for a new market. As they discovered, an onslaught launch in a new market with few customers is a huge expenditure of money with very little return. PhotosToYou survived, but most startups in new markets that used an onslaught launch are out of business.

For Resegmenting a Market: Niche Launch

If you are trying to resegment an existing market, the launch choices are a lot harder. New Lanchester Strategy rules still apply, but by segmenting the market, you've diluted the power of your competitors' sales and marketing budgets since you are now in an adjacent market. The relevant question is: "Are there customers ready to buy in the segment we've defined?" If so, proceed with an all-out launch to capture market share (as in an onslaught launch), but target the launch to the customers in your new niche. In a niche launch, the company puts all its demand-creation dollars into acquiring a single identifiable market segment and customer. However, if the new segment you are defining is speculative—that is, you are creating the market segment and its customers—then treat this market as you would a new market and execute an early adopter launch.

B. Launch: Select the Customer Audiences

Having chosen your launch strategy, you next select the customer audiences—that is, who your launch messages are intended to reach. This is the first step in creating demand for the product. Later, in the Company Building step, when your company starts broad-based demand-creation spending on advertising, trade shows, etc., the audience may broaden, but for now, you want to know who will be the first recipients of the messages.

One pitfall startups often fall into is selecting an audience with whom they are comfortable and familiar, rather than the one most likely to buy their product. The Customer Development process should help you avoid looking in the wrong place for your audience. In the past, startups would launch products before they had talked to customers, and so would have little knowledge of customers' needs and desires. In contrast, if you have followed the Customer Development process you have already sold to earlyvangelist customers. By the time you get to company and product launch, you have gained extensive knowledge about the problems customers want solved. Moreover, in Customer Validation, you spent an inordinate amount of time not only understanding your customers' needs, but learning exactly who buys and assembling an influence map of everyone involved in the buying process.

In addition, you have made enough actual sales to perceive whether your customers display any strong demographic or geographic purchase patterns. For example, you may have found that the majority of your earlyvangelist customers were under age 35 (demographic) or that customers on the West Coast purchased more frequently than those on the East Coast (geographic).

To define the audience for the launch, select the people on the influence map your launch messages need to reach. However, beware of another trap startups fall into: thinking everyone on the influence map is a target for the launch messages. Everyone can't be in the audience, or the message will get diluted. To be successful the audience must be a small group (or even an individual) that carries the most influence. More specifically:

- In an existing market the launch audience is the user or organization responsible for choosing (not necessarily using) the product
- In a new market, the launch audience consists of potential earlyvangelists who recognize they have a problem and have been actively looking for a solution
- In a resegmented market, the launch audience is made up of users or organizations that will appreciate the segment you've selected

C. Launch: Select the Messengers

Now that you have an idea of who your launch audience is, think about one other group that will receive the launch messages. As shown in Figure 5.4, at launch the company must educate not just its customer audience, but its messengers -- the people or organizations that will convey the message to that audience.

Message ⟶ Messenger ⟶ Audience

Multiple Audiences: Your Target Audience Is Reached Via Messengers *(Figure 5.4)*

PR people sometimes use the term "industry influencers." However, in *The Tipping Point*, Malcolm Gladwell articulates a theory that there are certain personality types who can create change by word-of-mouth, which he calls the "law of the few." Captivate these critical people, he says, and your message becomes contagious. The example he uses are epidemics; dramatic changes build slowly to a critical mass and then explode overnight -- seemingly in response to the smallest of changes.

One of Gladwell's personality types includes "messengers." His hypothesis, which is borne out by empirical evidence from new company and product launches, is this: To communicate a new idea or product you only need to reach a few well-placed and highly leveraged individuals called messengers. Messengers have a special gift for bringing the world together. Because of their influence and connections, this small group is single-handedly capable of igniting a revolution in the marketplace. As part of your launch, it's critical to identify these people and communicate the company message and positioning to them.

There are three types of messengers your company needs to educate: Experts, evangelists, and connectors. Experts are exactly what they sound like. They know your industry or product in detail, and others rely on them for their opinions. Experts may be industry analysts in private research firms (Gartner, NPD, AMR), Wall Street analysts (Morgan Stanley, Goldman Sachs), or consultants who provide advice for your particular industry. Experts may even be potential customers who run user groups other potential customers turn to for advice.

Some experts will not proselytize about any individual product and will charge for their generic advice and counsel. However, an important segment of experts talk about "best products." These are the product reviewers in what are nominally paid media. Walt Mossberg, the technology columnist for *The Wall Street Journal*, David Pogue at *The New York Times*, and Stewart Alsop at Fortune are examples of experts who discuss and recommend products. Experts lay great store on their independence. During company and product launch, the press and early customers call on experts to help them obtain an independent view of your company's claims. In Customer Discovery and Customer Validation, you identified the experts in your industry or segment and developed relationships with them. As a prerequisite to launch, you must know what they believe and educate them about your company and product.

The second classes of messengers, evangelists, are unabashed cheerleaders and salespeople for your product and, if yours is a new or resegmented market, for your Market Type. They tell everyone how great the product is and about the unlimited potential of your product and market. While nominally carrying less credibility than experts, evangelists have two advantages: typically they are paying customers, and they are incredibly enthusiastic about what they have to say. As you've seen in signing up early customers, earlyvangelists had to share in the company's vision to take a risk to purchase before the product had even shipped. Emotionally they have as much on the line as you do. Most are more than willing to stand up and tell others why they bought.

At times startups confuse evangelists with customers who will give a reference. They are not the same. A customer reference is something you have to arm twist to get; an evangelist is someone you can't get off the phone. By launch time, earlyvangelists need to be happy enough with your company and product to enthusiastically tell others about it.

Connectors are a sometimes unrecognized type of messenger. They are not product or industry experts, nor have they bought anything from your company. They are individuals who seem to know everyone; each industry has a few. They may be bloggers who expound on the general state of your industry and write magazine or newspaper columns. They may be individuals who organize and hold conferences where the key industry thought leaders gather. Often they are the thought leaders. The other interesting point about connectors is their ability to bridge multiple worlds. Your relationships with connectors should be the same as the ones you've developed with the experts. You need to have already established a relationship and at minimum educated them about your company and product before you get to this phase. Hopefully by launch connectors find your company and product interesting enough to write about in their newsgroups or to want you to speak at their conferences.

Great public relations firms know how to influence the messengers. They may have their own language describing who the messengers are (e.g., "influencers") and how they manage the "information chain," but a competent PR firm can add tremendous value at this step.

D. Launch: Craft the Messages

The messages the company delivers at launch are the cumulative result of all the positioning work you've done to date. Here I want to add just one more thought as you craft the final messages: messages need to be memorable and "sticky." Why? Because the more memorable or sticky a message, the greater its ability to create change. And in the case of a company and product launch, not only do we want people to change their buying behavior; we want them to change how they think.

Great PR people know that tinkering with how they present information can dramatically change its impact. My favorite example of how a slight change in a message could have prevented a PR debacle was when Silicon Valley ran into a tenacious bug that took over all of Santa Clara County. No, it wasn't a software bug or a glitch in Microsoft Windows. It was the Mediterranean fruit fly, a huge threat to California agriculture, the largest business in the state. In 1981 it had infested the home of high tech. The state decided the most expeditious way to eradicate this pest would be to use helicopters to spray a pesticide. Unfortunately, chemicals designed for total death to insects do not have consumer-friendly names. Rather than realize this, the state announced it was going to saturate the area with "Malathion," a pesticide that would wipe out the Medfly. This decision was a political hairball for the governor, as California produces 25% of the country's agricultural goods, and the spread of this Medfly would have a devastating impact on crops. Moreover, the notion of something called "Malathion—which resonated with fear and death—raining from the skies over their homes and children did not exactly bring screams of joy from the residents. People were outraged this toxic chemical was going to be sprayed on them.

Now imagine that someone in the governor's office had given the choice of the "message" two minutes of thought. A subtle change in the presentation of the message could have reduced the outcry and fear dramatically. Envisage the state had announced it was spraying "Spring Mist" or "Summer Dew," or even "Bugs Away," every evening rather than "Malathion." The subtle alteration in the message would have had a dramatic impact. People would have been standing outside soaking up the spray rather than sealing their windows with plastic. You may laugh, thinking no one would change his or her perceptions based on semantics, but in fact people do every day. Think about a hamburger. You may eat a lot of them, but if McDonald's message was "dead cow, slaughtered by the millions, butchered by minimum wage-earners, sometimes contaminated with E-coli, then ground into patties, frozen into solid blocks, and reheated when you order them," instead of "You deserve a break today," sales might be a tad lower.

For companies entering a new market, it's almost a Silicon Valley axiom to give a new market its own TLA (three-letter acronym) or memorable phrase. The message it delivers is that the company is inventing something significant enough to have its own name. In enterprise software Sales Automation, CRM, and ERP have entered the lexicon. In consumer products, phrases like PDA, e-commerce, fast food, and Home Theater have meaning where none existed before. If you doubt the power of a memorable phrase to shape a debate, think about the battle of carefully crafted messages on each side of the abortion debate. You're not "anti-abortion," you're "pro-life"; you're not "pro-abortion," you're "pro-choice." Each of these messages powerfully influences perceptions. For a company entering an existing market or attempting to resegment one, the messages are about, "There's got to be a better way, and our company has it." The messages answer the questions you posed when you talked to earlyvangelists: "What pain does this alleviate? What value does it deliver? And why should I care?"

E. Launch: Understand the Message Context

A message that is brilliant today and gets customers begging to buy your product could have fallen flat two years ago and may be obsolete in three years. Why? Because "no message is an island." In crafting your messages, remember that all messages operate in a context. (Another idea from *The Tipping Point*.)

They don't just show up in a potential customer's ear by themselves. Messages are accompanied by lots of other messages that can radically increase (or decrease) how memorable or sticky your message is. Satellite TV (DirecTV, EchoStar) messages caught on when cable companies' service became abysmal and pricing went through the roof. U.S. corporations paid a lot more attention to the security of their infrastructure after 9/11. The huge Y2K concerns of December 2000 were moot on Jan. 2, 2001.

In all these cases the message didn't change, the context around it did. Another example is the collapse of the dot-com and telecom bubbles at the start of the 21st century. The same e-commerce or telecom messages presented at the height of the bubble could raise a company $50 million and gain it access to almost any corporate executive suite. Not only would new startups get access, but the recipients of those messages felt smart if they passed on the information to their associates. Today, those messages wouldn't get a phone call returned, and people would feel embarrassed if they repeated them. The messages in this new context were not only ineffective, they were toxic to anyone who passed them on. Ponder this for a minute: it's the same message, same company, but a new context. The checklist in Table 5.6 will help you adjust your message to the context.

Message Context Checklist

☐ What problem are you solving for your customer?
☐ Is the problem related to other problems that have garnered press?
☐ What's changed in your market? If so, what are others saying about it?
☐ What hot topics are industry analysts and relevant press (technical/business/consumer) talking about that are relevant to your company and/or product?

Message Context Checklist *(Table 5.6)*

F. Launch: Understand the Media for the Message

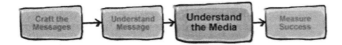

Media are part of any launch strategy; in effect, they are another type of messenger (see Figure 5.4). Think of paid media as paid messengers. Purchased media is one traditional way a company can deliver its messages directly. Media can be magazines, the U.S. Postal Service, or email. The message format may be ads, direct mail, or trade shows. While paid media are a key part of any marketing communications strategy, remember that customers tend to see messages from unpaid messengers as much more credible. In fact, for most startups in the business-to-business space the use of paid media is overkill at launch.

Your company needs to formulate a media strategy—a plan that describes what media will be used to reach your customers and, more importantly, which media won't. Rather than picking the cheapest media on the basis of readership, remember your hard work in the Customer Discovery and Customer Validation steps has already told you a lot about what media your early customers rely on. If you forgot to ask them, now is a good time to go back and iterate. The checklist in Table 5.7 will help formulate your questions.

Media Checklist
☐ Which media did earlyvangelists tell me they rely on?
☐ Which media do I believe my potential mainstream customers rely on? Are they the same as the media that reach earlyvangelists?
☐ Which media do others in the influence and Organization Map rely on?
☐ Which medium offers the best return on investments?

Media Checklist (Table 5.7)

G. Launch: Measure Success

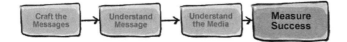

One of the words I've been hard-pressed to find in the lexicon of marketers is "measurement." "Measurement" is the bane of most marketing communications executives because they think keeping score belongs in accounting. Startups have found it difficult to measure the results of marketing expenditures in large part because they have had no concrete objectives. In Customer Creation we started with a series of strategic objectives (get market share, educate customers about the new market, etc.) so it would be easier to furnish a set of measurable objectives. In this phase you want to answer the question, "How do you know whether you have succeeded?" To do that, you need to first answer another question, namely, "What are the specific success criteria?"

To establish criteria for a successful launch, the Customer Development team needs to agree on its goals. For an existing market the metrics are pretty clear—leads that will ultimately result in market share. But what about when you are redefining a market or entering a new market? How do you measure how much you've affected target customers' perceptions? You already have a baseline: the customer and external audits you ran before the launch. After the launch, call the people on both audit lists and ask them the same questions again. Compare the results to find out how effective you were in reaching and influencing customers and key messengers.

Now expand the notion of an audit to include the press coverage your launch received. Do a press audit to gauge the extent to which the messages you thought you were communicating were actually picked up and repeated by the press. Are they using your three-letter acronym or phrase to describe the market? Are they describing the issues as your company has positioned them? Finally, how deep and wide was the coverage? Did you get brief mentions in two obscure trade magazines or a substantial notice in *The Wall Street Journal*? (Table 5.8 summarizes the techniques you can use to measure the success of your launch activities.)

	Existing Market	**New Market**	**Resegmenting a Market**
Leads	Number of qualified leads	Number of inquiries	Number of leads & inquiries
Messengers' Perception of Change	External audit	External audit	External audit
Audience's Perception of Change	Customer audit	Customer audit	Customer audit
Messages on Target	Press audit	Press audit	Press audit
Depth of Coverage	Press audit	Press audit	Press audit

Techniques for Measuring the Success of a Launch (Table 5.8)

Phase 4: Create Demand

Demand creation encompasses all the marketing activities that "Get" customers and drive customer awareness and desire for your products. They include public relations, advertising, trade shows, seminars, and collateral (brochures, data sheets). Demand creation, the last phase in the Customer Creation step, is typically the first phase most marketing communications executives want to execute. However, the place for demand creation is at the end of a thoughtful process, not at the beginning. In this phase you:

- Select a demand-creation strategy matching the company's first-year objectives
- Agree on demand-creation measurements
- Iterate, return, or exit

A. Create Demand:
Select a Strategy Matching First-Year Objectives

At times marketing departments remind me of the adage, "When you're up to your neck in alligators, it's hard to remember the goal was to drain the swamp." The primary mistake most marketing groups make is having goals for demand creation that are not the same as the goal for sales—in other words, to help the company make its revenue projection. For example, if your sales goals are to capture 10% market share and $3M in sales revenue in year one, then your demand-creation goals are the same. Once that is understood, then what follows is a demand-creation strategy that lists the steps you will take and the activities you will deploy to accomplish that goal. Traditionally, marketing and its communications programs have lots of moving parts, and it's easy to let the complexity confuse the reason why they really exist.

So as a reminder in the Customer Development model, once the sales and demand creation goals are in sync:

- For companies entering an existing market, the function of demand creation is to create qualified end-user demand and drive it into the sales channel
- For companies resegmenting a market, the function of demand creation is to educate customers about the new benefits resegmenting the market has created and drive demand into the sales channel
- For companies entering a new market, the function of demand creation is to educate customers about the market and drive the early or niche adopters into the sales channel. (See Table 5.9)

Existing Market	New Market	Resegmenting a Market
Leads/orders	Perception/market growth/leads/orders	Leads/orders/perception

Selecting a Demand Creation Strategy *(Table 5.9)*

When I ran Marketing, to ensure my team understood their role in demand creation, I used to have them chant, "Our job is to create end-user demand and drive it into our channel" as an opening to my staff meeting (we were in an existing market). I also kept reminding them that demand-creation activities (advertising, trade shows) were in addition to the ongoing PR activities with the messengers that started with the company and product launch.

B. Create Demand: Agree on Measurements

Demand-creation budgets are the largest component of an ongoing marketing department. While picking the right media, trade show, or direct mail piece is still sometimes as much an art as a science, a process needs to be in place to measure results and course correct if necessary. In my marketing departments, we accomplished this by admitting not every demand-creation activity would be successful. We took ownership when they failed, and we course corrected when necessary. Mistakes were accepted as part of the normal learning process. However, covering them up or not having a method to measure and correct mistakes were grounds for termination.

The best way to keep demand-creation activities and sales in sync is to agree on a set of goals for each stage in the pipeline and measure them. (Remember, you created this sales roadmap in Customer Validation.) Looking at the sales roadmap in Figure 5.5, you could simply say, "We need to pour leads into the sales funnel so orders come out." However, that would be an indiscriminate use of scarce dollars.

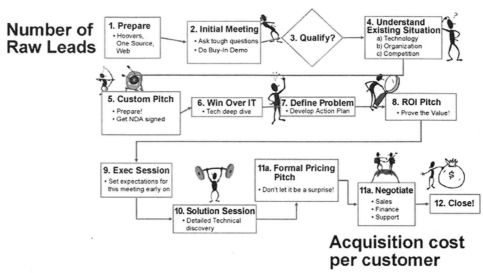

Number of Qualified Leads

Number of Raw Leads

Acquisition cost per customer

Demand Creation's Role in the Sales Roadmap (Figure 5.5)

Let's use as an example the startup in an existing market with a goal of capturing 10% market share and $3M in sales revenue in year one. If the average selling price of the product is $500, then Sales must sell 6,000 units to bring in $3M in the first year. Work backwards from the 6,000 units at the end of the roadmap and calculate how many active customers are needed in the front of the roadmap. How many qualified leads (i.e., a potential customer who has expressed interest in your product and meets your buying criteria) turn into active customers? How many raw leads (i.e., a potential customer who has expressed interest in your product but has not yet been tested to see if they are potential buyers) are needed to get those qualified leads? What is the cost of each lead? What is the cost of acquiring each customer? Once these metrics are in place, you can begin to measure how effective your demand-creation spending is in relationship to these metrics. Then you have a baseline for course correction.

While setting goals for leads seems like a measurable activity, understanding how your marketing communications activities affect perception seems more difficult. I've been amazed at how often I've heard, "It's impossible to measure customer perception." The reality is much different; you can even measure it at a trade show. I used to have my trade show manager ask people coming into our booth whether they had ever heard of our company. He took their contact information at the show and followed up with a phone call or an email afterward.

Then he would ask again if they had ever heard of our company. Over 78% of the show attendees who had said they had never heard of us when they first walked into our booth could now correctly describe our company and what it did. That's measuring awareness.

C. Iterate, Return, or Exit

With Customer Creation under way, you are almost at the beginning of the end. With the company and product launch you have gotten the rocket off the pad in a very public way. You have conducted external audits, positioned the company and product, developed a set of messages to communicate the positioning, and launched your company and product with a series of messengers to carry the story. Demand creation is driving end-user demand into the sales channel. Finally, you are using and refining the metrics you've created to measure the marketing dollars you are spending. As sales begin to scale, you are probably feeling the hard part of creating a startup may be over.

However, as exhausting as the Customer Creation process has been, you may need to iterate parts of it again. Has the positioning made sense to real live customers out in the field? Do the messengers buy the story? Has demand creation driven hordes of customers to the feet of your salespeople? If not, don't despair. As you have seen, every step in Customer Development is a learning and discovery process. It may be that your failures in positioning and messaging will bring new understanding as you analyze what didn't work. Recall that even subtle changes in messages can make enormous differences. (When it was first introduced, "Diet-Beer" was laughed off the marketplace shelves. It took nerve and panache to reintroduce it as "Lite-Beer" and create an enormously profitable market.) Take everything you learned in Phases 1 through 3, modify your positioning based on feedback, go back to Phase 1 and do it again.

However, in some cases there may be nothing wrong with the your positioning, messages, or demand-creation activities. The problem may be in the Market Type. If you are getting creamed by competitors, or if you cannot generate demand, it's time to step back and ask, "Are we in the right Market Type?"

Some signs that you're ready to move forward are positive answers to questions like these: Do sales go up as demand creation efforts become more effective? Are competitors beginning to take notice or even starting to copy your positioning? Does the financial model still work? If the answers are yes, you get to look yourself and your staff in the eye for the most personally trying part of the entire Customer Development process: building the company.

Customer Creation Summary

Phase	Goals	Deliverables
1. Get ready to Launch		
A. Construct Market-Type Questionnaire	Market type customers think the company fits	Market-Type Questionnaire
B. Choose Market Type	Pick the "Market Type"	Consensus on "Market Type"
C. Agree on First-Year Customer Creation and Sales Objectives	Set sales and marcomm goals for first year	Sales/Marketing Numbers; Customer Creation Budget
2. Position the Company & Product		
A. Select a Public Relations Agency	Interview and select a PR agency that understands strategy	PR Agency Selected
B. Conduct Internal and External Audits	Assess how you see yourself, and how customers, analysts, influencers, and press see your company	Audit Summary
C. Match Positioning to Market Type	Position the company and product	Positioning Statements
3. Launch the Company & Product		
A. Select a Launch by Market Type	Choose onslaught, niche or early adopter strategy	Launch Strategy
B. Select Customer Audience	Determine audience you are trying to reach at launch	Audience Description
C. Select Messengers	Identify experts, evangelists, and connectors	Messengers by Name
D. Craft Messages	Emotively message the value proposition	Key Messages
E. Understand Message Context	Identify external issues that establish message context	Context Summary
F. Understand Media for Message	Formulate media strategy	Media Based on Target Customers
G. Measure Success	Define what's important about the launch, and tie to goals	Metrics: Leads, Perception, on Target, Depth of Coverage
4. Create Demand		
A. Select First-Year Strategy	Formulate demand creation strategy for 1st-year objectives	Strategy Summary and Plan
B. Agree on Measurement	Establish criteria to measure demand creation success	Metrics: Qualified Leads, Sales Pipeline, Orders, Reduced Sales Cycle Time
C. Iterate, Return, or Exit	Determine whether demand creation been successful for the chosen market type	Robust Sales Pipeline and Customer Interest

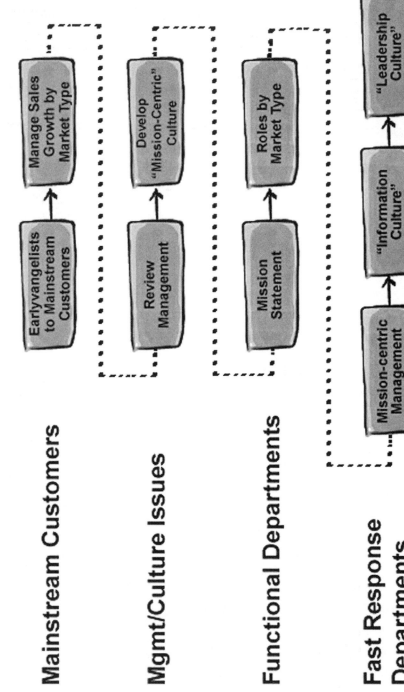

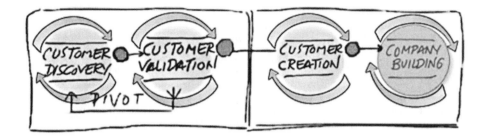

CHAPTER 6

Company Building

The essential thing is action. Action has three stages: the decision born of thought, the order or preparation for execution, and the execution itself. All three stages are governed by the will. The will is rooted in character, and for the man of action character is of more critical importance than intellect. Intellect without will is worthless, will without intellect is dangerous.
— Sun Tzu, as quoted in the Marine Corps Warfighting Doctrine

MARK AND DAVE WERE THE CO-FOUNDERS of BetaSheet, a pharmaceutical drug discovery company. Before starting BetaSheet, Mark had been the VP of Computational Chemistry of a startup acquired by Genentech. At Genentech Mark realized it was possible to revolutionize drug discovery by using computational methods rather than traditional wet labs. He passionately believed scalable drug discovery was going to be the new direction for the pharmaceutical and biotech industries, and he tried to convince the company to fund a new lab inside the company. After Genentech said his idea was not big enough to be of interest to the company, he decided to start a company himself. He took Dave, his Director of Computer Methods Engineering, with him.

After some initial fund-raising, Mark became a first-time CEO, with Dave as his VP of Development. I'd been introduced to Mark by one of his VCs and sat on his board from the beginning. From my front-row seat I watched BetaSheet go through all the startup ups and downs, made even harder by a market glutted with products, a collapsing biotechnology industry, and a complicated internal organization. Not only was BetaSheet trying to develop a complex piece of software to predict which drugs might be active, it was taking its own predictions and attempting to make active drug compounds. The idea was that potential customers would turn from skeptics to believers if BetaSheet walked into a sales presentation with a new, until now unknown, version of one of their commercial drugs.

One of the first crises occurred nine months into the company's existence. For the fourth consecutive month, Product Development seemed to be going nowhere. Mark had already shared his opinion that Dave was not up to running an entire engineering department. After some heart-to-heart conversations with VCs over the next several weeks, Dave agreed to step aside and stay with the company as Chief Technology Officer. While the search went on for a new VP of Engineering, Mark jumped in and took charge. In the eyes of the board, he performed a small miracle by improving morale and getting a working product headed out the door. By the time the new VP came on board, all the hard technical problems had been solved.

Meanwhile, at the prompting of one of the VCs, an experienced VP of Sales from a big company was hired despite Mark's misgivings he didn't "feel right" for a startup. Eleven months later, the VP and the national sales force he had hired were burning money like there was no tomorrow. There was embarrassed silence at the board meeting when the VP said for the sixth month in a row, "We have lots of activity in the pipeline, but it's real tough for a startup to close an order in a major drug company. I don't know when we'll close our first order." At Mark's urging, the VP was let go. With strong reservations (as Mark had no sales management expertise), the board agreed to have Sales report directly to Mark until a replacement was found.

In the following six months, Mark delighted us by personally selling the product to the first three top pharmaceutical companies he approached and helping the sales team build a solid sales pipeline. Later, we didn't say much when we found out he had promised these early customers the moon, since our competitors were turning into piles of rubble. The company was moving forward, the sales team was pumped, and the new VP of Sales came on board with a running start.

Next to go was Bob, the Chief Scientist and head of the chemistry group. After Mark fired him, Bob unloaded. "Mark has a new idea a day," he said, "and it's impossible to complete a project before he changes his mind. And when things aren't the way he wants them, he starts screaming at you. He doesn't want any discussion; it's his way or the highway. In the end you are either going to have your entire exec staff quit, or Mark will end up replacing us all with execs who simply do what he says." Those turned out to be prophetic words.

Despite the bumps in the road, the next few board meetings were pleasant. Sales seemed to be looking better and better. Yet Mark sounded more and more frustrated. Over lunch one day all Mark could talk about was that competitors were going to put the company out of business if we didn't follow up on his new ideas. I asked him if Sales was as worried as he was about competition. His response caught me off guard. "The VP of Sales won't let me talk to our salespeople or customers anymore." On hearing this I sat up and leaned across the table to hear the rest. "Yeah, our VP of Sales told me we can't start selling products we don't have or we'll never make money."

The rest of the lunch was a blur. As soon as I got to my car, I called the VP of Sales and got an earful. Mark was trying to convince the sales force what they really ought to be selling was his next great vision. Any time the salespeople tried to take Mark in to help close a customer, he tried to convince them it was the next product, not this one, they would want to buy. This was not good.

There was more. Mark, the Sales VP told me, was driving her crazy, coming in daily with a list of new sales opportunities she should be pursuing and badgering her to use sales presentations full of technical features, not solutions to what the customers had said were their problems. On top of that, she couldn't even use the new BetaSheet company literature to train the 12 salespeople she had hired since Mark had rewritten all the new data sheets to push his new product ideas. She asked whether I knew the new VP of Marketing was spending all his time on PR and trade shows since Mark had taken on product strategy and the new product requirements documents himself. I promised the board would talk to Mark.

The next week, two board members met with Mark about his relationship with Sales. Mark believed BetaSheet needed to keep pushing the edge of innovation, not get used to being settled in. BetaSheet, he complained, was turning into a company of "don't rock the boat" people in suits. He was going to keep rocking the boat because that was his job as CEO. The consensus around the board was that Mark needed to be managed. We agreed to wait and see how the situation at BetaSheet developed.

What we didn't understand was that back in the company life was anything but pleasant, as I was to learn from Sally, the CFO. Sally had been with BetaSheet since the beginning and was a gray-haired veteran of many startups. Her observations were dispassionate yet pointed. She said Mark thrived on chaos and managed well in it. The problem was BetaSheet needed to become a company that moved beyond chaos. It was getting bigger, and since the span of control was beyond Mark's reach, it needed process and procedures. Yet Mark had derisively rejected all of her proposals on how to put processes in place to manage the size the company would become. "We have a dysfunctional company. The exec staff is now split between people who have given up thinking for themselves and just do what Mark tells them to do, and those who still can think for themselves and are going to leave. The company has grown past Mark, and the board needs to make a choice." I left the restaurant hearing a stark call to action.

Perhaps my admiration for what Mark had accomplished as an entrepreneur blinded me to his limitations, but I thought it was worth a few more lunches to see if I could get him to realize he needed to change. Mark listened and nodded in the right places as I tried to explain that needing a modicum of process and procedures was a sign of success, not failure. I thought I had made some progress until Mark repeated that he was the only one in the company who was trying to see what was coming next in our market and no one in the company wanted to go there.

Over subsequent lunches I broached the subject of a transition. Taking one last shot at helping Mark understand, I observed that fixation on the next-generation products and customers was the role of a Chief Scientist or VP of Product Strategy. Mark should think about whether he truly enjoyed being CEO of a company that had grown beyond being a startup. Perhaps, I suggested, we could hire a COO to help Mark worry about the day-to-day operations. Or perhaps Mark might want to be both chairman and head of product strategy. Or could he think of some other roles that might work? None of these alternatives meant Mark had to give up control—just look at Bill Gates at Microsoft or Larry Ellison at Oracle. They each had people around them to manage the things they weren't great at. Mark promised to consider a transition, but judging from what happened next, he must have dismissed the idea as soon as he left the restaurant.

Things finally came to a head when the entire BetaSheet exec staff went to the office of the lead VC and said they were resigning en masse unless Mark was removed. Not surprisingly, the VCs concluded it was time for a new CEO.

The next board meeting was as difficult as I feared it would be. Mark complained bitterly, "How come none of you ever told me we were going to hire a new CEO?" I winced as Mark's lead VC recounted how Mark had said from day one he understood the company would someday hire a CEO. "You always said you'd do what's right for the company. I can't believe you're acting like you never heard this before."

I listened as Mark vented. "Telling me that needing to hire professional management is good news for the company is just a crock. After three years of working 80-hour weeks and doing such a great job building my company, the board is going to take it all away from me! I haven't done anything wrong and the company is running just fine. Making me Chairman is just a polite way of getting rid of me. You don't realize how badly someone from the outside will screw up our business. No one could possibly ever know our company as well as I do."

The result happened as if it was preordained. I won't forget the conversation I had with Mark after the meeting. "Steve, how did it ever come to this? Should I fight my dismissal? Do I have enough shares to throw my board members out? Will you help me get rid of them? What if I quit and took all the key scientists and engineers? They'd follow me, wouldn't they? Those damn VCs are stealing my company, and they're going to screw it up and ruin everything."

The names have been changed to protect the innocent, but I have sat through too many painful board meetings like this. In the world of startups, some form of this meeting is probably occurring every day.

At first blush the questions this story, and the countless others like it, raises are these: Was Mark being unfairly jettisoned from the company he built? Or were the VCs doing what they were supposed to do to build value in the company? The answers are almost a litmus test of the beliefs you bring to reading this book. However, there is another, deeper set of questions. Could Mark have grown into a better CEO with more coaching? Did I let him down? What type of CEO should the company hire? What should Mark's role be? Would BetaSheet be better off without Mark in six months? In a year? In two years? Why? After you're done with this chapter, I think you'll understand why both Mark and his board could be right and dead wrong.

The Company-Building Philosophy

The first three steps in this book focused on developing and understanding customers, validating sales with earlyvangelists, and creating a market and demand for the product. The next challenge, and the final step in the Customer Development model, is to build the company.

One of the mysteries about startups is this: Why does staffing heavily early on in some companies generate momentum and success while in others it leads to chaos, layoffs, and a death spiral? Why do some companies catch fire and others enter the land of the living dead or run out of money? When do you crank up the burn rate and hire, and when should you cut spending and go into survival mode?

Another of the puzzles of entrepreneurship is why some of the largest and most successful companies are still run by their founders long after they have become established. Ford, Microsoft, Nike, Polaroid, Oracle, Amazon, and Apple all belie the conventional investor wisdom that entrepreneurs eventually are outgrown by the companies they create. In fact, these companies prove a very different point: The long-term success of a startup requires founder continuity long past the point when conventional wisdom says the founders should be replaced. Startups at the end of the Customer Development process are not just nascent large companies waiting to shed their founders so they can grow. They are small companies that need to innovate continually so they can become large, sustainable businesses.

This makes the demise of an entrepreneur just as his or her company begins to succeed a Shakespearean tragedy. Why do some founders do so well in building a company but fail to grow with it? Why do some companies survive the Customer Development process but never manage to capitalize on their initial success? What do the winners have that the losers don't? Can we quantify and describe those characteristics?

Entrepreneurs like Mark believe getting the company to the next stage means simply doing more of the same. As Mark found out, an entrepreneur's tenure can have a more ignominious end. On the other hand, many investors believe all they need to do is bring in professional management to implement process and harvest the bounty. Both are wrong. The irony is that just when investors need to keep the company's momentum and flexibility going to reach mainstream customers, they stumble by substituting bureaucracy, while entrepreneurs fail to adapt their management style to the very success they have created.

Mark's debacle at BetaSheet reflects the lack of deliberation on the part of both the founding entrepreneur and the board about the company-building steps that transform a startup from a company focused on Customer Development into a larger company with mainstream customers. This evolution requires three actions:

- Build a mainstream customer base beyond the first earlyvangelist customers
- Build the company's organization, management, and culture to support greater scale
- Create fast-response departments to sustain the climate of learning and discovery that got the company to this stage

Concurrently, the company cannot rest on its laurels and become internally focused. To stay alive, it must remain alert and responsive to changes in its external environment, including competition, customers, and the market.

Building a Mainstream Customer Base

At first glance, the only apparent difference between a startup and a large company is the amount of customer revenue. If only it were that simple. The transition from small startup to larger company is not always represented by a linear sales graph. Growing sales revenue requires reaching a much broader group of customers beyond the earlyvangelists. And building this mainstream customer base requires shaping your sales, marketing, and business strategies on the basis of the Market Type in which you are competing.

Once again, Market Type is key. Just as this fundamental strategic choice shaped your choices in finding and reaching earlyvangelists, it will now shape how your company will grow and how you will allocate resources to do this. That's because each of the four Market Types has a distinctive sales growth curve shaped by the degree of difficulty involved in transitioning sales from the earlyvangelists to mainstream customers.

The sales growth curves in Figure 6.1 for a new market and an existing market illustrate the difference. Even after finding and successfully selling to earlyvangelists, the rate of sales differs in later years because of the different adoption rates of mainstream customers.

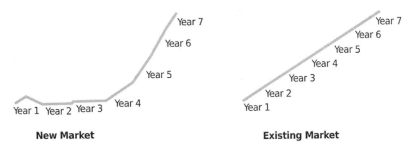

New Market Versus Existing Market Sales Growth Curves (Figure 6.1)

This means that the activities you perform in Company Building, just like the activities in earlier steps, depend on the Market Type. Most entrepreneurs whose companies have reached this stage breathe a sigh of relief, thinking their journey is over and the hard work is behind them. They have found their customers and created a repeatable sales roadmap. Now all they need to do is hire additional sales staff. This common wisdom is incorrect. The most dangerous trap is a lack of understanding about Market Types. Market Type predicts not only how this transition will occur but also the type of staffing, hiring, and spending you will need.

Moore's insight is that early adopters (earlyvangelists, in our lingo) are not high-volume mainstream buyers. So success with early sales does not provide the sales roadmap for later mainstream buyers. Moore posits that a company must come up with new sales strategies in order to bridge the chasm. (See Figure 6.2.)

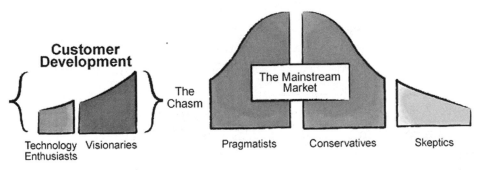

Technology Life Cycle Adoption Curve and Customer Development (Figure 6.2)

Customer Development is on the left-hand side of the adoption curve. The chasm is the gap in sales revenue that occurs when sales to earlyvangelists do not smoothly transition into mainstream sales. The width of the gap varies dramatically with the Market Type, which explains the different sales growth curves for each Market Type.

So why did we spend all this time in Customer Development if most of our customers will be in the mainstream market? You'll see Moore's chasm-crossing strategy builds on what was learned from these early customers to develop a much larger, mainstream customer base. We'll see how this works with Market Type in the discussion of Phase 1.

Building the Company's Organization and Management

As a company scales its revenue and transitions from early to mainstream customers, the company itself needs to grow and change as well. The most important changes are, first, in the overall corporate management and culture and, second, in the creation of functional departments.

Mission-centric Organization and Culture

Most startups don't give much thought to organization and culture, and if they do, it may have something to do with Friday beer bashes, refrigerators full of soft drinks, or an iconoclastic founder. Entrepreneurs and their investors tend to assume success means they must transform themselves as quickly as possible into a large company, complete with all the accoutrements of a large-company organization and culture: a hierarchical, command-driven management style, process-driven decision-making, an HR-driven employee handbook, and an "execution" mindset. The result is typically a bureaucracy imposed way too early. Such a system stems from the belief that imposing order and certainty on a disorderly, uncertain marketplace will result in predictable and repeatable success. (Paradoxically, pursuing order and certainty as a goal from the beginning would have meant the startup would never have gotten off the ground.)

In this final stage of Customer Development, the CEO, executives, and board need to recognize that with the uncertainty of the mainstream market still ahead of the company, just mimicking the culture and organization of a large company can be the beginning of the end for a promising startup. Consider what happened to BetaSheet four years after Mark left. With BetaSheet's early and visible success, the board was able to hire a traditional CEO experienced in the pharmaceutical business. She arrived just as the sales team missed its numbers. Customers were simply not adopting the product as rapidly as expected. The new CEO cut back the sales staff dramatically and replaced the VP of Sales. Then she looked at the rest of Mark's management team and replaced them one-by-one with a new team of experienced sales, marketing, and Product Development executives from much larger companies.

After that rocky start, sales and the company continued to grow for the next 18 months. BetaSheet's once radical ideas garnered acceptance in the pharmaceutical industry, and revenue was once again meeting plan. The board and investment bankers began to talk about an IPO. However, unseen by the BetaSheet management team, dark clouds were gathering on the horizon.

As large BetaSheet customers understood how strategically important this drug discovery software was, they began to set up their own in-house groups to provide it for themselves. Further, BetaSheet's new market creation activities had not only educated customers but also helped competitors understand how lucrative this new opportunity could be. Finally, while early customers were enthusiastic and supportive, revenue wasn't growing at the rate early sales successes had predicted. At the same time, new competitors and existing companies were starting to develop and offer similar products.

Internally, things were also changing. Not only had Mark left the company, but after 18 months an exodus of the most innovative engineering and sales talent began. The word among employees was that initiative and innovation were not appreciated; all decisions needed senior management approval. It became understood "not going by the book" was now a career-limiting move at BetaSheet. Moreover, by the third year, infighting between Sales and Product Development, and between Sales and Marketing, was almost as intense as battles with competitors. The BetaSheet departments each had their own agendas, at times mutually exclusive. New products never seemed to make it to market as priorities changed monthly. The sales decline, which began in year three, became a rapid death spiral in the fourth year. By its fifth anniversary the company shut its doors.

For a startup on such a fast track the BetaSheet story is depressing, but it's not unique. Replacing entrepreneurial management with process-oriented executives who crater the company happens all the time. The problem is that most founders and investors seem to have no alternative for organization and culture than the extremes of startup chaos and corporate rigidity.

In this chapter I propose a third alternative. As it grows, a successful startup moves its company organization and culture through three distinct stages (see Figure 6.3).

Stages in the Evolution from Startup to Large Company (Figure 6.3)

The first stage, which spans Customer Discovery, Customer Validation, and Customer Creation, is centered on the Customer and Product Development teams. The second stage happens in Company Building: The organization becomes mission-centric in order to scale up and cross the chasm between early and mainstream customers. When the company grows larger, it becomes process-centric to build repeatable and scalable processes.

Experienced executives understand process, but few of them understand what it means to be mission-centric. To make the transition to a large organization and cross the chasm, your startup must become an agile company, one that can still respond with entrepreneurial speed, but do so with a much larger group of people. Creating that agility requires a written and widely understood corporate mission that drives the day-to-day operations of the departments and the employees. As you'll see in Phases 2 and 3, this mission-centric mantra must pervade the culture of the entire company.

For the organization to grow, these transitions must occur. If the members of the founding team want to continue their tenure with the company, they must also make these transitions. They need to recognize the shifts in emphasis, embrace them, and lead the change in management style. At BetaSheet, Mark failed to understand this evolution, and both he and the company paid the price.

Transforming the Customer Development Team into Functional Organizations

If you've followed the Customer Development model to this point, you've already built your first mission-centric team. In Phase 3 of this step you will transform the mission-oriented culture of the Customer Development team into departments organized to execute and support the corporate mission.

Don't mistake this as building departments that then invent missions to justify their existence. Too many startups interpret growth as a call to build, staff, and scale traditional departments according to a cookie-cutter model (thinking all companies must have Sales, Marketing, Business Development) rather than building a structure from a clear strategic need. In contrast, in the Customer Development model, the next step is to add a layer of management and organization still focused on the customer-centric mission, not just on building departments and headcount. You want to achieve a management system and departments that communicate and delegate strategic objectives to the staff so they can operate without direct daily control while still pursuing the same mission.

This can be achieved only if executives are selected because they share the same values, not just because their resumes show lots of experience. At the same time, this next layer of management needs to be made up of people who are leaders in their own right, not just yes-men to a charismatic founder. As leaders, they transmit the company's vision to all the people who help carry it out. I learned this principle early on in my career, when I took over as VP of Marketing at SuperMac, a company just exiting Chapter 11. I asked my department managers what their mission was. Their responses were disconcerting. Our head of the trade show department responded, "My mission is to set up our trade show booths." The other managers gave the same kinds of answers. The head of the public relations group said he was there to write press releases. The leader of the Product Marketing Department said his job was to write data sheets and price lists. When I pressed them to think why Marketing was going to trade shows, or writing press releases or penning data sheets, the best I could get was "because that's our job." A lack of clarity about mission is always a leadership failure. Soon thereafter, I began to educate my staff about their mission. It took a year to get a department of people who understood their business card title might be their daily function, but it wasn't their job. The mission of Marketing at SuperMac was to:

- Generate end-user demand
- Drive that demand into our sales channels
- Educate our sales channels
- Help Engineering understand customer needs

These four simple statements helped Marketing organize around a shared mission (which we all recited at the beginning of our staff meetings). Everyone else in the company knew what we in Marketing were going to do all day, and how to tell whether we succeeded. You'll see how the Customer Development team morphs into mission-driven functional organizations in Phase 3.

Creating Fast-Response Departments

Customer Development and a mission-centric organization call for doing different things from day to day, because in a learning and discovery organization, change and the reaction to change are the only constants. In contrast, "a process-driven organization" is designed to repeat things that have been found to work with little change. When it's successful its constant is sameness from day to day—no surprises, no rapid shifts.

Process is essential for setting measurable goals and establishing repeatable procedures that do not require experts to implement. Process is how large companies can grow larger, how they can scale departments and the company without hiring superstars. Large companies can hire thousands of average employees who can follow the rules and check to see whether the business is proceeding according to plan. Process in an organization means procedures, rules, measurements, goals and stability.

Everything about process is anathema to most entrepreneurs, who in their gut believe success shouldn't require process. Yet they rarely have anything to offer in its place. Now they do: the "fast-response" department.

Creating fast-response departments offers a natural evolution from the learning and discovery stage to the functional departments a large company needs. Fast-response departments keep the company agile and avoid rigor mortis. We'll look at fast-response departments in detail in the discussion of Phase 4.

Overview of Company Building

Company Building: Overview of the Process (Figure 6.4)

Company Building has four phases. In Phase 1, you set the company up for its next big hurdle, transitioning sales from earlyvangelists to mainstream customers, by matching the appropriate sales growth curve to hiring, spending and relentless execution.

In Phase 2, you review the current executive management and assess whether the current team can scale. In this phase you devote a lot of attention to creating a mission-centric organization and culture as an essential means of scaling the company.

In Phase 3, capitalizing on all the learning and discovery the company has done to date, the Customer Development team realigns into departments by business function. Each department gets reoriented to support the corporate mission by developing its own departmental mission.

Finally, in Phase 4, at the end of Customer Development, the company works to create fast-response departments for scale, speed, and agility. Here you use the military concept of OODA (Observe, Orient, Decide, and Act) by moving and responding to competitors and customers at a tempo much faster than your competition. This requires departments to have at their fingertips up-to-date customer information and to be able to rapidly disseminate that information across the company.

Phase 1: Reach Mainstream Customers

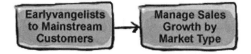

It's been a long journey through Customer Development. This phase is the culmination of all your hard work in building a successful startup. By now you have early customers, you've positioned your company and product, and you're on the way to creating demand for what you're selling. All this is in preparation for reaching the high-volume mainstream customers who can transform your startup into a dominant player in your market.

As I've noted, the extremely useful notion of a chasm between early adopters and mainstream customers needs to be supplemented with the understanding that the width of the chasm and the time frame for crossing it depend on the Market Type in which you're operating. Accordingly, this section describes the differences in customer transitions and sales-growth curves in a new market, an existing market, and a resegmented market. An understanding of the customer transition and sales growth by Market Type will allow your company to forecast the timing of mass market adoption, hiring and cash-burn needs, and other essential factors in growing the company appropriately. The sales-growth curve describes the how; the chasm explains the why.

This understanding is essential to your efforts to reach mainstream customers. In this phase you will:

- Manage the transition from earlyvangelists to mainstream customers, understanding how the transition differs by Market Type
- Manage the sales-growth curve appropriate for your company and Market Type

The outcome of this phase is twofold: (1) a chasm-crossing strategy that fits the Market Type and (2) a revenue/expenses plan and a cash-needs plan matching the Market Type.

A. Transitioning from Earlyvangelists to the Mainstream in a New Market

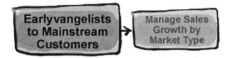

In a new market, the motivations of early buyers and mainstream customers are substantially different. The earlyvangelists you've targeted in Customer Validation want to solve some immediate and painful problem or, in the case of companies, gain a large competitive advantage by purchasing a revolutionary breakthrough. The majority of customers, however, aren't earlyvangelists; they're pragmatists. Unlike earlyvangelists, they typically want evolutionary change. Consequently, the effort you have put into building a repeatable and scalable sales process for earlyvangelists will not lead you to volume sales. Visionaries will put up with a product that doesn't quite work; pragmatists need something that doesn't require heroics to use. Further, pragmatists do not care for or trust the visionaries as references. Pragmatists want references from other pragmatists. The chasm between earlyvangelists and volume sales to mainstream customers occurs because these two groups of customers have little in common.

In a new market, the gap between visionary enthusiasm and mainstream acceptance is at its widest point (see Figure 6.5). The width of the gap explains the hockey-stick sales growth curve often seen in a new market: a small blip of revenue in the first year or so from sales to earlyvangelists and then a long, flat period, or even a dip, until the sales force learns how to sell to a completely different class of customers and Marketing convinces pragmatists your new product is worth adopting.

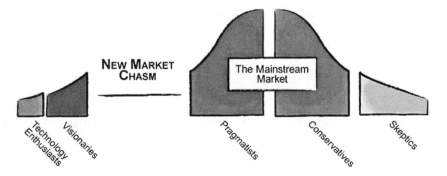

The Chasm in a New Market (Figure 6.5)

In addition to the long hiatus until sales take off, a new market has the most serious sales risks on either side of the chasm. On the near side of the chasm, finding a repeatable sales process for earlyvangelists might succeed all too well. Your sales organization might become content with the relatively low level of repeatable business. In fact, the sales force may exhaust the visionary market by selling to all potential earlyvangelists without having prepared to learn the new sales roadmap for reaching mainstream customers.

The risk on the other side of the chasm is that you may never get there. Mainstream pragmatists in a new market may see no reason to start adopting your product. Especially in tough economic times, few customers want to be innovators if they can help it. When spending is tight, new companies with innovative ideas find the mainstream a formidable and sometimes impenetrable customer base.

There is another risk as well—your competition. After years of investing in educating a new market about the benefits of your product, your startup could lose to a "fast-follower"—a company that enters the market, piggybacks on top of all your market education, crosses the chasm, and reaps the rewards. Usually, startups lose to a company that has implemented a fast-response organization and is learning and discovering faster than they can.

While these risks may sound catastrophic, they don't have to be. The biggest danger is not understanding the characteristics of new-market customers—or worse, recognizing them but refusing to risk changing the sales model that has produced your earlyvangelist sales in order to go after the volume customers. That can be a first-order tragedy for your investors and company.

To reach mainstream customers in a new market, your company must devise selling and marketing strategies that differ from those used in an existing or resegmented market. For example, rather than simply hiring lots of salespeople to capture hordes of customers (as in an existing market), you must find the sparse population of earlyvangelists and use them to gain a foothold in the mainstream market. Rather than spending large sums on a branding campaign (as in a market you are trying to resegment) to an audience that is not ready to listen, you need to use the few yet potent earlyvangelists to woo and win the mainstream market.

Two of the best-known strategies are (1) "crossing the chasm" by finding niche markets[7] and (2) creating a "tipping point."[8] These strategies are summarized in Table 6.1.

---

[7] Geoff Moore. 2002 (August 20). *Crossing the Chasm: Marketing and Selling Technology Products to Mainstream Customers,* rev. ed. New York: HarperBusiness.

[8] Malcolm Gladwell. 2000 (February). *The Tipping Point: How Little Things Can Make a Big Difference.* Boston: Little & Brown.

Strategy	Implementation
Crossing the Chasm by Creating Niche Markets	Focus narrow sales efforts on earlyvangelists in one specific market, application, or company type. Use word of mouth as references. Develop "whole products" for mainstream appeal.
Creating Tipping Points[7]	Focus on individual sales until a critical mass of early adopters are reached. Then a further small charge "tips" the customer base, and a large effect is observed. "Viral marketing" is one example of a tipping point strategy.

Earlyvangelist to Mainstream Customer Strategies in a New Market (Table 6.1)

While both strategies have been widely discussed, their implementation by startups has not always been successful. My contention is these strategies work best when applied in new markets, not all markets. Chasm-crossing and tipping point are best suited for converting a small cadre of true believers into a mass movement. Chasm-crossing builds upon initial earlyvangelist sales by targeting your sales force to focus on a single reference market, application, industry, or company type (the niche), then selling to the mainstream economic buyers. These mainstream buyers need a "whole product" (a complete solution). Tipping point strategies work differently (they are sometimes compared to how epidemics spread). They capitalize on the observation that just a few "right" people can create a change in customer and market behavior. That once a critical mass of these right people endorse a product, particularly one that is "sticky," mass adoption can occur at an exponential rate. When the tipping point strategy is applied to a company or product, the goal is to artificially create the herd effect by managing customer perceptions of an inexorable trend.

B. Managing Sales Growth in a New Market

For years venture capitalists have realized startups in new markets take an extended time to reap the rewards. VCs refer to these startups as having a hockey-stick rate of sales growth. As illustrated in Figure 6.6, while there may be a blip in sales revenue from earlyvangelist orders, in a new market sales can be close to zero during the first few years. Revenue accelerates to exponential growth only when the company successfully educates customers, creates new sales and channel roadmaps that reach mainstream customers, and has the staying power and resources for the long haul.

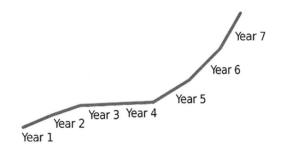

New Market Sales Growth—The Hockey Stick (Figure 6.6)

Besides being a sobering predictor of life without much revenue, this sales growth curve sets several important parameters for a startup in a new market with no sales revenue coming in:

- Capital requirements: How much money will the company need to raise until revenue starts coming?
- Cash flow/burn rate: How does the company manage its cash and burn rate?
- Market education/adoption plan: How much education will it take, and how long will it take for the market to grow to sufficient size?
- Hiring plan: If infinite marketing dollars will not affect demand in a new market, why and when does the company need to staff a marketing department? The same question applies to the sales staff. If revenue is not elastic based on the number of salespeople in the field (but rather depends on the creation of the market), why and when does the company staff the sales organization?

The implication of these questions is that in a new market Company Building is all about husbanding resources and passionately evangelizing and growing the market until the market grows large enough for sales revenue to appear. Your experience of selling to earlyvangelists during Customer Validation will help you answer, "How many of these early customers can your company really find in the first few years?" That question will help you set your sales revenue and expense model, and give you a feeling of the cash needed until the "hockey stick" sales curve driven by mainstream customers kicks in.

One last risk in entering a new market is the market itself turns out to be a chimera. In other words, there may simply not be enough customers past the initial early adopters to sustain a large business. Worse, most companies don't find out they were wrong until years later when they are out of money. By then it is too late to reposition the company. Some examples of new markets that never materialized are home dry-cleaning products, low-fat substitutes for snack products, "smart cards" (credit cards with a computer chip in them), the artificial intelligence market in the early 1980s, and the pen computing market in the early 1990s. Therefore before selecting a new market as a positioning choice, entrepreneurs and their companies ought to look at their projected burn rate, look deep into the eyes of their investors and cofounders, and make sure this is the path everyone agrees to travel together willingly.

C. Moving from Earlyvangelists to the Mainstream in an Existing Market

In an existing market, the chasm between earlyvangelists and mainstream customers is small or may not exist (see Figure 6.7). That's because the visionaries and pragmatists are the same type of customer. In an established market, all customers will readily understand your product and its benefits.

There is no long interregnum as the sales organization learns a new sales roadmap and a new class of customers gets educated. The only limits on sales growth are market share and differentiation. The absence of a chasm is a signal that this market is ripe for exploitation and relentless execution. The challenge is while customers may understand your product and benefits, they may not understand why they should buy your product rather than one from a familiar existing company.

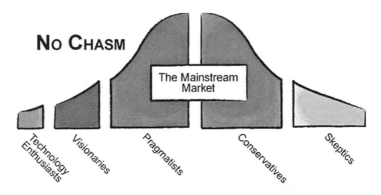

The Chasm in an Existing Market (Figure 6.7)

This is where positioning[9] and branding [10] come into play. Positioning and branding are well-known strategies for differentiating companies and products. At times these two words are used synonymously, which is a problem since they are different, and the difference matters. In an existing market, where market share is the objective and there is little distinction among competitors, the fastest and least expensive way to differentiate your company and product is to establish positioning, or value (i.e., everyone knows why your product is better and wants it) rather than pursuing branding (everyone knows about your product and thinks your company is wonderful). Positioning can be considered successful when customers not only recognize the product or service but can recite its attributes. When positioning is executed correctly, it creates end-user demand for the product. For example, *Starbucks is the No. 1 place for coffee* is the Starbucks positioning. In contrast, branding works best when you are resegmenting a market. *Starbucks is a great company and treats its employees well* is Starbucks positioning the company. Spending money on branding in an existing market may mean potential customers know who your company is, but still end up buying from a competitor.

D. Managing Sales Growth in an Existing Market

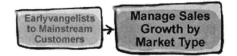

In an existing market, Customer Validation and Creation should have already proven there are willing customers who understand your startup's unique advantages. Hopefully, Marketing has differentiated the product and is now creating end-user demand and driving it into your sales channel. The sales organization is scaling to reap the rewards. If all goes well, the graph of year-to-year sales in an existing market is a nice straight line (Figure 6.8). And the table you put together is a standard sales and marketing forecasting and hiring plan.

---

[9] Al Ries and Jack Trout. Positioning: *The Battle for Your Mind.*
[10] Al Ries. 1998 (October). *The 22 Immutable Laws of Branding.* New York: HarperCollins.

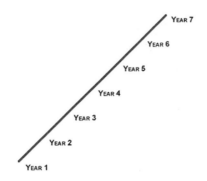

Sales Growth in an Existing Market *(Figure 6.8)*

If you're lucky enough to be in this Market Type and at this stage, scaling means worrying about:

- Capital requirements: How much money needed until cash flow break even?
- Hiring plan: Can the company scale rapidly enough to exploit the market?
- Product lifecycle: Your nice linear sales curve is true only as long as your product remains competitive. Are there follow-on products in your pipeline?
- Competitive responses: Most competitors will not stay unresponsive forever. What happens when they respond?

In an existing market, then, Company Building is about pursuing relentless execution and exploitation of the market, while simultaneously being intensely paranoid about your product lifecycle and the responses of competitors. (Think of the myriad car manufacturers who began producing SUVs after the Chrysler Minivan created a mass market in the 1970s.) The density and intensity of this Market Type means the linear upward sales curve can easily reverse direction.

E. Moving from Earlyvangelists to Mainstream Customers in a Resegmented Market

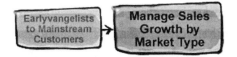

A resegmented market strategy lands your company somewhere between a new market and an existing market. Although the chasm between earlyvangelists and mainstream customers is not as wide as in a new market (Figure 6.9), it takes time to convince mainstream customers that what you have defined as unique about your product or company is a compelling selling proposition. As a result, in the early years, sales may be low.

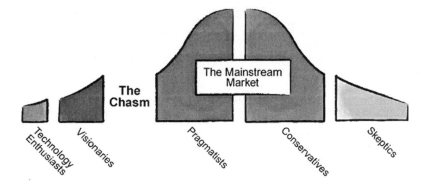

The Chasm in a Resegmented Market *(Figure 6.9)*

There are two chasm risks in this Market Type. First, is the seductive nature of sales to early adopters. In this Market Type, there are sufficient visionary customers to generate revenue, albeit at a small scale, to make the company think it has built a scalable business model. The reality is the company is skimming a low volume of sales from a competitive existing market. Crossing the chasm in this Market Type means attracting masses of mainstream customers who need to be educated to what's new and different about the way you've redefined the market. In other words, you have some of the same issues as a company entering a new market. However, instead of using niche marketing and tipping point strategies as you would in a new market, you use branding and positioning to reach mainstream customers. It is here, in a resegmented market, that all the conventional wisdom about branding and positioning is actually valid. Marketers use these tactical tools to differentiate their company and product from those in an existing market. For example, in the home appliance market, Subzero, Miele and Bosch created a new segment of kitchen appliances: high-end and feature-laden. Consumers (at least in the U.S.) were perplexed about why they should pay exorbitant prices for what were "just" refrigerators, washers, and dryers. However, after some time, adroit marketing and positioning took hold, and these previously mundane appliances turned into status symbols. Similar examples of successful resegmentation can be found across a wide variety of industries: Starbucks transforming the 49-cent cup of coffee into the $3 latte; Dell turning commodity personal computers into build-your-own, custom-designed products; Perrier and Calistoga turning water, the ultimate commodity, into a high-end purchase that costs more than gas.

This litany of success stories brings us to the second risk in a resegmented market—resegmenting an existing market typically is expensive, and companies require sufficient capital for seeing an adroit marketing and positioning through to completion. While there may be a ready existing market for your company to reach and resegment, your messages need to be heard above the cacophony of the incumbents. Startups that resegment typically underestimate the dollar and time commitments necessary to make a lasting impression on the consumer psyche.

In Customer Creation, I pointed out that one of the key marketing mistakes is having an ad or PR campaign that lacks an underlying positioning strategy. Having a positioning strategy is the prerequisite to branding. Too many VPs of Marketing choose a branding campaign when they cannot even articulate a position. Branding is expensive, time-consuming, and designed to elicit a visceral reaction. The key in a market you are resegmenting is to use positioning to establish the value of the new segment and create demand for a product. Then you can use branding to reinforce the value of that segment and grow demand exponentially into the hockey-stick part of the sales curve.

To reiterate: Branding and positioning strategies, while widely popularized, have been misused by many startups. In a new market, these strategies are expensive and deadly (they were the sinkhole for most dot-coms). They are critical, however, in a market you are resegmenting. In a resegmented market, you use branding and positioning to turn a small cadre of early evangelists into a mass market, yet have the customers in that mass market believe they remain a small, elite group.

F. Managing Sales Growth in a Resegmented Market

Sales growth in a resegmented market is a complicated balancing act, since it combines the sales growth models of new and existing markets. The good news is there is an existing market of customers who will readily understand what the product is. This allows the company to immediately generate some level of sales even amid stiff competition. However, these early sales should not be confused with success. The company won't achieve explosive sales growth until the market understands and adopts its resegmentation. The result is the sales curve shown in Figure 6.10. The sales-growth issues that need to be managed in a resegmented market are these:

- Capital requirements: How much money is needed until cash flow break-even?
- Market education costs: Can the company afford the continued cost of educating and creating this new segment?
- Positioning and branding costs: Unlike a new market, a resegmented market offers a clear target to be different from. This positioning and branding are costly. Is there a budget?
- Hiring plan: Can the company balance early sales without overhiring before the ramp appears?
- Market evaluation: What happens if resegmentation doesn't work? Most startups end up in the land of the living dead. How do you avoid it?

Sales Growth in a Resegmented Market (Figure 6.10)

In short, Company Building in a resegmented market is similar to Company Building in a new market. It is about husbanding resources and passionately evangelizing and growing the new market segment until the segment is large enough for hockey-stick sales revenue to appear. As with a new market, one of the risks is the new segment can be a chimera. In this case, you're left trying to make it against multiple competitors in an existing market with a product that isn't significantly unique.

Phase 2: Review Management and Build a Mission-Centric Organization

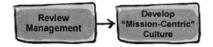

Company Building prepares the company to move from an organization focused on learning, discovery and attracting earlyvangelist customers to one putting all its resources into finding and acquiring mainstream customers. For this to happen, you need to ensure your senior management can lead this critical transition.

The appraisal of the executive team may be a wrenching shift for individuals and the entire company. The process must be guided and managed by the board. In this phase, you will:

- Ask the board to review the CEO and the executive staff
- Develop a mission-centric culture and organization

A. The Board Reviews the CEO and Executive Staff

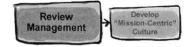

When you reach the company-building step, it's time for the board to look inward and decide whether the current CEO and executive staff are capable of scaling the company. To get here, the company needed people like Mark at BetaSheet: passionate visionaries capable of articulating a compelling vision, agile enough to learn and discover as they went, resilient enough to deal with countless failures, and responsive enough to capitalize on what they learned in order to get early customers. What lies ahead, however, is a different set of challenges: finding the new set of mainstream customers on the other side of the chasm and managing the sales growth curve. These new challenges require a different set of skills. Critical for this transition are a CEO and executive staff who are clear-eyed pragmatists, capable of crafting and articulating a coherent mission for the company and distributing authority down to departments that are all driving toward the same goal.

	Entreprenurial-Driven Learning & Discovery	Mission-Oriented Management	Process-Managed Execution & Growth
Personal Contribution	Superstar	Leader	Manager of plans, goals, process, and personnel
Time Commitment	24/7	As needed	Long term 9 to 5
Planning	Opportunistic and agile	Mission- and goal-driven	Process- and goal-driven
Process	Hates and eliminates	As needed, driven by mission	Implements and uses
Management Style	Autocratic, star system	Distributed to departments	May be bureaucratic
Span of Control	Hands-on	Mission-driven, synchronized	Distributed down the organization
Focus	High and passionate vision	Mission	Execution
Uncertainty/Chaos	Brings order out of chaos	Focuses on fast response	Focuses on repeatability

CEO/Executive Characteristics by Stage of the Company (Table 6.2)

By now, the board has a good sense of the skill set of the CEO and executive team as entrepreneurs. What makes the current evaluation hard is that it is based not on an assessment of what they have done, but on a forecast of what they are capable of. This is the irony of successful entrepreneurial executives: Their very success may predicate their demise.

Table 6.2 helps elucidate some of the characteristics of entrepreneurial executives by stage of the company. (Looking at this table, what should the BetaSheet board have done about Mark?) One of the most striking attributes of founding entrepreneurial executives is their individual contribution to the company, be it in Sales or Product Development. As technical or business visionaries, these founding executives are leaders by the dint of their personal achievements. As the company grows, however, it needs less of an iconoclastic superstar and more of a leader who is mission- and goal-driven. Leaders at this stage must be comfortable driving the company goals down the organization, and building and encouraging mission-oriented leadership on the departmental level. This stage also needs less of a 24/7 commitment from its CEO and more of an as-needed time commitment to prevent burnout.

Planning is another key distinction. The learning and discovery stage called for opportunistic and agile leadership. As the company scales, it needs leaders who can keep a larger team focused on a single-minded mission. In this mission-centric stage, hierarchy is added, but responsibility and decision-making become more widely distributed as the span of control gets larger than one individual can manage. Keeping this larger organization agile and responsive is a hallmark of mission-oriented management.

This shift from Customer Development team to mission-centric organization may be beyond the scope or understanding of a first-time CEO and team. Some never make the transition from visionary autocrats to leaders. Others understand the need for a transition and adapt accordingly. It's up to the board to decide which group the current executive team falls into.

This assessment involves a careful consideration of the risks and rewards of discarding the founders. Looking at the abrupt change in skills needed in the transitions from Customer Development to mission-centric organization to process-driven growth and execution, it's tempting for a board to say, "Maybe it's time to get more experienced executives. If the founders and early executives leave, that's OK; we don't need them anymore. The learning and discovery phase is over. Founders are too individualistic and cantankerous, and the company would be much easier to run and calmer without them." All this is often true -- particularly in a company in an existing market, where the gap between early customers and the mainstream market is nonexistent, and execution and process are paramount. A founding CEO who wants to chase new markets rather than reap the rewards of the existing one is the bane of investors, and an unwitting candidate for unemployment.

Nevertheless, the jury is out on whether more startups fail in the long run from getting the founders completely out of the company or from keeping founders in place too long. In some startups (technology startups, especially), product lifecycles are painfully short. Regardless of whether a company is in a new market, an existing market, or a resegmented market, the one certainty is that within three years the company will face a competitive challenge. The challenge may come from small competitors grown bigger, from large companies that now find the market big enough to enter, or from an underlying shift in core technology. Facing these new competitive threats requires all the resourceful, creative, and entrepreneurial skills the company needed as a startup. Time after time startups that have grown into adolescence stumble and succumb to voracious competitors large and small because they have lost the corporate DNA for innovation, and learning and discovery. The reason? The new management team brought in to build the company into a profitable business could not see the value of founders who kept talking about the next new thing and could not adapt to a process-driven organization. So they tossed the founders out. And paid the price later.

In an overheated economic climate, where investors could get their investments liquid early via a public offering, merger or acquisition, none of this was their concern. Investors could take a short-term view of the company and reap their profit by selling their stake in the company long before the next crisis of innovation occurred. However, in an economy where startups need to build for lasting value, boards and investors may want to consider the consequences of not finding a productive home to hibernate the creative talent for the competitive storm that is bound to come.

The concepts of mission-oriented leadership and fast-response organization developed in this chapter offer investors and entrepreneurs another path to consider. Instead of viewing the management choices in a startup as binary—entrepreneur-driven on Monday, dressed up in suits and processes on Tuesday—mission-oriented leadership offers a middle path that can extend the life of the initial management team, focus the company on its immediate objectives, and build sufficient momentum to cross the chasm.

B. Developing a Mission-Centric Organization and Culture

The consequence of not having a common mission was clear at BetaSheet. Mark led the company through Customer Discovery and Customer Validation, and he had the scars to prove it. In Mark's mind, he had a singular vision for BetaSheet and was keeping his eyes fixed on where he saw the company going. However, one of his fundamental mistakes was in failing to ensure that his board and executive staff, to say nothing of the rest of the company, shared his vision. The new executives Mark hired to run Sales, Marketing, and Engineering acted like hired guns rather than committed owners. Part of this was Mark's fault in not selecting his hires for commitment to his vision rather than the length of their resume. Part of it was the fault of Mark's board in not teaching him the value of hiring executives who shared his vision. In fact, one of Mark's board members reinforced this lack of commitment in the executive staff by offering up a candidate for VP of Sales whose main qualification was that he was marking time in the board member's office. Finally, part of the problem was Mark should have been communicating and evangelizing his vision inside the company as effectively as he was doing outside. As BetaSheet scaled up, Mark's board, his executive staff, and his employees all could have shared the same worldview. Instead, the end was marked by dissonance not only about style, but about what made the company unique.

Stating Your Corporate Mission

So how do you avoid Mark's error and make the mission part of the lifeblood of your company? At the heart of the mission-centric organization is the corporate mission statement. Most startups put together a mission statement because the executive staff remembered seeing one at their last job, and somehow it felt important. Or perhaps their investors told them they needed a mission statement for their PowerPoint presentations. In neither case was a mission statement something the company lived on a daily basis.

Where does a "lived" mission statement come from? You just finished the long, laborious process of Customer Discovery, Validation, and Creation deriving, testing, and executing your mission. The mission statement you craft now is a further refinement of one you first proposed in Customer Discovery, revisited in Customer Validation, and tested with customers in Customer Creation. The goal of the earlier mission statements was to help customers understand how your company and products are unique. You may have embedded this mission on your company website, and your salespeople may have put it in their presentations. The mission statement you need in the company-building stage is different. It's for you and your company, not your customers. It consists of a paragraph or two that tells you, your board and your employees how you will cross the chasm from earlyvangelists to mainstream customers and manage the sales growth curve. It tells everyone in specific terms why they come to work, what they need to do, and how they will know they have succeeded. And it mentions the two dirty words that never get presented in mission statements that customers see: revenue and profit.

An example of a clearly written mission statement is the one "lived" at CafePress, a company that allows individuals and groups to easily create their own store to sell T-shirts, coffee cups, books and CDs.

- At CafePress our mission is to allow customers to set up stores to sell a wide range of custom products. (Our goal is to make sure they say we are the best place to go on the Web to make and sell CDs, book, and promotional items.) Here's how we are going to do that:
- We are going to give them a variety of high-quality products and good service in an easy-to-use website. (We will know we succeed if an average store sells $45 per month.). At the same time we will help these customers sell by giving them marketing tools to reach their customers
- We are going to do it for what they would consider a fair price (yet maintain 40% margins.) Next year our plan is to grow to $30 million in revenue and be profitable. (Therefore we need 25,000 new customers a month)
- We are going to try to be a good citizen of our community. (We are going to print on recyclable materials, use environmentally friendly packaging, and use non-toxic inks wherever practical)
- We are going to take good care of our employees (full medical and dental) because the longer they stick around, the better our company will become
- We are also going to offer stock options to all employees, because if they're interested in our profits and long-term success we'll all make money

Read this mission statement sentence by sentence. It tells the employees why they come to work, what they need to do, and how they will know when they're successful.

Crafting Your Corporate Mission Statement

Most companies spend an inordinate amount of time crafting a finely honed corporate mission statement for external consumption and then do nothing internally to make it happen. What I'm describing here is quite different. First, the corporate mission statement you develop now is for use inside the company. You may use some version of it to make your customers and investors happy, but that is not its purpose. Second, the mission statement is action-oriented. It is written to provide daily guidance for all employees. For that reason, it is focused on execution and what the company is trying to achieve. If you do it right, your corporate mission statement will help employees decide and act locally while being guided by an understanding of the big picture.

Crafting this "operational" mission statement is a visible sign of the transition in management from entrepreneurial to mission-centric. The CEO uses this opportunity to get commitment and buy-in from all the operating executives (as well as any of the remaining founders who may be in non-operational roles). If needed, the CEO may bring in other employees to ensure the statement is both shared and grounded. The board needs to be involved in the process as well, both to provide input and give final approval.

Mission Element	Specifics
Why your employees come to work	• To build CafePress into the world's largest retailer of customized goods
What they need to do all day	• Make sure customers say we are the only place to go on the web to make and sell CDs, books, and promotional items • Give sellers marketing tools to reach their customers • Try to be a good citizen of our community. Print on recyclable materials, use enviromentally friendly packaging, and use non-toxic inks whenever practical
How they will know they have succeeded	• Customers say CafePress is the world's best place to sell and buy custom items • Customers get great service for what they consider a fair price • Customers come back often (on average once every three weeks)
Corporate revenue and profit goals	• An average store sells $45 per month • Acquire 25,000 new customers per month • Grow to $30 million in revenue by the end of next year • Maintain 40% profit margin • Take good care of employees. Provide stock options and full medical and dental benefits

Template for Drafting a Corporate Mission Statement (Figure 6.11)

Figure 6.11 shows a rough template for drafting a corporate mission statement based on the one for CafePress. As you write (and rewrite) your mission statement, remember there are no right and wrong answers. The litmus test is this: Can new hires read the corporate mission statement and understand the company, their job, and what they need to do to succeed?

Keep in mind a mission statement for a company executing in an existing market will be quite different from a company in a new or resegmented market. In an existing market, the mission statement reflects the goal of straight-line sales growth. It describes how the company executes relentlessly to exploit the market while remaining paranoid about product lifecycle and competitors. In a new market, the company mission statement reflects the hockey-stick growth curve, and it emphasizes husbanding resources and passionately evangelizing and growing the market. In a resegmented market the mission statement describes the branding and positioning work necessary to create a unique and differentiated image of the company.

Following Through

The corporate mission statement is essential, but it's just a start. The mission-centric culture must embrace the entire company, not just the departments dealing with customers. For this reason the executive team needs to make an intense effort to ensure members of all departments feel they share a common purpose. This requires constant communication across the company. In Phase 4, you'll carry the mission-centric process further by having each department craft its own departmental mission statement. These departmental statements will answer the same three questions as the corporate mission statement—why people come to work, what they are going to do all day, and how they will know they have succeeded— in terms of the goals and activities of the specific department.

Phase 3: Transition the Customer Development Team into Functional Departments

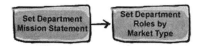

Phase 3 of Company Building signals the end of Customer Development teams and the shift to formal departments. Through constant interaction with earlyvangelist customers in Steps 1 through 3, the Customer Development team has discovered how to build repeatable sales and channel roadmaps. With these completed, the focus shifts to acquiring mainstream customers. This requires more than a small group of people to execute. Unfortunately, a Customer Development team without functional organization cannot scale. To remedy this, the company now needs to organize into departments that aggregate specific business functions that would have been counterproductive in earlier stages—principally sales, marketing, and business development—and organize them appropriately to match the needs of the company's Market Type. Accordingly, in this phase, you will:

- Craft mission statements for departments organized around business functions
- Define departmental roles according to the Market Type

A. Crafting Departmental Mission Statements

Before you set up Sales, Marketing, Business Development, and other customer-facing departments, you must figure out what these departments should do. That might sound like a facetious statement. We all know what departments do: Sales hires people to go out and sell, Marketing hires a staff and writes data sheets and runs advertisements, and so on. But that's simply not true, because the goals of each department are different depending on the Market Type, as will be clear from the discussion in this section.

Before you formally set up those departments, therefore, it's incumbent on the executive staff to think through what each department's goals will be and to articulate those goals in the form of departmental mission statements. The reason for doing this before you start hiring and staffing is that existing departments tend to rationalize their own existence and activities. Very few vice presidents in the annals of corporate history have ever said, "I think my department and staff are superfluous; let's get rid of all of them."

In Phase 2 you assembled a corporate mission statement that matched your Market Type. Your task now is to translate that corporate mission into departmental mission statements with objectives that are department- and task-specific. For example, a mission statement for a marketing department in an existing market might look like this:

The mission of our Marketing Department is to create end-user demand and drive it into the sales channel, educate the channel and customers about why our products are superior, and help Engineering understand customer needs and desires. We will accomplish this through demand-creation activities (advertising, PR, trade shows, seminars, websites, etc.), competitive analyses, channel and customer collateral (white papers, data sheets, product reviews), customer surveys, and market requirements documents.

Our goals are 40,000 active and accepted leads into the sales channel, company and product name recognition over 65% in our target market, and five positive product reviews per quarter. We will reach 35% market share in year one of sales with a headcount of five people, spending less than $750,000.

Figure 6.12 shows how the mission statement fits the template provided earlier for a corporate mission statement.

Mission Element	Specifics
Why department members come to work	• Create end-user demand and drive it into the sales channel • Educate the channel and customers about why our products are superior • Help Engineering understand customer needs and desires
What they need to do all day	• Demand-creation activities (advertising, PR, tradeshows, seminars, web sites, etc.) • Competitive analyses, channel and customer collateral (white papers, data sheets, product reviews) • Customer survey, market requirements documents
How they will know they have succeeded	• 40,000 active and accepted leads into the sales channel, company and product name recognition over 65% in target market • Five positive product reviews per quarter
Contribution to corporate profit goals	• 35% market share in year one • Headcount of five people, spend under $750K

Sample Mission Statement for a Marketing Department in a New Market (Figure 6.12)

It specifies exactly why people in this department come to work, what they need to do all day, how they will know they have succeeded, and what their contribution is to the company's profit goals. With this statement, I don't think employees will have any doubt about their mission.

B. Defining Departmental Roles by Market Type

Now that you have the mission statements for the departments, you can organize the departments themselves. Keep in mind the underlying risk in simply setting up departments by function. Now that you have a proven process for earlyvangelist sales and departments are being set up, the natural tendency is for senior executives to revert to form. The head of Sales says, "Finally, I can build my sales force"; the head of Marketing says, "Now I can hire a PR agency, run ads, and generate marketing requirements documents for Engineering"; and the head of Business Development says, "Time to do deals." Nothing could be further from the truth. Each department needs to consider how its role is defined by the Market Type the company is facing. The following discussion considers the roles of Sales, Marketing, and Business Development in each Market Type.

Department Roles in an Existing Market

Until now, the role of Sales as part of the Customer Development team has been to confirm product/market fit, find repeatable sales and channel roadmaps, and secure the earlyvangelist customers and orders to prove the roadmaps and business model work. Now that you have a critical mass of early customers, the role of a sales department is, "Get more of those customers to scale revenue and the company." That's because only in an existing market are the earlyvangelists and mainstream customers quite similar. Therefore you need to build a sales organization that can repeatedly and reliably execute from a known roadmap. This implies a sales compensation program that will incentivize the correct behavior—no wild swings for the fence, no new market forays, just day-to-day, relentless execution.

Organizing the marketing department presents the same challenges as Sales. Up until now, Marketing's role in Customer Development has been in learning and discovery—searching for new customer segments and niches, and testing positioning, pricing, promotion, and product features. Now Marketing's role shifts from creativity to execution. Since the sales organization at this point is all about repeatability and scale, all it wants from the marketing department are the materials that will support getting more customers. This means Marketing needs to drive demand into the sales channel by providing qualified customer leads, competitive analyses, customer case studies, sales training, channel support, and the like. This shift from strategist to tactical spear-carrier can be traumatic for the individual marketer or small marketing team that literally a month before was leading the Customer Development process, but it must be accomplished if Sales is to grab market share.

As Sales demands tactical execution, there's a danger Marketing will move its creative efforts to either marketing communications or product management. In the first case, the risk is that Marketing confuses its new function with simply being a marketing communications department, hiring PR agencies, branding the company, and so on. If the marketers are more technically oriented, the risk is that they will begin acting like product managers and start developing the Marketing Requirements Document (MRD) for the next product release. Mistakes like these are the natural tendency of creative people who no longer have a creative job. These mistakes are much more likely to happen in the absence of a clearly understood departmental mission tied to the corporate mission.

Regrettably, the dot-com bubble mutated the title "Business Development" into a barely recognizable role. Let's set one thing straight: Business development is not a 21st-century term for "sales." Any time I find people in a company using it that way I stay far away, since if they are imprecise about this role, they are usually fuzzy about their financial numbers and the rest of their business. The real function of a business development group is to assemble the strategic relationships necessary to build the "whole product" via partnerships and deals so the company can sell to mainstream customers.

The "whole product" is a concept defined by Bill Davidow[11] in the early years of technology marketing. It says that mainstream customers and late adopters on the technology lifecycle adoption curve need an off-the-shelf, no-risk, complete solution. They do not want to assemble piece parts from startups.

In an existing market, your competitors define how complete your product offering needs to be. If your competitors have "whole products," you need the same. In the computer business, for example, IBM is currently the ultimate supplier of whole products. It provides the hardware, software, systems integration support, and all the ancillary software to support a business solution. There is no way a startup just scaling up to compete in this space could offer a whole product. That wasn't a liability in the earlier stages of Customer Development, when the company was selling to earlyvangelists who were happy to assemble a whole product themselves. No mainstream customer, however, is going to buy a half-finished product. Consequently, the strategic mission of Business Development is to assemble a whole product to acquire mainstream customers. This means Business Development is a partnering and deal function, not a sales activity. Table 6.3 summarizes the objectives of each department in an existing market and the main ways those objectives are achieved.

---

[11] William H. Davidow. 1986 (June). *Marketing High Technology: An Insider's View.* New York: Free Press.

	Objectives	How Achieved
Sales	• Relentless execution • Market share	• Hire, staff, train • Use roadmap to guide "cookbook" execution
Marketing	• Create end-user demand and drive it into the sales channel • Ensure channel has sales tools	• Demand creation (PR, shows, ads, etc.) • Channel collateral, competitive analyses
Business Development	• Build and deliver the "whole product"	• Deals that minimally match competitors' solutions

Roles of Departments in an Existing Market (Table 6.3)

Department Roles in a New Market

For Sales in a new market this is a confusing time. The hard-won lessons learned in Customer Validation are not transferable, since the mainstream customers are not the same as the earlyvangelists you've been selling to. Therefore, even with an infinite number of salespeople, sales revenue will not scale without a change in strategy.

A real risk for a sales department in a new market is to continue to believe that earlyvangelists represent the mainstream market. Earlyvangelist sales cannot provide the hockey-stick growth curve that will turn the startup into a large company. At this stage earlyvangelists sales shouldn't be discouraged (they provide the ongoing revenue), but they should be thought of as a segment the sales department must outgrow if the company is to succeed. As discussed in Phase 1 of this chapter, the task now is to use the earlyvangelists as a "beachhead" into a narrow market segment or niche, or as the fulcrum for a tipping point.

The job of Marketing in a new market is to identify the potential mainstream customers, understand how they differ from the earlyvangelists, and come up with a chasm-crossing strategy to reach them. The danger here is that Marketing will act as if it is in an existing market and begin heavy demand-creation spending or worse, believe it can accelerate customer adoption by "branding." In a new market, there is no demand to create. Until the mainstream customers are identified and a plan to affect their behavior is agreed upon, spending infinite marketing dollars will not change sales revenue. In this Market Type, marketing is still a strategic function focused on helping Sales find the mainstream market, not on demand-creation activities.

The role of Business Development in a new market is to help Sales and Marketing bridge the perceptual gap between a company that is of interest only to earlyvangelists and one that makes sense for mainstream customers. Business Development does so by forming alliances and partnerships that are congruent with the "beachhead" markets being targeted by Sales. The goal is to make the company appear more palatable to mainstream customers by building the "whole product." Table 6.4 summarizes department roles in a new market.

	Objectives	How Achieved
Sales	• Identify and sell to "beachhead" customers • Sell to narrow market	• Pursue niche selling to mainstream customers • Continue low-level earlyvangelist sales
Marketing	• Adopt niche market or tipping point strategy • Identify and create new market with mainstream customers	• Develop mainstream customer roadmap • Avoid demand-creation spending until new market scales
Business Development	• Build "whole product"	• Establish relationships that enable "whole product" first niche by niche, then for the broad mainstream

Roles of Departments in a New Market (Table 6.4)

Department Roles in a Resegmented Market

A resegmented market requires strategies and departmental missions that combine the features of departments in existing and new markets. For this reason, departments in this type of company can sometimes feel and act schizophrenic. You start competing in an existing market where competition is fierce, with the goal of uniquely differentiating the product into a space where no one currently resides, but where you hope lots of customers will follow. At times Sales may act like it is in an existing marketing while Marketing plans new-market tactics. This confusion is par for the course, but requires close and frequent synchronization of missions and tactics.

The sales department in a resegmented market follows two tracks: selling to customers in an existing and very competitive environment (with a product that has fewer features than the competition) while simultaneously attempting to find new customers, as if in a new market. However, unlike a new market where the move to mainstream customers was predicated on chasm-crossing or tipping-point strategies (i.e., niche-at-a-time or epidemic), in a resegmented market Sales is counting on Marketing to use positioning and branding to "peel off" substantial numbers of existing customers by creating a differentiated segment. One of the risks is Sales becoming beguiled by the existing customers in the market you are attempting to resegment. Continuing low-level sales to address these customers is just a part of the sales strategy. Sales executives must remember the real goal is to change the perception of the current base of customers in order to create a new, much more valuable market segment—one where your product is the market leader.

	Objectives	How Achieved
Sales	• Generate revenue from an existing market • Identify and sell to "beachhead" customers in the new market segement • Hit hockey stick by exploiting new market segment	• Scale sales force to generate revenue in existing market (few hires) • Add new hires to focus on new market segment • Transition sales to new segment and scale sales staff
Marketing	• Help sales generate revenue in existing market • Create new segment from an existing market	• Use guerilla Marketing tactics, minimize expenditures • Use positioning and branding to create new segment, differentiation, and awareness
Business Development	• Build and deliver whole product to differentiate company and product in new segment	• Establish relationships that enable "whole product" for mainstream customers in the new segment

Roles of Departments in a Resegmented Market (Table 6.5)

The same temptations face Marketing, as the sales group will be pressuring it for demand-creation activities in the existing market segment. While some demand creation is necessary, Marketing's primary objective should be to find the way to uniquely differentiate the company and its product into a new category—taking a large group of existing customers with them. As described in Phase 1 of this chapter, branding and positioning are the appropriate marketing tools for differentiation. Similarly, Business Development needs to find the unique partnerships and relationships that constitute the "whole product," required to differentiate the company from other vendors. Table 6.5 summarizes department roles in a resegmented market.

Phase 4: Build Fast-response Departments

The mantra of Phase 4 of Company Building is provided by the war-fighting doctrine of the U.S. Marine Corps: Whoever can make and implement his decisions consistently faster gains a tremendous, often decisive, advantage. Decision-making thus becomes a time-competitive process, and timeliness of decisions becomes essential to generating tempo.[12]

In business, no less than in war, fast decision-making has lethal consequences for the laggards. To sell to mainstream customers and build long-term success for your company, you need to create an agile organization that can respond to customers, competitors, and market opportunities as rapidly as possible. You've made a start by organizing departments around clearly articulated missions. Now your task is to turn those departments into fast-response departments. To do that, you need to carry the learning and discovery culture you cultivated in Phases 1 through 3 into your functional departments. Two organizing principles, decentralized decision-making and the OODA loop (Observe, Orient, Decide, Act), provide the foundation for this phase.

During the Customer Discovery, Validation, and Creation steps, the Customer Development team was a flat organization and included founders who could make on-the-spot strategic decisions. As you transition to functional departments, you must decentralize decision-making so each department can react in real time to changes in customers, markets, and competition.

No organizational habit is more insidious and dangerous to a small company than constant formal, upward review and the need to wait for the big decision. In some companies the phrase "executive leadership" is oxymoronic as everyone knows that employees who are at the point of decision appreciate the true situation better than the executive sitting behind a desk, far removed from the facts. To ensure this doesn't describe your company, you need a mission-driven culture and bottom-up decentralized management style that pushes decisions down the corporate ladder.

The second principle of a fast response department is the OODA loop. This concept is crucial in this stage of the company's life, when you are trying to grow while maintaining

---

[12] U.S. Marine Corps. 1989. Warfighting Doctrine FMFM 1. Pub # PCN 139-000050-00.

speed and agility. Speed in management means shortening the time needed to make decisions, plan, coordinate, and communicate, and the time to incorporate feedback. In an existing market, it is speed relative to the competition and customers. In a new or resegmented market, it is speed relative to your cash flow and profitability. The aim is to be faster than your competitors (or faster than your cash-burn rate) and react quickly to customer needs or opportunities. The speed difference doesn't have to be large, even a small improvement frequently taken advantage of can lead to significant results.

A company set up to use and exploit OODA loops for its departments would have the following characteristics:

Observe:

- Is information-gathering and dissemination an integral part of the department culture?
- Does bad news travel as fast or faster than good news? Or is information hoarded?
- Are messengers rewarded or punished?

Orient:

- Does the department have a culture for understanding the market? Customers? Competitors?
- Is there a dispassionate process for reviewing competitors' products and your own?
- Are the company and departmental missions well understood?

Decide:

- Can individual managers and executives make independent decisions?
- Are decisions made in the context of the corporate and departmental mission?

Act:

- Is there an efficient process for executing tactical decisions immediately?
- Is there a process for synchronizing actions?
- Is there a lessons-learned process for reviewing past decisions?

Making decentralized decision-making and OODA loops part of your company culture requires three main steps. In this phase, you will:

- Implement mission-centric management
- Create a culture for information gathering and dissemination
- Build a leadership culture

A. Implementing Mission-Centric Management

In 1982 Andy Bechtolsheim, a graduate student at Stanford University, built a computer out of a readily available commercial microprocessor and an operating system designed by AT&T and enhanced by students at U.C. Berkeley. Bechtolsheim's design was lean, powerful, and unique. While it was less powerful than the existing minicomputers, it was affordable enough to be used by only one person. Bechtolsheim's computer also had the ability to connect to other computers through a then-new network called Ethernet and included TCP/IP, now known as the Internet protocol suite.

Stanford University licensed Bechtolsheim's computer design to anyone who was interested. Bechtolsheim and a fellow graduate student, Vinod Khosla, formed one of the nine startups that licensed the design. The company relentlessly pursued business deals (it signed a $40 million OEM deal in its second year) and created new versions of its computer at an astonishing pace. Within six years the company's sales had grown to $1 billion, and the eight other licensees disappeared from the market. Twenty years later Bechtolsheim and Khosla's company (eponymously named Sun, after the Stanford University Network) had become a $15 billion company.

What differentiated Bechtolsheim and Khosla's company from the other entrants in this new market? Was it, as some would argue, a clear case of first-mover advantage? Not really. While Sun had the benefit of having the computer's designer as a founder, all the other startups had innovative and competent technical staffs. Sun succeeded, I believe, because it focused relentlessly on its mission and built an organization that could execute faster than its competitors—so much faster that Sun's decisions looked like a blur to its competitors.

Mission-centric management is the foundation on which agile companies like Sun build fast-response departments. Unlike relatively inflexible, process-driven management, mission-centric management deals better with the two fundamental problems a startup continually faces: uncertainty and time. For a small company, precision and certainty are unattainable in most competitive or customer situations. Consequently, the company and its departments must build on what is attainable— speed and agility. Mission-centric management offers the flexibility to deal with rapidly changing situations and exploit fleeting windows of customer and market opportunity. It builds a system in which even Type A executives can cooperate (at least to the extent of coordinating their efforts) yet executives at all levels get what they would kill for at most companies: the charter and latitude to act with initiative and boldness.

Mission-centric management tactics support decentralized decision-making. Once in position, this type of decision-making results in an agile, sped-up, and informed decision-making process that makes a company flexible, cohesive, and responsive—in other words, a growing company that kicks butt.

Creating mission-centric management requires a conscious shift in thinking on the part of managers and employees. The process begins with the departmental missions you created in Phase 3. Beyond those, mission-centric management has five unique parts:

- Mission intention
- Employee initiative
- Mutual trust and communication
- "Good enough" decision-making
- Mission synchronization

Let's consider each of these in turn.

Mission Intention

Earlier in this chapter I described the mission statement as a paragraph or two that lets you and your employees know why you come to work, what you are going to do, and how you will know you've succeeded. Yet that description of the mission only details the tasks to be done. In reality there are two parts to any mission: the tasks to be accomplished and the reason, or intention, for executing those tasks. A task statement describes what action needs to be taken ("We are going to reach $10 million in sales with 45% gross margin this year"), while the intention describes the desired result of the action: "$10 million in sales is our cash flow break-even and 45% gross margin makes us profitable. Both are of equal importance to us this year. Do not sacrifice one for the other." Of the two, the intention is more important. While a situation may change, making the task obsolete (your sales group can't make the $10 million in revenue), the intention is more enduring and continues to guide the company's actions ("Let's see, we are trying to achieve cash flow break-even and profitability. If we can't make $10 million in sales, how much do we have to cut expenses to still achieve cash flow break-even, and what effect will that have on profitability?"). For mission-centric management to work, you need to ensure the intentions of all missions (corporate and departmental) are understood, not just by a few key executives, but by everyone, top to bottom, in the company. At this point in a company's life, disseminating the intention of the corporate and departmental missions is an important way of leading the organization. Accordingly, it is a prime responsibility of all executives.

While mission-centric management relies on the executives to explain the underlying intention of the corporate and departmental mission, it leaves employees as free as possible to choose how the missions get accomplished. For example, the sales department might put together a sales plan to reach the goal that says, "We will achieve $10 million in revenue with 200 new orders at an average selling price of $50,000 with a cost of sales of $2.7 million." The idea of intention implies once employees understand the thinking behind the mission, they can work collaboratively to achieve it. Think of intention as the answer to the aphorism, "When you are up to your neck in alligators it's hard to remember you were supposed to drain the swamp."

Intention also goes a level deeper. Imagine that the head of Sales and the other department heads, seeing they may not make the revenue number, understand the consequences and have contingency plans in place. "If we fail to make $10 million in revenue this year, we can't keep spending like we are on a $10 million revenue plan," should be an automatic consequence of intention in a mission-centric department. Of course, this requires implicit trust and high-bandwidth communications among the executives, an issue we'll take up a bit later in this section. The alternative is the finger-pointing that happens in other startups. "Well, Marketing did what it was supposed to, why should we have to cut our budget?"

By making the mission intention widely known across the company, the CEO and departmental VPs exercise leadership not by providing explicit directives and detailed directions, but by sending out broad guidance. In this style of management, all executives and employees down the line have the ability to exercise full authority and apply their judgment and imagination.[13] The higher an executive sits in the corporate hierarchy, the more general should be the supervision he or she exercises, and the less the burden of detail. The CEO and VPs should intervene in a subordinate's actions only in exceptional cases when irreparable harm is imminent.

In summary, mission-centric management maximizes low-level initiative while achieving a high level of cooperation in order to obtain better results. This is the

[13] Spenser Wilkinson. 1895. *The Brain of an Army: A Popular Account of the German General Staff*, p. 106. Westminster, UK: A. Constable.

antithesis of micromanagement. It requires entrepreneurs to think clearly about who they are, who they have hired (and why), and how well they have communicated this policy. Mission-centric management turns into a corporate debacle when executives believe they're managing this way and employees believe the opposite—they should wait for executive direction because they will be punished if they make a mistake. To avoid such failures, the company leadership needs to communicate the mission-centric policy clearly and consistently—and act accordingly.

Employee Initiative

One reason for BetaSheet's demise was the imposition of top-down management. After Mark's departure, all new ideas had to be vetted by committee, sent up the organization for approval, then passed back down to the employees for implementation. It's no wonder the best second- and third-level managers and employees soon followed Mark out of the company. The new leadership at BetaSheet was operating under the assumption that once the company achieved a certain size, a hierarchical command and process-driven organization would suffice to help it grow larger. Unfortunately, BetaSheet's unique, new market was immediately crowded with competitors who could see the opportunity BetaSheet had pioneered. And the employees who could have saved the company with innovative and creative product and market ideas had long since left.

Success in a startup is all about searching, finding, and exploiting ephemeral opportunities. This is possible only when all employees—not just the founders— take initiative. Employees must accept that taking initiative and acting on their own authority is part of their implicit employment contract. Simply showing up and doing the job is characteristic of work in a process-centric organization but anathema to a mission-centric one.

The mandate to show initiative does not mean employees are free to act any way they please. In fact, it places a special responsibility on employees to (1) always keep the mission and intent in mind and (2) coordinate their actions within their departmental and corporate missions. Conversely, delegating authority to employees does not absolve the CEO and department executives of ultimate responsibility for results. They must learn to articulate their missions and intentions in such a way that employees understand the objectives without feeling restricted in their freedom of action. Executives must be adept at expressing their desires clearly and forcefully without micromanaging—a skill that requires practice. Creating a culture of employee initiative depends on selecting, hiring, and retaining employees who work best in this type of environment. You do not have the basis for fast-response departments if you hire (or tolerate) employees or executives who wait for orders, believe they must do everything by the book, learn never to tell the boss anything that will make him or her uncomfortable, or are used to being superstars who never have to cooperate with their peers. At this stage of your company's life, your competitors or your own inertia will soon put you out of business.

Mutual Trust and Communication

A successful mission-centric organization demands mutual trust and confidence in the abilities and judgment of employees and executives. Executives trust their employees to perform their missions competently and with minimal supervision, to work in concert with the overall intention, and to communicate news about customers, competitors, success, and failures between the various departments. (Good news should travel fast, but bad news should travel faster.) Employees, meanwhile, trust executives to provide the necessary leadership and support them loyally and fully, even when they make mistakes. This is a big order in a startup, where in some cases large egos and equally large political agendas seem to be the norm. Mutual trust and communication simply cannot exist in an environment where an admission of failure or a request for help is looked down upon as a career-limiting move, or where information is hoarded as a source of power. For cooperation to be maintained, the company must establish a culture of quickly removing employees or executives who do not earn the respect and trust of their peers.

Trust has a flip side; it must be earned as well as given. Since a mission-centric department is decentralized and spontaneous rather than centralized and coercive, discipline is not only imposed from above, it must also be generated from within. In order to earn executives' trust, employees must demonstrate the self-discipline to accomplish their missions with minimal supervision and to always act in accordance with the mission intention. Executives and managers, in order to earn employees' trust, must demonstrate they will support and protect employees as they exercise initiative.

A great side effect of mutual trust is its positive effect on morale. Trust increases the individual's identity with the company, department, and mission. Employees in this type of company not only wear their company T-shirts with pride, but talk incessantly about the organization's prospects and achievements.

"Good Enough" Decision-Making

Gen. George Patton said, "A good plan violently executed now is better than a perfect plan next week." The same is true in your company. Most decisions in a small company must be made in the face of uncertainty. Since every situation is unique, there is no perfect solution to any customer or competitor problem, and you shouldn't agonize over trying to find one. This doesn't mean gambling the company's fortunes on a whim. It means adopting plans with an acceptable degree of risk, and doing it quickly. In general, the company that consistently makes and implements decisions rapidly gains a tremendous, often decisive, competitive advantage.

Timely decisions also demand efficient meetings with the agenda and deliberations limited to the issues at hand. It's painful to see an executive staff meeting that should be focused on making a quick business decision sidetracked by every HR, legal, PR, and Product Development objection. In every company a reason can be found not to do anything. Company cultures that allow the sideshows to derail the decision process don't make rapid decisions. Naturally, there are situations in which time is not a limiting factor, such as long-term strategic, engineering, and product planning, and you should not rush these decisions unreasonably. That said, strive to cultivate a culture of tightly focused meetings with clear decision-making objectives. The result should be a "Good Enough" decision-making culture.

Mission Synchronization

Even with well-written mission statements and the best intentions, a mission-centric process can fail without a way to formally keep departmental missions synchronized. Mission synchronization is akin to the synchronization process that the Customer Development and Product Development groups employed during Customer Discovery, Validation, and Creation. In those steps Customer Development and Product Development teams regularly updated each other about the realities of the marketplace and the product schedule and features. Together both teams could react to customer needs by shifting Product Development or business strategies to accommodate those realities.

As you move to a mission-centric process, all departments need to stay in sync and move in concert with the corporate mission and intent. This means synchronization meetings now have three functions, to ensure: (1) all departments still understand the corporate mission, (2) all the departmental missions are mutually supportive, and (3) the CEO understands and approves the way each department will execute its mission.

There's a striking contrast between a synchronization meeting in a mission-centric organization and a staff meeting in a larger, process-driven company. As shown in Table 6.6, in a process-driven company, orders and goals come from the top down, while status reports flow from the bottom up. In a mission-centric organization, synchronization meetings are peer-wise, cross-departmental coordinating sessions that allow the entire company to respond to changing conditions.

	Customer Development Organization	Mission-Centric Organization	Process-Driven Organization
Who	• Customer-facing teams & product development teams	• Department-to-department • Corporate-to-department • Department-to-corporate	• Corporate-to-department
Why	• Update hypothesis versus reality • Allow entire company to understand and react to change	• Keep departmental missions aligned with corporate mission • Ensure that departmental missions are mutually supportive • Ensure that departments tactical moves are in step with the corporate objective(s)	• Transmit orders and goals from top of the organization downwards • Report status from bottom of organization upwards

Synchronization Strategies by Type of Organization (Table 6.6)

B. Creating a Culture for Information Gathering and Dissemination

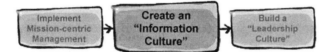

A fast-response department requires a constant stream of information. In Customer Discovery, Validation, and Creation, the way to ensure that flow of timely information was through personal observation and experience—getting out from behind your desk and into the field to get close to customers, competitors, and the market. Now that the company has grown past its first few customers, executives need three basic views of information to understand what is going on:

- First-hand knowledge
- An overall view
- The view from the eyes of customers and competitors

First-hand knowledge is the "getting down and dirty outside the building" method you've used until now. Executives need to continue this activity even while the company grows. They need to hear what customers are saying, what competitors are doing, and what the sales staff is experiencing. From this view, executives can get a sense of what they can and cannot demand of their people in the field.

In companies I'm involved with this means, first, that all executives (not just the head of Sales) are out talking to customers and the sales channel frequently—at least once a quarter. A summary of everyone's impressions and findings should be circulated widely after each trip. Second, anyone who talks to customers and the sales channel needs to communicate company-wide at least weekly—with both bad news and good. (I prefer the bad news since it requires action to fix. Good news just means that you collect a check from a customer.) Part of the cultural shift that differentiates a mission-centric organization is acknowledging that this type of information sharing goes against the natural sunny-side-up outlook of every salesperson on the planet. "Share bad news?! Are you crazy, I'm not going to tell anyone I lost an account, let alone why I lost it!" Yet, that honestly is exactly what the company needs.

The second picture is a synthesized "bird's-eye view" of the customer and competitive environment. You assemble this view by gathering information from a variety of sources: sales data, win/loss information, market research data, competitive analyses, and so on. From this big-picture view, executives try to make sense of the shape of the market and the overall patterns in the unfolding competitive and customer situation. At the same time, they can gauge how well industry data and actual sales in the field match the company's revenue and market-share expectations.

All this requires having a formal market and customer intelligence function in each department. This doesn't require a full-time dedicated person, just someone who realizes it's his or her job. Your intelligence scouts need to gather first- and second-hand data and issue reports on a regular basis, at least monthly. Intelligence reports should be devoid of political agendas and focus on facts: market-share data, win/loss summaries, customer quality reports, tech support calls.

The third view is of the action as seen through the eyes of customers and competitors. Put yourself in your customers' and competitors' shoes in order to deduce possible competitors' moves and anticipate customer needs. In an existing market this is where you ask yourself, "If I were my own competitor and had its resources, what would my next move be?" In looking through the eyes of a customer, the question might be, "Why should I buy from this company versus another one? What do I see that will convince me to give them an order?" In a new or resegmented market, the questions might be, "Why would more than a few techno junkies buy this product? How would I get my 90-year-old grandmother to understand and buy this product? How would I explain it to her and her friends?"

Think of this technique as playing chess. You need to look at all the likely moves from both sides of the chessboard. This is a game that ought to be played out at executive and departmental staff meetings: What would we do if we were our competitors? How would we react? What would we be planning? After a while this type of role-playing will become an integral part of everyone's thinking and planning.

Of the three pictures, first-hand knowledge is clearly the most detailed, but now that your company is bigger it usually offers a very narrow field of vision. Executives who focus only on this image risk losing sight of the big picture. The bird's-eye view provides an overall image but lacks the critical detail, just as a status report captures only a broad impression of the events in the marketplace. Executives who focus only on this image are out of touch with reality. The third picture is largely a mental exercise limited by the fact that you can never be sure what your customers and competitors are up to. The combination of all three views helps executives form an accurate picture of what is going on in their business.

Even with information from all three views, executives and managers need to remember two points. First, there will never be enough information to make a perfect decision. Second, wherever possible, decisions should be made by the individual on the spot who has direct observation of the situation.

Don't lose sight of the most important element of data gathering: what to do with the information once you collect it. Information dissemination is another cornerstone of agile companies and fast-response departments. Information, whether good or bad, must not be guarded like some precious commodity. Some company cultures reward executives who hoard knowledge or suppress bad news. In any of my companies, that is a firing offense. All news, but especially bad news, needs to be dissected, understood, and acted upon. This means understanding sales losses is more important than understanding sales wins; understanding why a competitor's products are better is more important than rationalizing ways in which yours is still superior. Information dissemination also means confronting the "dead moose on the conference table" issue—the unmentionable subject everyone knows about but no one wants to address. This kind of issue is often personnel related. It could be someone not pulling his or her weight as part of the team, unethical behavior, or any other subject that typically goes unspoken and unaddressed. If problematic behavior appears and does not get dealt with quickly, the death knell is already sounding for your fast-response organization.

C. Building a Leadership Culture

Southwest Airlines started as a small regional airline in 1973. Thirty years later, it was the most profitable airline in the United States. It did not achieve this striking growth through better planes (all airlines had access to everything Boeing or Airbus could supply), nor did it have better or more profitable routes. Southwest achieved its success by building an agile company with the ultimate fast-response departments. Its people worked as a team to turn around planes for the next flight in 25 minutes (their competitors took hours). The company cut costs by listening to every imaginable employee suggestion until the cost of a seat on one of Southwest's planes was 24% lower than on its nearest competitor. In return for listening to employees, the company commanded an unusual degree of loyalty.

All this is to say that Southwest Airlines created a leadership culture. Its managers were focused on inspiring, guiding, and supporting committed employees and encouraging them to perform freely within modest limits. Over time, Southwest became known for employees who exhibited a high degree of independence, self-discipline, and initiative.

Southwest is living proof that with the right culture, employees not only accept responsibility but actively seek it. In this type of company, exercising imagination, ingenuity, and creativity is widespread.

So how do you create a culture of leadership? It takes more than preaching

So how do you create a culture of leadership? It takes more than preaching responsibility and initiative. Your company's philosophy of leadership is expressed in the things you do (or don't do) to push responsibility down the organization. For example, trying to micromanage employees slows decisions and kills individual initiative. Attempting to impose precise order on how a project in a department is accomplished stifles creativity and leads to a formulistic approach to business problems. Insisting on certainty and all the facts before you act forces you to pass up opportunities and creates a "no risk" culture. Clinging to preset business plans that have outlived their usefulness destroys the company's ability to adapt to changing circumstances and exploit opportunities as they come. Instead, let your people know that you want them to exercise leadership, and back them up when they do. When you give direction on how a task gets done, do so only to the degree needed to provide coordination that can't be achieved any other way. Keep direction as brief and simple as possible, relying on employees to work out the details of execution. Be continually open to feedback that the plan isn't working and needs adjustment. Needless to say, this way of sharing responsibility and leadership depends upon all the work you've done to make sure everyone understands the mission and its intent.

While this might sound obvious in a company where the CEO can no longer manage every detail, many entrepreneurs have a hard time letting go when it's their brilliance and vision that created the idea of the company in the first place. This inability to delegate was one of Mark's downfalls at BetaSheet and is one of the common issues when a founder is removed by the board.

None of this delegation downward means an abrogation or diminishing of the CEO's responsibility. On the contrary, executives should always begin delegating with a "trust but verify" philosophy. The first few times a job or mission is assigned, check to see that the work has been performed to your satisfaction. If it has been carried out, then reduce the amount of verification until it becomes part of the synchronization meetings. If the job didn't get done, or wasn't done correctly, provide direction, training, and guidance to make sure employees have the knowledge and understanding to perform the task. Then back off and let them do their jobs.

Another important aspect of leadership culture is a close-knit sense of being part of a team. The organization's formal leaders should reinforce the common values that make employees feel good about their organization and company. This means creating a supportive atmosphere in which initiative is encouraged and rewarded, provided it advances the shared mission of the team.

A leadership culture also depends upon developing employee maturity—engendering in employees a willingness to exercise initiative, the judgment to act wisely, and an eagerness to accept responsibility. Maturity in this sense is not necessarily linked to age or seniority. I've seen 20-somethings step up to the plate and grab all the responsibility they can get their hands on, while those twice their age shrug and say, "It's not my job."

One way to nurture maturity is to transition the "superstars" found in every corner of a startup into coaches and role models. When the company was a small startup, it looked for those world-class individuals who were 10 times more productive than average. Now, when you need to scale and grow, you'll find there are not enough superstars in the job market to match the caliber of your existing staff. In a traditional startup, as processes, procedures, and rules begin to get added, jobs are redefined so "average" hires can do them. The superstars, who tend to be individualist and iconoclastic, look at all this with dismay, lamenting, "the company is going downhill." Like the elves in the *Lord of the Rings* stories, they realize that their time has passed and quietly leave the company. One way to keep and motivate superstars is to integrate them into larger teams as role models and coaches. If they can teach, make them coaches. If they prefer isolation, let them be revered role models. And if they are outspoken, they can become the voices in the wilderness that will sometimes be prophetic—as long as your culture protects the mavericks. However you deploy them, the long-term tenure, motivation, and contribution of iconoclastic superstars and founders are the ultimate tests of a leadership culture.

Fast Response Departments and the Agile Company

The result of building fast response departments is an agile company. As this Company Building phase ends, you have assembled a company and management processes that can scale, yet is more responsive than competitors', and relentless and ruthless in its execution. Figure 6.13 summarizes all of the components of the agile company.

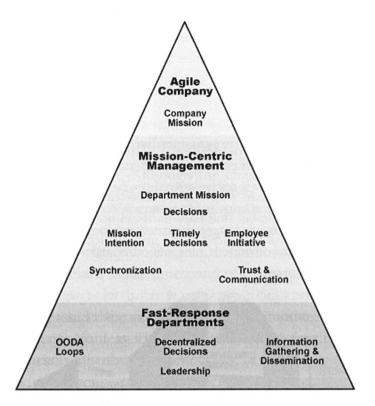

Fast-Response Departments, Mission-Centric Management
& the Agile Company *(Figure 6.13)*

Iterate and Grow

The end of this company-building phase brings to mind a quote from Winston Churchill in World War II after the British finally won their first major land victory over the Germans at el Alamein in North Africa: "Now this is not the end. It is not even the beginning of the end. But it is, perhaps, the end of the beginning."[14]

The same can now certainly be said for you and your company—it is the end of the beginning.

By the end of this phase your company has gone through some major and irreversible structural changes. It will never be the small startup you once knew. You have moved from selling to earlyvangelists to setting your sights on mainstream customers, you've reviewed your management team and built a mission-centric

---

[14] Speech in November 1942.

organization, and you've transitioned the Customer Development team into functional, fast-response departments.

Now it's time to honestly assess whether these company-building activities provide a sound footing for moving forward.

- Has Sales crossed into the mainstream and hit the hockey stick or is each order still a heroic effort?
- Is the company on its revenue and expense plan?
- If so, do you have a viable and profitable business model?
- Is there a management team in place that can grow and build the company?
- Is there a mission-centric culture in place—company and department wide?

As grueling as the company-building process was, you may need to iterate parts of it again. Typically, finding mainstream customers is hardest to get right the first time in new and resegmented markets. Finding the right mix of positioning and branding is difficult, and if the company doesn't get it right, sales won't take off as expected. However, if you've been following the Customer Development model, the consequences are not fatal to the company (and may not be career limiting for you). Provided you've kept the headcount and expenses low, you can afford to try again.

As difficult as it is to find mainstream customers, the tectonic shifts changing cultures bring are equally wrenching. That's why agility is so important, and why there can be a huge payoff from implementing a mission-centric company and fast-response departments. Just remember that changing people's behaviors and expectations is hard, and you need to work at it constantly.

The payoff for successfully executing this company-building step is a set of words that any founder or CEO would be proud to hear: a profitable, successful, relentless, driven, and tenacious company with satisfied employees on the path to an IPO.

COMPANY-BUILDING SUMMARY

Phase	Goals	Deliverables
1. Reach Mainstream Customers	Move the company from early sales into a scalable business	
A. Transition from Earlyvangelists to Mainstream Customers	Select the appropriate strategy to reach mainstream customers.	Written chasm-crossing plan that matches Market Type
B. Manage Sales Growth	Develop a sales, marketing, and business development revenue and expense plan that matches Market Type.	Written plan matches Market Type
2. Review Management and Build a Mission-Centric Organization	Grow past the Customer Development team	
A. The Board Reviews the CEO and Executive Staff	Evaluate whether current management can transition in the new company-building roles.	Management team that can build the company
B. Develop a Mission-Centric Organization and Culture	Evolve management style from visionary founder to one that can scale with more people.	Corporate mission statement Mission-centric culture across company
3. Customer Development Team into Functional Departments	Set up functional departments that are mission driven	
A. Craft Departmental Mission Statements	Set up mission-driven goals for new departments.	Departmental mission statements
B. Define Department Roles	Define the department roles by Market Type.	Written departmental objectives and responsibilities that match Market Type
4. Build Fast-Response Departments	Create agile and responsive departments that can still operate like a small startup	
A. Implement Mission-Centric Management	Build the components of mission-centric management; intention, initiative, trust and communication, good-enough decision-making, mission synchronization.	Mission-centric rolled out across departments
B. Create a Culture for Information Gathering and Dissemination	Departments with multiple views of information; firsthand knowledge, overall view, view through customers' eyes.	Written plan for acquiring the three views of market and customers
C. Build a Leadership Culture	Lead by delegation, build mission-driven culture.	Superstar transition, mavericks protected
D. Iterate and Grow	Verify that sales have crossed into the mainstream. Management team that can grow and build the company.	Predict revenue and expenses Viable and profitable business model Mission-centric culture, executives suited to mission

Bibliography

Entrepreneurial Management Stack

Over the last few years we've discovered that startups are not smaller versions of large companies. The skills founders need are not covered by traditional books for MBAs and large company managers. There are now a few books that specifically address founders' needs. Alexander Osterwalder's *Business Model Generation* is the first book that allows you to answer "What's your business model?" intelligently and with precision. Make sure this one is on your shelf.

Eric Ries was the best student I ever had. He took the Customer Development process, combined it with Agile Engineering, and actually did the first implementation in a startup. His insights about the combined Customer Development/Agile process and its implications past startups into large corporations is a sea change in thinking. His book, *The Lean Startup,* is a "must-have" for your shelf.

It's impossible to implement any of this if you don't understand Agile Development. *Extreme Programming Explained* by one of the pioneers of Agile, Kent Beck, is a great tutorial. If you don't understand Values, Principles and Practices in XP it makes Customer Development almost impossible.

If you're in a large company, *the other side of innovation* makes sense of how to insert innovation into an execution organization. If you're starting a medical device company *Biodesign: The Process of Innovating Medical Technologies* is a must-have. It has a great customer discovery process.

- *Business Model Generation* – Alexander Osterwalder
- *The Lean Startup* – Eric Ries
- *Extreme Programming Explained* – Kent Beck
- *The other side of innovation* – Vijay Govindarajan & Chris Trimble
- *Biodesign: The Process of Innovating Medical Technologies* – Zenios, Makower, Yock, et al
- *The Four Steps to the Epiphany* – Steve Blank
- *The Startup Owner's Manual* – Steve Blank and Bob Dorf
- *The Startup Owner's Manual Founder's Workbook*, a digital workbook companion to *The Startup Owner's Manual*

Must-Read Books

The other side of innovation is the closest recipe I've read for getting entrepreneurship right in large companies. *Innovator's Dilemma* and *Innovator's Solution* helped me refine the notion of the Four Types of Startup Markets. I read these books as the handbook for startups trying to disrupt an established company. *The Innovators DNA* rings true about the skills founders need to have. *Crossing the Chasm* made me understand that there are repeatable patterns in early stage companies. It started my search for the repeatable set of patterns that preceded the chasm. The *Tipping Point* has made me realize that marketing communications strategies for companies in New Markets often follow the Tipping Point. *Blue Ocean Strategy* is a great way to look at what I've called "market type."

- *the other side of innovation* – Vijay Govindarajan & Chris Trimble
- *The Innovator's Dilemma* & *The Innovator's Solution* – Clayton M. Christensen
- *The Innovator's DNA: Mastering the Five Skills of Disruptive Innovators* – Jeff Dyer, Hal Gregersen, Clayton M. Christensen
- *Crossing the Chasm: Marketing and Selling High-Tech Products to Mainstream Customers*
- *Inside the Tornado: Marketing Strategies from Silicon Valley's Cutting Edge*
- *Dealing with Darwin: How Great Companies Innovate at Every Phase of Their Evolution* – all three by Geoffrey A. Moore
- *The Tipping Point: How Little Things Can Make a Big Difference* – Malcolm Gladwell
- *Blue Ocean Strategy: How to Create Uncontested Market Space and Make Competition Irrelevant* – R. Mauborgne and W. C. Kim

Strategy Books for Startups

The Marketing Playbook gives marketers five strategy options, teaches gap analysis and offer tactical marketing campaign advice. *Do More Faster* identifies issues that first-time entrepreneurs encounter and offers useful advice. *Getting Real* is web-focused. Noam Wasserman's *Founders Dilemma* is essential reading to building a great startup team.

These books are timeless classics. *The Entrepreneurial Mindset* articulates the critically important idea that there are different types of startup opportunities. The notion of three Market Types springs from here and Christensen's work. The book provides a framework for the early marketing/sales strategies essential in a startup. *Delivering Profitable Value* talks more about value propositions and value delivery systems than you ever want to hear again. However, this is one of the books you struggle through and then realize you learned something valuable. Schumpeter's book *Theory of Economic Development* is famous for his phrase "creative destruction" and its relevance to entrepreneurship. Peter Drucker's *Concept of the Corporation* was the first insider's view of how a decentralized company (GM) works. His *Innovation and Entrepreneurship* is a classic. While written for a corporate audience, read it for the sources of innovation. If you write software, you already know about Fred Brooks' time-honored text, *The Mythical Man Month*. If you manage a software company you need to read it so you don't act like Dilbert's pointy-haired boss. Peppers & Rogers, *The One to One Future* opened my eyes to concepts of lifetime value, most profitable customers and the entire customer lifecycle of "get, keep and grow." Bill Davidow's *Marketing High Technology* introduced me to the concept of "whole product" and the unique needs of mainstream customers. Michael Porter is the father of competitive strategy. His books *Competitive Strategy, Competitive Advantage*, and *On Competition* are still the standards.

- *The Marketing Playbook* – John Zagula and Richard Tong
- *Do More Faster: Techstar lessons to accelerate your startup* – David Cohen and Brad Feld
- *Getting Real: The smarter, faster, easier way to build a successful web application* – Jason Fried
- *The Founder's Dilemma: Anticipating and Avoiding the Pitfalls that Can Sink a Startup* – Noam Wasserman
- *The Entrepreneurial Mindset: Strategies for Continuously Creating Opportunity in an Age of Uncertainty* – R. McGrath and I. MacMillan
- *Delivering Profitable Value* – Michael J. Lanning.
- *Theory of Economic Development* – Joseph Schumpeter
- *Concept of the Corporation and Innovation and Entrepreneurship* – Peter Drucker
- *The Mythical Man Month* – Fred Brooks
- *The One to One Future: Building Relationships One Customer at a Time* – Don Peppers, Martha Rogers
- *Marketing High Technology: An Insider's View* and *Total Customer Service: The Ultimate Weapon* – William H. Davidow
- *Competitive Strategy, Competitive Advantage,* and *On Competition* – all by Michael Porter

Innovation and Entrepreneurship in the Enterprise

How large companies can stay innovative and entrepreneurial has been the Holy Grail for authors of business books, business schools, consulting firms, etc. There's some great work from lots of authors in this area but I'd start by reading *the other side of innovation*. Next I'd read *The Future of Management* and consider its implications.

Then I'd read the short Harvard Business Review articles. Eric Von Hippel's work on new product introduction methodologies and the notion of "Lead Users" offer many parallels with Customer Discovery and Validation. But like most books on the subject it's written from the point of view of a large company. Von Hippel's four steps of 1) goal generation and team formation, 2) trend research, 3) lead user pyramid networking and 4) lead user workshop and idea improvement is a more rigorous and disciplined approach than suggested in my book, *The Four Steps to the Epiphany*.

Books

- *the other side of innovation* – Vijay Govindarajan and Chris Trimble
- *Innovator's Dilemma* & *The Innovator's Solution* – Clayton Christensen
- *The Future of Management* – Gary Hamel
- *Winning Through Innovation: A Practical Guide to Leading Organizational Change and Renewal* – Charles O'Reilly
- *Breakthrough Products with Lead User Research* – Eric Von Hippel and Mary Sonnack
- *The Sources of Innovation* – Eric Von Hippel

Harvard Business Review Articles

- *Meeting the Challenge of Disruptive Change* – Clayton Christensen/Michael Overdorf: March/April 2000
- *The Quest for Resilience* – Gary Hamel/Liisa Valikangas: Sept. 2003
- *The Ambidextrous Organization* – Charles O'Reilly/Michael Tushman: April 2004
- *Darwin and the Demon: Innovating Within Established Enterprises* – Geoffrey Moore: July/August 2004
- *Meeting the Challenge of Corporate Entrepreneurship* – David Garvin/Lynne Levesque: Oct. 2006
- The Innovator's DNA – Jeffrey Dyer, Hal Gregersen, Clayton Christensen: Dec. 2009

"War as Strategy" Books

The metaphor that business is war is a cliché that points to a deeper truth. Many basic business concepts; competition, leadership, strategy versus tactics, logistics, etc. have their roots in military affairs. The difference is that in business no one dies. At some time in your business life you need to study war or become a casualty. Sun Tzu covered all the basics of strategy in *The Art of War* until the advent of technology temporarily superseded him. Also, in the same vein try *The Book of Five Rings* by Miyamoto Musashi. These two books have unfortunately become business clichés but they remain timeless reading. Carl Von Clausewitz's *On War* is a 19th-century western attempt to understand war. The "Boyd" book, *The Fighter Pilot Who Changed the Art of War,* is a biography and may seem out of place here, but John Boyd's OODA loop is at the core of Customer Development and the Pivot. Read it and then look at all the websites for Boyd papers, particularly *Patterns of Conflict. The New Lanchester Strategy* is so offbeat that it tends to be overlooked. Its ratios of what you require to attack or defend a market keep coming up so often in real life that I've found it hard to ignore.

- *The Art of War by Sun Tzu* – translated by Thomas Cleary, or the one by Griffith
- *The Book of Five Rings* – Miyamoto Musashi
- *On War* – Carl Von Clausewitz's Everyman's Library Series
- *Boyd: The Fighter Pilot Who Changed the Art of War* – Robert Coram
- *The Mind of War: John Boyd and American Security* – Grant T. Hammond
- *Lanchester Strategy: An Introduction* – Taoka
- *New Lanchester Strategy: Sales and Marketing Strategy for the Weak (New Lanchester Strategy)* – Shinichi Yano, Kenichi Sato, Connie Prener

Marketing Communications Books

Ries and Trout positioning books can be read in a plane ride, yet after all these years they are still a smack on the side of the head. Regis McKenna has always been a favorite of mine. However, as you read *Relationship Marketing* separate out the examples McKenna uses into either startups or large sustainable businesses. What worked in one won't necessarily work in another. Read these books first before you dive into the 21st-century stuff like Seth Godin.

Godin "gets deeply" the profound changes the Internet is having in the way we think about customers and communicating with them. Godin's *All Marketers are Liars* talks about the power of storytelling in marketing. His *Permission Marketing* book crystallized a direct marketing technique (permission marketing), which was simply impossible to achieve pre-Internet. Read his *Ideavirus* after you've read *Permission Marketing. Made to Stick* gives you the tools to make your messages "sticky." I put *Sway* here because great marketers know how to find these irrational behaviors Lakoff's book, *Don't Think of an Elephant!* while written for a political audience has some valuable insights on framing communications.

- *Positioning: The Battle for Your Mind The 20th Anniversary Edition and The 22 Immutable Laws of Marketing: Violate Them at Your Own Risk* – Al Ries, Jack Trout
- *All Marketers Are Liars* – Seth Godin
- *Made to Stick: Why Some Ideas Survive and Others Die* – Chip and Dan Heath
- *Relationship Marketing: Successful Strategies for the Age of the Customer* – Regis McKenna
- *Permission Marketing: Turning Strangers Into Friends, and Friends into Customers and Unleashing the Ideavirus* – Seth Godin
- *Don't Think of an Elephant!* – George Lakoff
- *Sway: The Irresistible Pull of Irrational Behavior* – Ori Brafman

Sales

Predictable Revenue is one of those short, smart, tactical books that you need to read if you have a direct sales force. Thomas Freese is the master of consultative selling. Both his books offer a great start in understanding how a pro sells. Jeff Thull's *Mastering the Complex* Sale has a lot of elements of Customer Discovery and Validation, but skip the first 50 pages. Many of the ideas of Customer Validation are based on the principles articulated by Bosworth, Heiman and Rackham. Bosworth's *Solution Selling* and its successor, *The New Solution Selling* are must-reads for any executive launching a new product. Their articulation of the hierarchy of buyers' needs as well their descriptions of how to get customers to articulate their needs, makes this a "must-read," particularly those selling to businesses. Yet in his new book, *What Great Salespeople Do,* he says: Ignore those books; follow this advice. Heiman's books are a bit more tactical and are part of a comprehensive sales training program from his company, Miller-Heiman. If you are in sales or have a sales background you can skip these. But if you aren't they are worth reading for the basic "blocking and tackling" advice. The only bad news is that

Heiman writes like a loud salesman – but the advice is sound. Rackham's *Spin Selling* is another series of books about major account, large-ticket item sales, with again the emphasis on selling the solution, not features. *Let's Get Real* is of the Sandler School of selling (another school of business-to-business sales methodology.) Jill Konrath has great strategies and insights for large sales. *Baseline Selling* uses baseball metaphors but it's an effective explanation of how to do consultative selling. I sure could have used the *Complete Idiots Guide to Cold Calling* when it was just me and the telephone. The *Strategy and Tactics of Pricing* provides a great framework for thinking about, "how much should I charge for this?"

- *Predictable Revenue* – Aaron Ross and MaryLou Tyler
- *Secrets of Question Based Selling: How the Most Powerful Tool in Business Can Double Your Sales Results and It Only Takes 1% to Have a Competitive Edge in Sales* – Thomas Freese
- *Mastering the Complex Sale* – Jeff Thull
- *What Great Salespeople Do* – Michael Bosworth
- *Solution Selling: Creating Buyers in Difficult Selling Markets* – Michael T. Bosworth
- *The New Solution Selling: The Revolutionary Process That is Changing the Way People Sell, The New Conceptual Selling: The Most Effective and Proven Method for Face-To-Face Sales Planning* and *The New Strategic Selling: The Unique Sales System Proven Successful by the World's Best Companies* – Stephen E. Heiman, et. al.
- *Spin Selling* and *The Spin Selling Fieldbook* – Neil Rackham
- *Let's Get Real or Let's Not Play* – Mahan Khalsa
- *Snap Selling – Speed Up Sales and Win More Business* and *Selling to Big Companies* – Jill Konrath
- Sandler Selling System – www.sandler.com
- Miller Heiman Sales Process Consulting & Training – www.millerheiman.com
- *Baseline Selling: How to Become A Sales Superstar* – Dave Kurlan
- *The Complete Idiot's Guide to Cold Calling* – Keith Rosen
- *The Strategy and Tactics of Pricing* – by Nagle, Hogan & Zale

Startup Law and Finance

If you don't pay attention to the law from the day you start your company it can kill you. But most books (and lawyers) speak in their own arcane language. David Weekly's *An Introduction to Stock and Options* should be your first read (unfortunately it's Kindle only.) *The Entrepreneur's Guide to Business Law* is the one book you ought to have on your shelf. While not written explicitly for Silicon Valley startups, it demystifies the most common areas you need to know. *Term Sheets & Valuations* is a great read if you're faced with a term sheet and staring at words like "liquidation preferences and conversion rights" and don't have a clue what they mean. Read this and you can act like you almost understand what you are giving away.

- *An Introduction to Stock and Options* – David Weekly
- *The Entrepreneur's Guide to Business Law* – by Constance Bagley and Craig Douchy
- *Term Sheets & Valuations – An Inside Look at the Intricacies of Venture Capital* – Alex Wilmerding; Aspatore Books Staff, Aspatore.com

Silicon Valley/Regional Clusters

Brad Feld's *Startup Communities* posits a big idea: Startup communities are driven by entrepreneurs who are the leaders and everyone else is a feeder. It's essential reading if you're trying to build your own cluster. Jessica Livingston's *Founders At Work* provides the best case studies/vignettes without a PR rewrite of how founders really start companies. An *Engineer's Guide to Silicon Valley Startups* is a quirky book that perfectly matches Silicon Valley culture. If you're an engineer in the Valley or coming out, this is a useful read. It describes what types of startups there are, how to get a job at one, negotiate your salary, stock options, etc. *Geek Silicon Valley* is part history and part travel guide. Also useful.

- *Startup Communities* – Brad Feld
- *Founders at Work* – Jessica Livingston
- *Geek Silicon Valley: The Inside Guide to Palo Alto, Stanford, et al.* – Ashlee Vance
- *The Visitor's Guide to Silicon Valley* – www.steveblank.com
- *An Engineer's Guide to Silicon Valley Startups* – Piaw Na

Venture Capital

If you buy one book to understand how VCs and fund-raising work, *Venture Deals* is the one. Wish I had it when I did startups. Same for *Mastering the VC Game*. If you read two books about how to deal with VCs, start here. The rest of the books are personal stories. Bill Draper's book is both history and advice from a VC pioneer. If you have never experienced a startup firsthand, Jerry Kaplan's book, *Startup,* and Michael Wolff's book, *Burn Rate,* are good reads of a founder's adventure with the venture capitalists. *Eboys* is the story of Benchmark Capital during the Internet Bubble. Ferguson's book is a great read for the first-time entrepreneur. His personality and views of the Venture Capitalists and "suits" offer a Rorschach ink blot test for the reader.

- *Venture Deals: Be Smarter than your Lawyer and Venture Capitalist* – by Brad Feld and Jason Mendelson
- *Mastering the VC Game* – Jeffrey Bussgang
- *The Startup Game: Inside the Partnership between Venture Capitalists and Entrepreneurs* – William H. Draper
- *Burn Rate: How I Survived the Gold Rush Years on the Internet* – Michael Wolff
- *Startup: A Silicon Valley Adventure* – Jerry Kaplan
- *Eboys: The First Inside Account of Venture Capitalists at Work* – Randall E. Stross
- *High Stakes, No Prisoners: A Winner's Tale of Greed and Glory in the Internet Wars* – Charles H. Ferguson
- *Pitching Hacks: The Book from Venture Hacks*

Venture Capital History
These books tell the story of the formation of the Venture Capital Industry.
- *Creative Capital: Georges Doriot and the Birth of Venture Capital* – Spencer E. Ante
- *Done Deals: Venture Capitalists Tell Their Stories* – Udayan Gupta
- *Semiconductor Timeline to 1976* –Semi and Don C. Hoefler
- *The Startup Game* – William Draper III

Startup Nuts & Bolts

Nesheim's book, *High Tech Start Up,* is the gold standard of the nuts and bolts of all the financing stages from venture capital to IPOs. If you promise to ignore the marketing advice he gives you, Baird's book, *Engineering Your Startup,* is the Cliff's Notes version in explaining the basics of financing, valuation, stock options, etc. Gordon Bells' book *High-Tech Ventures* is incomprehensible on the first, second or third reads. Yet it is simply the best "operating manual" for startups that has been written. (The only glaring flaw is Bell's assumption that a market exists for the product and that marketing's job is data sheets and trade shows.) Read it in doses for insight and revelation, and make notes (think of reading the Bible) rather than reading it straight through.

- *High Tech Start Up: The Complete Handbook for Creating Successful New High Tech Companies* – John L. Nesheim
- *Engineering Your Start-Up: A Guide for the High-Tech Entrepreneur* – Michael L. Baird
- *High-Tech Ventures: The Guide for Entrepreneurial Success* – Gordon Bell

Startup Textbooks

If you take an entrepreneurship class in a business school or university you'll probably encounter one of these textbooks. The reason you don't see them on the desks of working entrepreneurs is that at $100–$150+ they're all priced for a captive student audience. (Some have paperback versions for $50–$85.) The other uncomfortable fact is that most startups in Silicon Valley ignore these textbooks once they leave school. In the real world, startups are now built using the business model/customer development/ agile engineering stack. Not one of these textbooks teach that.

Of all the entrepreneurship texts, *Technology Ventures* is "the gold standard." Jeff Timmons' *New Venture Creation* has too much great stuff in it to ignore. At first read, it is simply overwhelming but tackle it a bit a time and use it to test your business plan for completeness. *Business Plans that Work* summarizes the relevant part of Timmons' *New Venture Creation* book and teaches how to write a document (the business plan) that no one ever reads. However, both books are worth having if you're in a large company and thinking about introducing follow-on products.

- *Technology Ventures* – Tom Byers, Richard Dorf, Andrew Nelson
- *New Venture Creation Entrepreneurship for the 21st Century and Business Plans That Work* – Jeffry A. Timmons
- *Entrepreneurship: Strategy and Resources* – Marc J. Dollinger
- *Launching New Ventures: An Entrepreneurial Approach* – Kathleen R. Allen
- *Entrepreneurship* – Robert Hisrich, Michael Peters, Dean Shepherd
- *Entrepreneurship* – William D. Bygrave , Andrew Zacharakis

- *Entrepreneurship: An Innovator's Guide to Startups and Corporate Ventures* – Marc H. Meyer, Frederick G. Crane
- *Entrepreneurship: Successfully Launching New Ventures* – Bruce R. Barringer
- *Entrepreneurial Small Business* – Jerome Katz
- *Entrepreneurship: In a European Perspective* – C.K. Volkmann, K.O. Tokarski and M. Granhagen
- *Patterns of Entrepreneurship Management* – Jack M. Kaplan, Anthony Warren
- *Technology Entrepreneurship: Creating, Capturing and Protecting Value* – Thomas N. Duening, Robert A. Hisrich, Michael A. Lechter
- *Nurturing Science-based Ventures: An International Case Perspective* – Ralf W. Seifert, Benoît F. Leleux, Chris L. Tucci
- *Venture Capital and Private Equity: A Casebook* – Josh Lerner, Felda Hardymon, Ann Leamon
- *Biodesign: The Process of Innovating Medical Technologies* – Zenios, Makower, Yock,Brinton, Kumar, Denend, Krummel

Manufacturing

I've yet to meet a manufacturing person who does not reference *The Goal* when talking about lean manufacturing principles first. It's a book inside a novel—so it humanizes the manufacturing experience. *Lean Thinking* is the best overall summary of the lean manufacturing genre. *Toyota Production System* is the father of all lean manufacturing—its simple tone is refreshing.

- *The Goal* – Eliyahu Goldratt
- *Lean Thinking* – James Womack
- *Toyota Production System: Beyond Large-Scale Production* – Taiicho Ohno
- *The Toyota Way* – Jeffrey Liker

Presentation and Product Design

Nancy Duarte's two books, *Slide:ology* and *Resonate*, are about presentation design. These are the two books I refer entrepreneurs to who want to build a killer customer presentation. The advice may not work for all audiences but it's a great place to start. Cooper's book, *The Inmates are Running the Asylum,* is about product design. It had the same impact on me as Moore's *Crossing the Chasm* – "why of course, that's what's wrong." It's important and articulate.

- *Slide:ology* and *Resonate* – Nancy Duarte
- *The Inmates Are Running the Asylum: Why High Tech Products Drive Us Crazy and How To Restore The Sanity* – Alan Cooper

Culture/Human Resources

What I Wish I Knew When I Was 20 and *InGenious* are the books I give all young entrepreneurs. If you are in a large company and wondering why your company isn't going anywhere, your answers might be found in *Good to Great*. Written by Jim Collins, the same author who wrote *Built to Last*, both are books that "you should be so lucky" to read. What differentiates good companies versus great? How do you institutionalize core values into a company that enable it to create value when the current management is long gone? When I first read these, I thought they were only for companies that were lucky enough to get big. Upon reflection, these books were the inspiration for the "Mission-Oriented Culture." Read them together.

Ironically, the best HR stuff for anyone in a startup to read is not a book. It is the work James Baron at Stanford has done. Download his slides on the Stanford Project on Emerging Companies. Baron's book, *Strategic Human Resources* – is a classic HR textbook. Finally, if you are working at a startup and wondering why the founder is nuts, *The Founder Factor* helps explain a few things.

I'm not sure how to characterize *The Checklist Manifesto* so I stuck it here. It's a quick read with some insights that match why Business Model strategy needs to be translated into Customer Development checklists.

- *What I Wish I Knew When I Was 20* and *InGenious* – Tina Seelig
- *Good To Great* and *Built to Last* – James C. Collins, Jerry I. Porras
- *The Human Equation: Building Profits by Putting People First* – Jeffrey Pfeffer
- *Strategic Human Resources: Frameworks for General Managers* – James N. Baron, David Kreps
- *The Founder Factor* – Nancy Truitt Pierce
- *The No Asshole Rule, Weird Ideas that Work* and *Good Boss, Bad Boss* – Robert I. Sutton
- *Hard Facts* and *The Knowing-Doing Gap* – Robert I. Sutton and Jeffrey Pfeffer
- *Competing on the Edge* – Shona L. Brown and Katheleen M. Eisenhardt
- *Confessions of a Serial Entrepreneur* – Stuart Skorman
- *The Checklist Manifesto* – Atul Gawande

Business History

Alfred Sloan's *My Years with General Motors* is a great read, but not for the traditional reasons. Read it from the point of view of an entrepreneur (Durant) who's built a great company by gut and instinct, got it to $200M and is replaced by the board. Then watches as a world-class bureaucrat grows into one of the largest and best run companies in the world. Make sure you read it in conjunction with *Sloan Rules* and *A Ghost's Memoir*. If you're an entrepreneur, the one founder you probably never heard of but should is William Durant. Read Madsen's biography. *The Nudist on the Late Shift* is a book you send to someone who lives outside of Silicon Valley and wants to know what life is like in a startup. If you want to understand how the modern corporation formed Chandlers' *Strategy and Structure* is the "Ur text."

- *My Years with General Motors* – Alfred Sloan
- *Not All Those Who Wander Are Lost* – Steve Blank
- *Sloan Rules: Alfred P. Sloan and the Triumph of General Motors* – David R. Farber
- *A Ghost's Memoir: The Making of Alfred P. Sloan's My Years with General Motors* – John McDonal
- *The Deal Maker: How William C. Durant Made General Motors* – Axel Madsen
- *Billy, Alfred and General Motors: The Story of Two Unique Men* – William Pelfrey
- *The Nudist on the Late Shift* – Po Bronson
- *The Facebook Effect: The Inside Story of the Company that is Connecting the World* – David Kirkpatrick
- *Strategy and Structure: Chapters in the History of the American Industrial Enterprise* – Alfred Chandler

Silicon Valley – Books

Terman/Shockley/Fairchild/Intel/National

- *Fred Terman at Stanford* – Stewart Gilmore
- *IEEE Oral History* – Fred Terman Associates
- *Broken Genius: The Rise and Fall of William Shockley* – Joel Shurkin
- *Makers of the Microchip: A Documentary History of Fairchild Semiconductor* – Christophe Lecuyer and David Brock
- *The Man Behind the Microchip: Robert Noyce* – Leslie Berlin
- *Spinoff: A Personal History of the Industry That Changed The World* – Charles Sporck

Silicon Valley History

- *Electronics in the West: The First Fifty Years* – Jane Morgan
- *The Origins of the Electronics Industry on the Pacific Coast* – A.L. Norberg
- *Revolution in Miniature: The History and Impact of Semiconductor Electronics* – Ernest Braun
- *Creating the Cold War University: The Transformation of Stanford* – Rebecca S. Lowen
- *The Closed World: Computers and the Politics of Discourse in Cold War America* – Paul Edwards
- *Understanding Silicon Valley* – Martin Kenney
- *The Man Who Invented the Computer: The Biography of John Atanasoff, Digital Pioneer* – Jane Smiley
- *How Silicon Valley Came to Be* – Timothy Sturgeon
- *The Inventor and the Pilot: Russell and Sigurd Varian* – Dorothy Varian
- *The Tube Guys* – Norman Pond
- *The Cold War and American Science: The Military-Industrial-Academic Complex at MIT and Stanford* – Stuart W. Leslie
- *Making Silicon Valley: Innovation & the Growth of High Tech* – Charles Lecuyer
- *Dealers of Lightning: Xerox PARC and the Dawn of the Computer Age* – Michael Hilzick
- *Regional Advantage: Culture and Competition in Silicon Valley and Route 128* – AnnaLee Saxenian
- *The New Argonauts: Regional Advantage in a Global Economy* – AnnaLee Saxenian
- *Bill and Dave: How Hewlett and Packard Built the World's Greatest Company* – Michael Malone

Books/Articles on the Entrepreneurial University

My friend, Stephen Spinelli, President of Philadelphia University, offered this great reading list on the activity of the university in tech transfer/collaborations with business, community and government. The list also covers the activity/behavior/leadership of the university president.

- *Engines of Innovation: The Entrepreneurial University in the Twenty-First Century* – Holden Thorp and Buck Goldstein
- *A University for the 21st Century* – Duderstadt, J. J.

- *Creating the Entrepreneurial University: The Case of MIT* – O'Shea, R., Allen, T. and Morse, K
- *How boards can balance demands for entrepreneurship and accountability* – Novak, R
- *Academic Capitalism and the New Economy: Markets, State, and Higher Education* – Sheila Slaughter and Gary Rhoades
- *The New Entrepreneurial University* – Trachtenberg, S. J. (1999) – Speech given to the American Association of University Administrators
- *The Entrepreneurial College President* – James L. Fisher and James V. Koch
- *Leaders in the Crossroads: Success and Failure in the College Presidency* – Stephen James Nelson
- *Creating Entrepreneurial Universities: Organizational Pathways of Transformation* – Burton Clark
- *Collegial Entrepreneurialism in Proactive Universities* – Burton Clark
- *Entrepreneurship and Small College Leadership. New Directions for Higher Education* –Robert Peck

All of the following four chapters are in the *Journal of the Programme* on *Institutional Management in Higher Education, Higher Education Management.* Vol. 13, No. 2, 2001. Organisation for Economic Co-operation and Development.

- *The Entrepreneurial University: New Foundations for Collegiality, Autonomy and Achievement* – Burton Clark
- *The Emergence of Entrepreneurial Cultures in European Universities* – John L. Davies
- *Promoting Academic Expertise and Authority in an Entrepreneurial Culture* – Craig McInnis
- *Structural Barriers to Innovation in Traditional Universities* – Jose-Gines Mora and Enrique Villarreal

Also see Tom Eisenmann's reading list from his Harvard Lean Startup class.

APPENDIX A:
THE CUSTOMER DEVELOPMENT TEAM

Background: The Death
Of The Departments

As we've seen early in this book, the first two steps in a startup, Customer Discovery and Customer Validation, require a task-oriented organization, not a functional one. And the task is unambiguous – learn and discover what problems customers have, and whether your product concept solves that problem; understand who will buy it; and use that knowledge to build a sales roadmap so a sales team can sell to them. And this organization (which we've been calling the Customer Development team) must have the agility to move with sudden and rapid shifts based on what customers have to say and the clout to reconfigure the company when the customer feedback requires it.

The need for a Customer Development team meant configuring the organizations that interacted with customers in a new and radical arrangement. I suggested (even insisted) that during Discovery and Validation there are no Sales, Marketing or Business Development organizations. And, even more painful for all the egos involved, there should be no executives with those titles. Finally, this Customer Development team must be led by one of the company's founders, or if not a founder someone with an equal vote and ability to radically change the company's direction, product or mission. This is not a job for a "hire" or someone's direct report. Optimally this group is headed by the founding CEO. Why do I feel so strongly about this?

Dance Like a Butterfly, Sting Like a Bee

Traditional Sales, Marketing and Business Development organizations are designed to execute a known process. My point all through this book is that during the Discovery and Validation phases nothing is known and everything is a working hypothesis. Traditional functional organizations and the job titles and job descriptions that work in a large company are worse than useless in a startup. Large companies typically have three customer-facing departments, and these departments have executive titles that describe an individual's role as the head of organizations: VP of Sales, VP of Marketing, and VP of Business Development. My belief is that these organizations and the executive titles that go with them are dangerous and dysfunctional in the first three phases of a startup. Why?

Sales

In an existing sales department the sales team knows how to sell to a well-understood group of customers using a standard corporate presentation, with an existing price-list and contract. If you want more revenue, add more salespeople. The conundrum is that during the Customer Discovery and Validation phases your startup doesn't know who its customers are, its presentations are changing daily, and the price lists and contracts are being made up on the spot. The worst thing that can happen to a startup is when the VP of Sales acts like he is in a big, existing company with lots of customer history. He brings his Rolodex, relationships and sales models from his last company and assumes this new startup is just another series of staffing and hiring. When a venture capitalist asks me to figure out what's wrong with sales at one of these startups (typically in a new or resegmented market and badly missing their revenue plan), the phone call with the VP of Sales usually goes like this. Me: "How's sales?" Sales VP: "Well we're just starting to ramp up the team." Me: "How many salespeople do you have?" Sales VP: "Six and we're interviewing for the last three slots." Me: "How many deals have you closed?" Sales VP: (Perceptible pause) "Well we have a quite good pipeline. But the problem is the presentation keeps changing." Me: "What do you mean?" Sales VP: "Well the company keeps changing its strategy and the corporate presentation sometimes changes twice a week." It's not that the Sales VP is foolish, he is just operating in an environment where all his experience and training have no relevance. In most cases it turns out he scaled the sales force prematurely. It's a startup. It's not IBM.

Ironically if you ask most startups if they would they hire the head of IBM's sales on day one most would leap at the chance. Yet consider what skills a world-class VP of Sales brings to a startup: an exceptional ability to hire, build, and motivate a worldwide sales organization; extreme competence in scaling a repeatable organization nationally and internationally, along with great forecasting and budgeting skills. In the first two steps of a startup none of these skills is relevant; in fact, these big-company skills are toxic. They have a startup building sales organizations before they are needed and staffing at the wrong time. Moreover, these executives are uncomfortable operating in the chaos and uncertainty that defines the opening days of the company.

What is needed in the Discovery and Validation phases are entrepreneurial sales skills; the ability to change presentations, customers and products daily, and to calmly process the news that the product features, schedules and functions have changed yet again; and the ability to listen to customer objections and understand whether they are issues about the product, the presentation, the pricing, or something else. No price list and product presentation will last more than a week. What's needed early on in sales is an individual comfortable with chaos and uncertainty who can close an order and not worry about building an organization. The goal of our first salesperson is to validate the business model by developing a sales roadmap, closing orders, and doing this without having a real product in hand. This may or may not be someone who can manage and build a sales department later.

Marketing

The same is true for marketing. Ask marketers in a startup what they do, and some will tell you their job is to brand the company so customers can understand what their company sells. Or it might be to create end-user demand and leads, and drive demand into the sales channel. Some may say the job is about strategic planning, while others will describe what they do is write Marketing Requirements Documents. And while all of that's correct in a company's later stages, none of it is accurate now. During Discovery and Validation the end users, markets, and channels are not known. So spending marketing dollars to create demand or write intricate product plans is futile and wasteful.

At times VCs ask if I would "take a look" at marketing at a startup missing their revenue plan. "We just think they need some help on positioning," is the request. If the company is in a new market or trying to redefine an existing one, the remainder of the phone call with the venture capitalist goes like this. Me: "Do they have a sales roadmap yet?" VC: "No." Me: "Hmm. So, what's marketing doing to help get one?" VC: "Well we can't quite tell exactly, it seems like lots of datasheets, brochures, trade shows, and webinars to generate leads and create demand. Oh, and they just hired an expensive PR agency, and have a new positioning and presentation." Me: "How many people are in the marketing department?" VC: "Don't know exactly, but it feels like four or five." As in the case of sales, when faced with chaos and confusion marketing people tend to revert to what they have successfully done before.

At least marketing and marketing communications are not as bad as in the heyday of the Internet Bubble when for awhile a new marketing title emerged, the VP of Branding. This title, essentially a renamed VP of Marketing Communications, sold a "bill of goods" to hundreds of gullible twenty-something CEOs promising to "create a brand," if only they could have $xx million ($xx million being equal to about 80% of whatever large pile of cash the new startup had raised). The sober reality after billions were spent was that branding is a marketing communications and demand-creation function that doesn't start until the company has figured out who its customers are at the end of the Validation step. You can't spend money on getting, keeping and growing customers until you know who your customers are.

Yet if you ask most startup CEOs if they would hire the head of Disney's Marketing department on day one most would leap at the chance. However, consider what skills a world-class VP of Marketing brings to a startup: positioning and branding skills at home on Madison Avenue. Or perhaps product management skills that would make Proctor & Gamble salivate. Or even strategic planning skills that McKinsey would love to hire. The bad news is the same as in Sales: None of these is relevant in the first two phases of a startup's life.

Business Development

If you want to get my blood pressure up when you invite me in to see your newly formed startup, introduce me to someone with a Business Development title. This is the most ill-used and abused title in a startup. By itself this function and title more than likely decreases the probability of success when used early in a startup more than any other single factor. When I hear it used in an early-stage company I question the competence of all involved. Does Business Development mean someone is involved with non-revenue producing partnerships? Does it means their group is responsible for revenue-producing deals, not done in the primary sales channel the company is using? Or did someone just want to use a fancy title for Sales?

Let's start simply. In the first two stages of a company's life there is no use for any Business Development function. None. Zero. You can cut your burn rate by either walking these people out the door or reassigning them to some productive use on the

Customer Development team. Until your startup has finished Validation you don't know who your customers, channel or partners will be. You cannot credibly have traction with any rational partner until you have proven your business yourself.

Eventually Business Development plays an important role in a company. The function of this group is to build the "whole product" so the company can sell to mainstream customers. The whole product is a concept defined by Bill Davidow in the early years of technology marketing. It says that mainstream customers and late adopters on the technology life cycle adoption curve need an off-the-shelf, no risk, complete solution. They do not want to assemble piece parts from startups. In the computer business IBM is the leading supplier of whole products. They provide the hardware, software, system integration support, and all the ancillary software to support your business problem. The theory is that an IBM customer needs to look no further than IBM for a complete business solution. But since you are a startup there is no way your company can currently offer a whole product. There will be pieces you just don't supply: system integration services, third-party software, configuration tools, applications, etc. The Business Development team's job is to assemble the "whole product" via partnerships and deals. This function was unnecessary in Customer Discovery and Validation because you realized that no mainstream customer would buy a half-finished product from your company. Instead you sold to earlyvangelists who not only did not need a whole product, but enjoyed assembling their own.

Viewed from the perspective of your erstwhile partners, before you have credible customers few of the vendors and suppliers you need to assemble your whole product will treat your company seriously. Therefore, during Customer Discovery and Validation the role of Business Development is superfluous and a distraction in a startup.

Engineering

The notion of a traditional engineering organization is also a detriment to the success of a startup. Not that you won't ultimately need an engineering department, but that having one in place before the first product is released is a mistake. Whoa! If there's no engineering, then how does the product get designed and built? I'm not advocating the dissolution of Product Development, just jettisoning the pieces that are not yet needed. The subgroups that make up fully staffed engineering departments found in large companies—an entire cadre of technical publications writers, huge quality assurance departments, detailed product specs the size of phone books, are all unnecessary—now. These accoutrements are as burdensome to getting the product built and shipped as the extra baggage was for sales and marketing.

A startup engineering strategy for the first two product releases is 1) execute against the technical vision of the founders, modified by customer feedback in Discovery and Validation. 2) Develop, then execute "a fast to market" (rather than first to market) plan that gets a first release (along with the vision of the product for the next 18 months) in the hands of the earlyvangelists as quickly as possible. 3) Use feedback from earlyvangelists who bought the product to flesh out the specification for the next release to a broader customer base.

The same rules for who you would want to run Engineering apply as they did for the other groups. Most software startups would probably be in heaven if they could hire Microsoft's VP of Windows Engineering. But as you can now fathom it would be the wrong choice. In a startup you don't need to hire and manage hundreds of engineers. Knowing how to schedule the resources for five-year software projects and run beta tests with tens of thousands of users is immaterial—at least right now. Instead, what a startup needs in someone with a keen product vision, an unerring eye for a minimal feature set, and an ear attuned to feedback from the Customer Development Team.

Titles Matter

One side effect of not having Sales, Marketing or Business Development departments is that you no longer have executives with those titles. Interestingly, the elimination of these titles is more important than getting rid of the departments themselves. If you're an executive in the midst of the confusion and stress of a startup it's easy to lose sight of what you are supposed to be doing (particularly if you aren't following a Customer Development methodology). The tendency is to default to what you have done before at other companies, and if you were a VP, it was to hire, staff and manage. For example, if a VP of Sales in a startup can't figure out how to achieve the revenue plan, the inclination is for them to think, "Let me go out and recruit a few more salespeople; that will solve our problem." Don't laugh, it happens all the time. Without a clear path to tell them that they should have been burning up the shoe leather and trying to assemble a sales roadmap before they hired anyone, people tend to revert to the roads they've traveled before.

Forming the Customer and Product Development Teams

For the first two steps in a startup's life (Discovery and Validation), the only functions or titles that exist are those that can be measured against this test: Does this department, title or new hire get your company closer to understanding:

- What the customers problems are?
- How your product matches those problems?
- How to build the sales roadmap?
- Getting orders to validate that roadmap?

If the function or title doesn't get you any closer to answering these questions then it is superfluous. Get rid of it. In place of the traditional Sales, Marketing and Business Development functions, a more effective way to organize in the Discovery and Validation stages of a startup is to assemble a Customer Development Team. This customer-oriented team has two roles: Customer Execution and Customer Vision. Alongside the customer-focused team is a Product Execution and Vision Team. Customer Execution and Vision is responsible for getting out and talking to customers, while Product Execution and Vision stay inside the company building and develop the product. "Vision" refers to those who can articulate the big picture. On the Customer side "vision" means someone who can articulately and passionately talk about the business or personal importance of the new product and company. On the product side vision refers to the individual that can describe the architecture and technology advantages to the customer, while simultaneously interpreting their complex technical requests for the Customer Execution Team. Frequently, the customer execution team will need to borrow technical resources to listen or talk to customers. In a startup's early stages up to 50% of the product visionaries' time may be spent in front of customers. The Customer and Product teams stay solidly in lock step via the synchronization meetings we've described. At times the Customer Execution group may need to borrow people from Product Execution and Vision.

The Customer Development Team serves as tactical shock troops for the Customer Discovery and Validation steps. At first, this "group" might be nothing more than a single founder out talking to customers to test the "problems" the company elucidated in its business plan (acting as the Customer Execution Team) while five engineers write code (the Technical Execution Team). Later, near the end of Customer Validation, the team might be much larger. There may be a team of five or more validating the sales roadmap, trying to close orders and testing the company positioning, while 20 engineers are about to ship the product.

If creating a Customer Development Team meant simply renaming the traditional sales, marketing and engineering departments and calling it a "Customer Development Team" it would be an exercise in futility. The organizations differ not only by the seamless integration of what are traditionally separate fiefdoms, but by virtue of the type of individuals you hire during Discovery and Validation.

Customer Development Team member characteristics:

- Experience moving between the customer and Product Development Team (Product marketing or product management background)
- Can they listen well? Or are they more interested in talking?
- Can they understand what they hear? Or do they report what they wanted to hear?
- Can they deal with constant change? Or are they more comfortable with doing the same thing day to day?
- Do they have the capacity to put themselves in their customers' shoes and understand how they work and what problems they have? Or are they more interested in talking about and selling a product?
- Are they self-starters or do they wait for direction?
- Are they innovators and creative or do they do what others tell them?

APPENDIX B:
CUSTOMER DEVELOPMENT CHECKLIST

The examples in this Appendix are used to illustrate the Customer Development methodology and process. Your process will differ depending on Market Type and company.

The example is of an Enterprise Software Company. Use it as a template to develop your own workbook specifically for your company/market.

CUSTOMER DISCOVERY STEP-BY-STEP

State Your Hypotheses

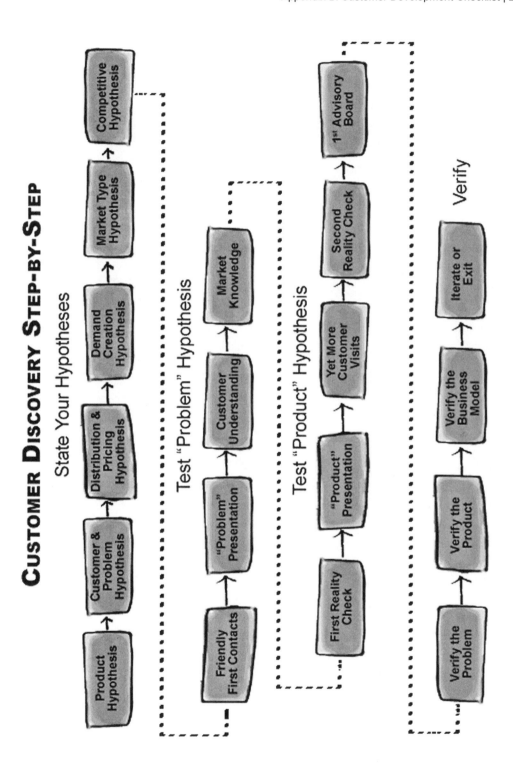

Test "Problem" Hypothesis

Test "Product" Hypothesis

Customer Validation Step-by-Step

Get Ready to Sell

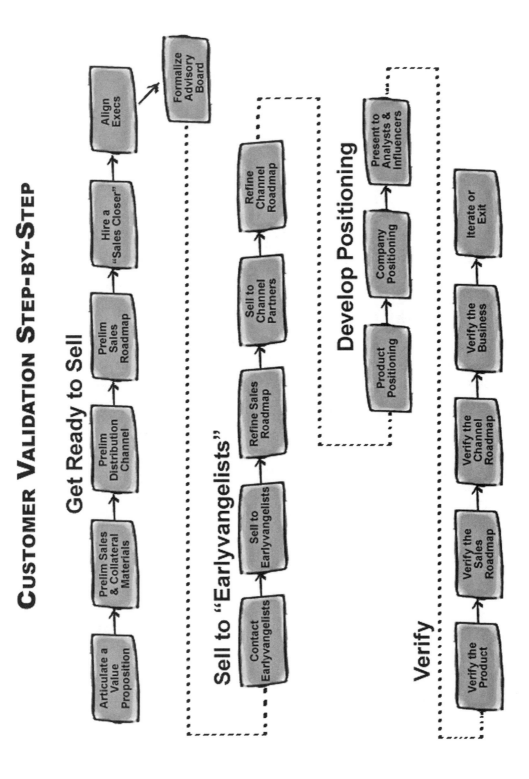

Articulate a Value Proposition → Prelim Sales & Collateral Materials → Prelim Distribution Channel → Prelim Sales Roadmap → Hire a "Sales Closer" → Align Execs → Formalize Advisory Board

Sell to "Earlyvangelists"

Contact Earlyvangelists → Sell to Earlyvangelists → Refine Sales Roadmap → Sell to Channel Partners → Refine Channel Roadmap

Develop Positioning

Product Positioning → Company Positioning → Present to Analysts & Influencers

Verify

Verify the Product → Verify the Sales Roadmap → Verify the Channel Roadmap → Verify the Business → Iterate or Exit

Customer Discovery   Board and Management Buy-In   Worksheet 0-a

Goal of Phase 0-a: Agreement between investors and founders on Customer Development process and Market Type. Understand the difference between Product Development and market development.

> *Author:*   Whoever is acting as CEO
> *Approval:*   Entire Founding Team/Board
> *Presenter:*   CEO
> *Time/Effort:* ½- to 1-day meeting of entire founding team and board

☐ Customer Development process emphasizes learning and discovery

1. Decide if there is board and founding team buy-in for this process
2. Ensure that there is enough funding for 2 to 3 passes through Customer Discovery and Validation

☐ Discuss Market Type

1. Existing, Resegmented or New
2. First pass with board on agreement of Market Type and different funding needs by type

☐ Agree on Customer Development Length

1. Board agreement on how long to stay in Discovery and Validation
2. Board agreement on Discovery and Validation exit criteria

Phase 0-a Exit Criteria: Buy-in of the team and board for Customer Development process, Market Type and exit criteria for each step.

Customer Discovery   The Team   Worksheet 0-b

Goal of Phase 0-b: Set up the Customer Development Team. Agree on Customer Development team methodology and goals.

> *Author:*   Whoever is acting as CEO
> *Approval:*   Entire Founding Team/Board
> *Presenter:*   CEO
> *Time/Effort:* ½- to 1-day meeting of entire founding team

☐ **Review the organizational differences between Product and Customer Development – traditional titles versus functional ones**

1. No VP of Sales
2. No VP of Marketing
3. No VP of Business Development

☐ **Identify the four key functional roles for the first four phases of a startup**

1. Who is the Business Visionary?
2. Who is the Business Executor?
3. Who is the Technical Visionary?
4. Who is the Technical Executor?

☐ **Review the goals of each role for each of the four Customer Development phases**

☐ **Enumerate 3 to 5 Core Values of the Founding Team**

1. Not a mission statement
2. Not about profit or products
3. Core ideology is about what the company believes in

Phase 0-b Exit Criteria: Buy-in of the team and board for functional job descriptions, right people in those jobs, core values.

Customer Discovery   **Hypothesis: The Product**   Worksheet 1-a

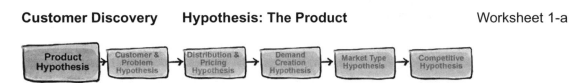

Goal of Phase 1a: The entire team must agree on the product features, benefits and release schedules.

> *Author:*   VP Technical Execution/VP Technical Vision
> *Approval:*   Founding Team and Executive Staff
> *Presenter:*   Business Execution, Technical Team
> *Time/Effort:* 2-4 days of authoring by VP Technical Execution, ½-day presentation/ strategy meeting with founding team and executive staff

☐ **What problem are you solving?**

☐ **One-Page Product Feature List: What are the technical attributes of the Product?**

1. What is the General Goal of the product?
2. Provide a simplified architectural diagram
3. Provide a feature list

☐ **Will these Features be well understood or do they require explanation?**

☐ **Benefit List: What do the features let a customer do?**

1. Something new?
2. Better?
3. More?
4. Faster?
5. Cheaper? Etc.
6. Underneath each of the features above, give a three-line summary of its benefits

☐ **Will these Benefits be accepted as such or do they need explanation?**

☐ **What is the initial Delivery Schedule? When will all of these features be available?**

1. Describe Release 1
2. Describe Release 2
3. Describe Release 3
4. All the way out as you can see (you will formalize this in Worksheet 4a)

☐ **What Intellectual Property (IP) of yours will be unique?**

1. What can you patent?
2. What is a trade secret that you need to protect?
3. What will you have to license?
4. Have you checked to see if you infringe on others' IP?

☐ **What is the Total Cost of Ownership of your Product?**

1. Training?
2. Deployment?
3. Additional technical infrastructure (more servers…)?
4. Additional personnel infrastructure..?

☐ **Dependency Analysis: Are you dependent on XXX to happen before your product can sell in volume?**

1. Workflow/lifestyle changes on the part of the customer?
2. Other products required?
3. Economic conditions?
4. Behavior changes?
5. Supply change modifications?
6. Laws to change?
7. Other infrastructure/products/change in behavior
8. If so, what?
9. When will it happen?
10. What happens to your company if it doesn't?
11. What metrics should be used to measure the change?

Phase 1a Exit Criteria: Product spec, written Feature and Benefit list, release description, dependency analysis.

Customer Discovery   Hypothesis: The Customer   Worksheet 1-b

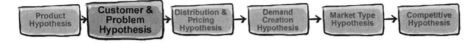

Goal of Phase 1b: Develop a hypothesis of who the customer is and what problems they have that will drive them to use your product, before you leave the building.

Author: Business Execution, Business Visionary
Approval: Founding Team and Executive Staff
Presenter: Founding Technical Team
Time/Effort: 3-5 days of authoring by VP Business Execution or Business Visionary, ½-day presentation/strategy meeting with founding team and executive staff

☐ **Define the different types of "customer"**

1. Who will be the product's day-to-day user?
2. Who are the influencers and recommenders?
3. Who is the "Economic Buyer?" (i.e. whose budget will pay for it?)
4. Do you think the Economic Buyer has an existing budget for this product or do they need to get one approved?
5. Who are the "Decision-makers?"
6. Who else needs to approve the purchase?

☐ **Customer Visionaries understand they have a pain and can visualize a solution. Where do you think you will find them?**

1. In what title or function?
2. In what company type?
3. In what industry segment?
4. Reminder: a visionary is a paying customer

☐ **Where in an organization do you think your first customers are?**

1. What departments?
2. What are their titles?
3. How do they differ from later customers? (Hint: Lots in a new market, little in an existing market.)

☐ **What problem does the customer have?**

☐ **What do you think the biggest pain is in how they work?**
1. Is it the same on all levels of the company?
2. If they could wave a magic wand and change anything what would it be?
3. Since your product doesn't exist, what do people do today to solve their problem?
   Don't do it? Do it badly? Don't recognize the need?

☐ **Where on the "problem recognition scale" is each type of customer (users, recommenders, economic buyers)?**
1. Latent Need (you recognize that the buyer needs your product but they don't... yet)?
2. Active Need – the buyer is in pain (they recognize a need but don't know how to solve it)?
3. Has a vision of a solution (the buyer has a vision of how to solve their problem)?

☐ **What is the organizational impact of this pain?**
1. Individual?
2. Departmental?
3. Corporate?

☐ **Define the magnitude of customer need – Is this a mission-critical product?**
1. Is this a have-to-have product?
2. Is this a nice-to-have product?
3. Is this product so important that the customers have built it themselves?
4. How well do the product features and benefits fit?

☐ **How does the potential user of the product spend their day now?**
1. What products do they use? How much time do they spend using them?
2. How would the world change for these users after they had your product?
3. How would it change their day? Their lives?
4. Would there be new users?
5. Summarize the "Day in the Life" of a customer

☐ **How would customers justify the Return On Investment (ROI) for this product?**
1. What will be measured?
2. Revenues? Costs - reduction or containment? Displaced costs? Avoided costs? Intangible?

☐ **What is the smallest/least complicated problem that can be solved for which the customer will pay for?**
1. What is the smallest feature set they will pay for in the first release?

Phase 1b Exit Criteria: A written description of a Customer and Problem Model. This includes hypothetical workflow and process. You then want to guess if the customer feels a pain, and if so how widespread is its organizational impact.

Customer Discovery   Hypothesis: Channel/Pricing   Worksheet 1-c

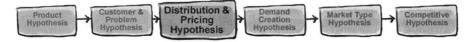

Goal of Phase 1c: Develop a distribution channel strategy (how the product will get to the customer) & pricing model.

> *Author:*   Business Execution, Business Visionary
>
> *Approval:*   Business Execution, Business Visionary
>
> *Presenter:*   Business Execution
>
> *Time/Effort:* 2-4 days of authoring by VP Business Execution or Business Visionary, ¼-day presentation/strategy meeting with founding team and executive staff

☐ **How will your users initially buy from you?**

1. From a salesman directly from the company?
2. From a rep or distributor?
3. Through a partner?
4. In a retail store? Mail order? On the Web?
5. Pick a distribution channel

☐ **Draw the distribution channel diagram**

1. How much will the channel cost (direct expenses or channel discounts)?
2. Are there indirect channel costs (presales support, channel promotional dollars…)?
3. What else is needed for customers to use/buy the product? How do they acquire those pieces?
4. What is the net revenue after channel costs?

☐ **If there are products somewhat like ours…**

1. How much do customers spend for them?

☐ **If users need a product like ours…**

1. How much do they pay to do the same thing today?

☐ **What is the economic basis for your pricing?**
1. Comparable products that already exist? (In an existing market)
2. The sum of the piece parts required to assemble the equivalent functionality?
3. An ROI analysis of saved time, money, expense (in a new market)?
4. Do you want to change the existing rules of pricing? Offer new pricing models?

☐ **How many copies/number of products can you sell at once?**
1. Per household or per company?
2. If the product was free, how many per household or per company?

☐ **How many can you sell?**
1. If you charged $1?
2. If you charged $1 million?
3. What is the price at which half of the customers say yes?

☐ **If users had your product…**
1. How much would they pay for your product?
2. Pick a preliminary price
3. Pick units for the first 2 years

☐ **Would it be easier to sell your product if it were…**
1. Sold in modules that individually cost less?
2. Configured as a complete solution?
3. Sold with other products?

Phase 1c Exit Criteria: Tentative pricing, tentative distribution channel model and demand creation activities. Analysis of comparative pricing.

Customer Discovery   Hypothesis: Demand Creation   Worksheet 1-d

Goal of Phase 1d: Develop a hypothesis of a) how you will reach customers and drive them into your distribution channel and b) who besides your company can reach and influence these customers.

> *Author:*   Business Execution, Business Visionary
> *Approval:*   Entire Founding Team
> *Presenter:*   Business Execution
> *Time/Effort :*   2-4 days of authoring by VP Business Execution or Business Visionary, ¼-day presentation/strategy meeting with founding team and executive staff

☐ **How will your users hear about you?**

1. Advertising
2. Word of mouth
3. Seminars
4. Partners
5. Pick a tentative demand creation activity

☐ **Begin to build a list of companies in adjacent markets/infrastructure (not competitors)**

1. Companies you would partner with/connect to
2. Professional service organizations
3. Understand their positioning/distribution/products

☐ **Begin to build a list of key industry influencers/recommenders**

1. Technically credible individuals
2. Key Industry analysts (Gartner, Yankee, Jupiter, etc.)
3. Key Wall Street Analysts who follow adjacent markets
4. Read their stuff – be able to draw their view of the world today and tomorrow
5. Modify their view of the future with your company/products

☐ **Begin to build a list of key conferences/trade shows**
1. Technical credibility
2. Key Industry analysts (Gartner, Yankee, Jupiter, etc.)

☐ **Begin to build a list of key press contacts**
1. Trade press
2. Technical press
3. Industry press
4. Business press
5. Keep track of the names of the authors of key articles

☐ **What key trends have customers/influencers/press identified?**
1. Infrastructure
2. Technical
3. Users
4. Distribution
5. Marketing

☐ **Begin to assemble an advisory board**
1. Begin to recruit members of the Technical Advisory board now. Initially for technical advice and pointers to technical talent. Later as a technical reference for customers
2. Understand needs for Customer, Business and Marketing advisory board members

Phase 1d Exit Criteria: Lists of adjacent companies, outside influencers, shows, press. Advisory board contacts. Key trend summary.

Customer Discovery   Hypothesis: Market Type   Worksheet 1-e

Goal of Phase 1e: Recognize that Market Type drives: sales curves, marketing strategies, revenue and cash flow needs. Test alternate Market Types on your company and product.

> *Author:*   Business Execution, Business Visionary
> *Approval:*   Entire Founding Team
> *Presenter:*   Founding Technical Team
> *Time/Effort:* 2-3 days of authoring by VP Business Execution or Business Visionary, ¼-day presentation/strategy meeting with founding team and executive staff

☐ **Do you have a new product in an existing market?**

☐ **Do you need to redefine/reframe a market?**

☐ **Do you want to create an entirely new market?**
1. Is your product/service a substitution for something customers already have?
2. Is it a replacement?
3. Is it a variant on something already out there, but can be "respun" into something new?
4. Is it something totally new?

Positioning in An Existing Market
☐ **If it's a new product in an existing market, define the basis of competition**
1. Positioning the product is the basis of competition
2. Picking the correct axis for the basis of competition is critical. For example:
   a. feature/technology axis
   b. price/performance axis
   c. channel/margin axis
3. What do the revenue and burn rate curves look like for this Market Type?

☐ **Who is driving the existing market?**

1. Are there existing standards? If so, whose agenda is driving them?
2. Do you want to embrace the standards, extend them, or replace them?
3. Are there different global issues from just national ones?

☐ **Do you have some advantage or appeal among any vertical or horizontal market segment?**

1. Which markets or segments?

Positioning in An Existing Market You Want to Resegment

☐ **If it's a new product in a market you want to resegment, define the basis of how you want to change the market**

1. Positioning the *change in the market* is the basis of competition
2. This is driven by some new feature of the product or service that redefines the market
3. Redraw the market map and show which new feature you offer that drives this
   For example:
   a. New customers
   b. New distribution channel
   c. Feature/technology axis
   d. Price/performance axis
   e. Channel/margin axis
4. Why would thousands of new customers believe in and move to this segment of the market?
5. What do the revenue and burn rate curves look like for this Market Type?

☐ **Who is driving the market you want to resegment?**

1. Are there existing standards? If so, whose agenda is driving them?
2. Do you want to embrace the standards, extend them, or replace them?
3. Are there different global issues from just national ones?

Positioning in a New Market

☐ **If it's a new market, create the market**

1. Positioning the creation of a *new market* is the basis of competition
   a. List the closest markets to yours (a market is a set of companies with common attributes)
   b. Draw the market map with you in the center
   c. Give your market a descriptive TLA (three-letter acronym)
2. Why would thousands of new customers believe in and move to this market?
3. What do the revenue and burn-rate curves look like for this Market Type?

Phase 1e Exit Criteria: A preliminary first hypothesis of the Market Type.

Customer Discovery   Hypothesis: Competition   Worksheet 1-f

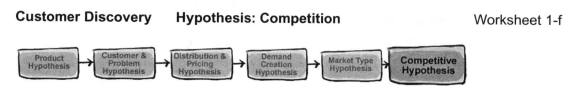

Goal of Phase 1f: As a precursor to devising company and product positioning you will ask some preliminary questions about the competitive environment.

Author: Business Execution, Business Visionary
Approval: Entire Founding Team
Presenter: Business Execution
Time/Effort: 2-3 days of authoring by VP Business Execution or Business Visionary, ¼-day presentation/strategy meeting with founding team and executive staff

☐ **Why will customers buy your product?**

1. Your product is something they need but they don't know it yet
2. Your product can do something they need and they can only get via multiple vendors
3. You solve a real, definable pain they cannot solve any other way. If so, how?
4. Your product is faster/cheaper/better than anything else out there. If so, you believe your superiority will last multiple generations because…?
5. Your product allow them to do something they could never do before

☐ **Why are you different?**

1. New Market (selling to new users who have no comparable product)
2. Better features?
3. Better performance?
4. Better channel?
5. Better price?

☐ **If this were in a grocery store, which products would be shelved next to it?**

☐ **Who are your closest competitors today?**

1. In features
2. In performance
3. In channel
4. In price

☐ **What do you like most about the competitors' products?**

1. What do your customers like most about the competitors' products?
2. If you could change one thing in a competitors' products, what would it be?

☐ **Who in a company uses the competitors' products today?**

1. By title? By function?

☐ **How do these competitive products get used?**

1. Describe the workflow/design flow for an end user
2. Describe how it affects the company
3. What percentage of their time is spent using the product?
4. How mission-critical is it?

Phase 1f Exit Criteria: A written description of the Competitive Environment.

Customer Discovery   Test the Problem: 1ˢᵗ Contacts   Worksheet 2-a

Goal of Phase 2a: Develop a customer list and schedule the first customer contacts.

> *Author:*   Business Execution
> *Approval:*   Business Execution, Business Vision
> *Presenter:* Business Execution, Business Vision
> *Time/Effort:* 5-10 days of calling by VP Business Execution

☐ **Make a list of 50 potential customers you can test your ideas on**

  1. You are less interested in brand names than you are in who will give you the time
  2. Don't be a title snob. But…
  3. Spend time on people you think fit your hypothesis of user profile

☐ **Get leads of who to call from:**

  1. Investors
  2. Founders
  3. Lawyers
  4. Headhunters, etc.
  5. Trade magazines
  6. Business reference books

☐ **Begin to develop an innovators' list. Ask others which are the most innovative:**

  1. Company
  2. Department in a company
  3. Individuals

☐ **Create an introductory email**

  1. Introduce yourself with a one-paragraph description of the company, a general description of what you are doing and what's in for them to spend time with you.
  2. Have the people who gave you the leads send the email

   3. Follow up with a call (see reference story below)

   4. 50 follow-up phone calls should yield 5-10 visits

☐ **Create a reference story/sales script (why are you calling/emailing)**

   1. Focus on the solution (not the features)

   2. What problems are you trying to solve?

   3. Why is it important to solve them?

   4. Say you are starting a company, were referred by X; you are building Y, but you don't want to sell them anything, you just want 20 minutes of their time to understand how they/their company work.

   5. Give them a reason to see you. What's in it for them?

☐ **Ten phone calls or emails a day**

   1. Call/email until you have your schedule booked with 3 customer visits a day

   2. Get used to being turned down but always ask, "If you're too busy, who should I talk to?"

   3. For this first meeting you are "level-insensitive"—you don't care about titles, you just want to gather data

   4. Keep hit-rate statistics (any pitch, leads or level better or worse than others?)

   5. Log all contacts into a database with enough to detail about the call

Phase 2a Exit Criteria: Reference story and 5 to 10 customer visits scheduled.

Customer Discovery   **Test the Problem: Presentation**   Worksheet 2-b

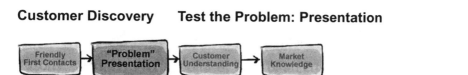

Goal of Phase 2b: In worksheet 1-b, you came up with a problem hypothesis. Now based on that hypothesis you will develop a presentation about this problem and test it with customers. In exchange for a customer talking to you, you need to give them something to talk about. You will assemble a "problem presentation" (in contrast to a product presentation). This presentation concatenates your hypothesis about the business problem you think is important for these customers, and some potential solutions. Your goal is not to convince the customer but to see if your assumptions are correct.

Author: Business Execution
Approval: Business Execution, Business Vision
Presenter: Business Execution, Business Vision
Time/Effort: 1-3 days by VP Business Execution or Business Visionary

☐ **Develop "problem" presentation**
   1. Describe the problem you are trying to solve (the pain, not the features)
   2. Problem/solution slide 1
   3. List problems in column 1
   4. Today's solution in column 2
   5. Your solution in column 3
   6. Ask why is it important to solve this problem

☐ **Do the customer segmentation**
   1. Who shares these problems? By company? By industry? By title?....
   2. A set of people with common problems = a common value proposition

☐ **Develop a questionnaire**
   1. List all the data you want to gather
   2. Now shorten the list to, "What are the three things I need to learn before I leave?"
   3. Be consistent across customers
   4. As you get confirmation on the key issues, begin to ask different questions

Phase 2b Exit Criteria: Problem Presentation with today's solution and your company's alternative. Capable of being given as a "chalk talk."

Customer Discovery   Test Problem: Customer Understanding   Worksheet 2-c

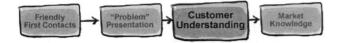

Goal of Phase 2c: Develop a deep understanding of a customer, how they work, their pain, and where it is felt. This first customer meeting is a "give-and-take": you have to give something for them to feel that it's worth a meeting. In exchange for them talking to you, you will share your problem presentation. You might carry a tape recorder and a notebook, or bring a digital camera and take pictures of the whiteboard as you make notes. Your goal is NOT to pitch your product but to validate your understanding of the problem.

Author: Business Execution
Approval: Business Execution, Business Vision
Presenter: Business Execution, Business Vision
Time/Effort: 5-15 days of customer visits by VP Business Execution or Business Visionary

☐ **The most important question to ask**
  1. What is the one thing you want to buy?
  2. Which leads to...
  3. How do you do it today (if at all)?
  4. How much does it cost you today?

☐ **How do your target customers work?**
  1. Ask how their job/life works today
  2. Ask them to describe the workflow/design flow
  3. Listen and understand
  4. Do not sell or even explain what you are doing; the goal is to understand what they are doing

☐ **What is the biggest *pain* in how they work?**
  1. If they could wave a magic wand and change anything in what they do what would it be?
  2. This is the IPO question – listen carefully
  3. Ask 3 variants around this question

☐ **What is the organizational impact of this pain?**
1. Individual?
2. Departmental?
3. Corporate?
4. Quantify the impact (dollars, time, costs, etc.)

☐ **What would make the customer change the current way they do things?**
1. Price?
2. Features?
3. New standard?

☐ **If they had a product like this ....(describe yours in conceptual terms) ...?**
1. What percentage of their time could be spent using the product?
2. How mission critical is it?
3. Would it solve the pain they mentioned earlier?
4. What would be the barriers to adopting a product like this?

☐ **Who do they think have similar products?**
1. Who else is an innovator in this space? (Other companies)
2. Where else in their company has this been tried?
3. Is anyone else inside their company trying to build this product?

☐ **How do they learn about new products?**
1. Trade shows. Do they go? Do others in their company go?
2. Magazines. What do they read? What do they trust? What do their bosses read?
3. Salespeople. Who are the best?
4. Who are the visionaries in the press/analyst community that they read/respect?

☐ **Can these customers be helpful in the future?**
1. For the next round of conversations?
2. For an advisory board?
3. As a paying customer?
4. Refer you to others to talk to?

Phase 2c Exit Criteria: Identical to Customer Hypothesis exit criteria, this time with facts.

Customer Discovery   Test Problem: Market Knowledge   Worksheet 2-d

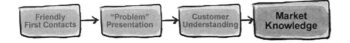

Goal of Phase 2d: Begin meeting with companies in adjacent markets, analysts, media, influencers and trade shows to understand the shape and direction of the market you are in or about to create.

Author: Business Execution
Approval: Business Execution, Business Vision
Presenter: Business Execution, Business Vision
Time/Effort: 5-10 days of company/analyst/conference visits by VP Business Execution or Business Visionary

☐ **Make contact with companies in adjacent markets/infrastructure (buy them lunch!)**

1. What are the industry trends?
2. What are key unresolved customer needs?
3. Who are the players?
4. What should you read?
5. Who should you know?
6. What should you ask?
7. What customers should you call on?
8. Just as you did with potential customers, don't present, don't sell, just listen and learn

☐ **Make contact with key industry influencers/recommenders (from Phase 1e)**

1. What are the trends?
2. Who are the players?
3. What should you read?
4. Just as you did with potential customers, don't present, don't sell; just listen and learn

☐ **Get copies of the Wall Street analyst reports on your market or adjacent markets (from Phase 1e)**
 1. What are the trends?
 2. Who are the players?
 3. Understand business models, key players, key metrics

☐ **Attend at least two key conferences or trade shows (from Phase 1e)**
 1. What are the trends?
 2. Who are the players?
 3. Who are the attendees?
 4. What are their visions of the future?
 5. How do they compare with yours?

Phase 2d Exit Criteria: Identical to Positioning Hypothesis exit criteria, this time with facts.

Customer Discovery   **Test Product Concept: 1st Reality Check**   Worksheet 3-a

Goal of Phase 3a: By now, you've talked to 5 or 10 customers in the market you think your product will fit. You *listened to how customers worked.* Before you go back out, review the customer and problem feedback with the Product Development Team and board, testing the initial hypothesis you made.

Author: Business Execution

Approval: All

Presenter: Business Execution, Business Vision

Time/Effort: 1 day of authoring by VP Business Execution or Business Visionary, ½-day presentation/strategy meeting with founding team, executive staff and board

☐ **Build a workflow map of your prototypical customer**

1. Diagram and describe how they do their job
2. Diagram and describe who they interact with
3. Do this until you can explain by going to the whiteboard, and understand how their business/life work today, how they spend their time, how they spend their money, etc.

☐ **Where on the "problem scale" were the customers you interviewed?**

1. You recognize that the buyer needs your product but they don't (…yet)
2. Buyer is in pain (the buyer recognizes a need but doesn't know how to solve it)
3. Has a vision of a solution (the buyer has a vision of how to solve their problem)
4. Buyer has cobbled together a solution out of inferior piece parts
5. Buyer has or can acquire a budget

☐ **Draw the customer workflow with and without your product/service**

1. Is the difference dramatic?
2. Will people pay for that difference?

☐ **What did you learn from your customer visits?**

1. What were the biggest surprises?
2. What were the biggest disappointments?

☐ **How do your preliminary product spec's (worksheet 1-a) meet these needs?**

1. Dead on
2. Somewhat
3. Not exactly

☐ **Re-review feature list and release schedule**

1. Prioritize feature list in terms of importance to the customer
2. Begin to put dates to 2-year release schedule

☐ **Why are you different?**

1. New Market (new users in with no single comparable product)
2. Better features?
3. Better performance?
4. Better channel?
5. Better price?

☐ **Review product spec**

1. Formalize and update the release schedule from Worksheet 1a into a 2-year plan
2. Do your current product plans meet the needs of the market?
3. Do you want to emphasize different features?
4. Is your pricing right?

Phase 3a Exit Criteria: Reality check. Map all you learned from customer visits against worksheets, initial hypotheses.

Customer Discovery   Test Product Concept: Presentation   Worksheet 3-b

Goal of Phase 3b: Now you are going to create the company's first customer presentation. It is emphatically not the presentation the company used for fund-raising or recruiting. Toss those slides out and start over. The goal is to test your assumptions about the pain you are solving, who you are solving it for, and whether the product solves that problem *in the mind of the customer.*

Author: Business Execution
Approval: Business Execution, Business Vision
Presenter: Business Execution, Business Vision
Time/Effort: 3-5 days of authoring by VP Business Execution or Business Visionary

☐ **Put together a questionnaire**
   1. List all the data you want to gather from this presentation (remember -- this is *not* a sales pitch)
   2. Be consistent across customers

☐ **Start with your "problem" presentation**
   1. Focus on why this product solves a real problem
   2. Describe the problem you are trying to solve (the pain, not the features)
   3. Describe why is it important to solve this problem
   4. Full stop – pause here and see if you get customer agreement on the pain

☐ **Then describe the product**
   1. If it's too early for a real product demo, go through the 5 (no more!) key features in slides
   2. Present all two years of features – broken down into releases
   3. Draw the customer workflow with and without your product/service
   4. Full stop – pause here and see if you get agreement on the before and after

5. Describe who else this might impact in the company
6. Full stop – pause here and see if you get agreement on the impact on the organization
7. No more than 20 minutes
8. Leave out all the marketing, positioning and fluff

☐ **Demo if you have one**

1. Even a prototype of a key concept can help a customer understand
2. Leave no materials with the customer

Phase 3b Exit Criteria: A *solutions* presentation with which you can test your understanding of the customer's pain, their workflow, and the organization impact of your product. And, oh yes, you get to test the product features as well.

Customer Discovery   Test Product Concept: More Visits   Worksheet 3-c

Goal of Phase 3c: Start with your original customer list and expand it to include 5 new potential customers. Now go back to those customers who were nice enough to talk to you as well as new prospects and *test your understanding of their needs as well as your product idea.* You are still not selling in this phase, you are trying to learn and understand. You want to see if your product meets a current or perceived need.

Author: Business Execution
Approval: Business Execution, Business Vision
Presenter: Business Execution, Business Vision
Time/Effort: 15-60 days of calling by VP Business Execution

☐ **Make a list of 50 potential customers to test your vision and product on**

1. In this phase you do want to test your assumptions about the title of who will buy
2. Target the appropriate titles/organization as if you were selling
3. This should include a good number of customers who saw you in Phase 2b

☐ **Create an introductory email**

1. A one-paragraph description of the product
2. Have the people who gave you the leads send the email
3. Follow up with a call (see reference story below)
4. 50 follow-up phone calls should yield 5-10 visits

☐ **Create a reference story/sales script (why are you calling/emailing)**

1. Focus on the solution (not the features)
2. What problems are you trying to solve?
3. Why is it important to solve them?
4. Say you are starting a company and you have just talked to …(companies in Phase 2a), were referred by X, you are building Y, but you don't want to sell them anything, you just want 20 minutes of their time to understand how they/their company work

☐ **Ten phone calls a day**

1. Call until you have your schedule booked with 3 customer visits a day
2. Get used to being turned down but always ask, "If you're too busy, who should I talk to?"
3. For this first meeting you don't care about titles, you just want to gather data
4. Keep hit-rate statistics (any pitch, leads or level better or worse than others?)

☐ **Validate your solution with the presentation**

1. Did you correctly identify a serious problem in their company?
2. Did you correctly identify who else in the company has this problem?
3. Would they buy a product to solve it?

☐ **Validate your product with the presentation**

1. Did your product solve a problem for them? For others?
2. What do they think of your product? Listen
3. Do your features match their needs?
4. What features should you have on day one? Later?

☐ **Validate your product positioning**

1. How do these customer think your product is different?
   a. Creating a New Market? (No other comparable product)
   b. Better than an existing product (Better features? Better performance? Better channel? Better price?)
   c. Somewhere in the middle (comparable to others, but changing the rules of the game)

☐ **What was the biggest *pain* in how they work?**

1. If they could wave a magic wand and change anything in what they do what would it be?
2. This is the IPO question – listen carefully
3. Ask 3 variants around this question

☐ **What is the organizational impact of this pain?**

1. Individual?
2. Departmental?
3. Corporate?
4. Quantify the impact (dollars, time, costs, etc.)

☐ **Where in the organization is the budget for this product?**
1. Is there a current budget for a product like this?
2. What department will pay for it?
3. Who else needs to approve it?

☐ **Validate your product pricing and distribution with the presentation**
1. Use the "if we gave it to you would you use it?" test to gauge interest
2. If it costs $1 million, would the customer buy it?
3. Test distribution alternatives by asking from what channel they would most likely buy

☐ **Validate customer's acquisition alternatives**
1. If they were interested in a product like this, how would you find out about it?
2. How do they find out about other new products like this?
3. Do they ask others (friends/Gartner Group) for an opinion before buying?

☐ **Understand the "whole product" requirements**
1. What is a "complete product" in the mind of the customer?
2. What other features are needed to move this into a mainstream product?
3. What other third-party software/integration are needed to move this into a mainstream product?

☐ **Validate customer's product acquisition process**
1. How does your company/you buy products like this?
2. What is the approval process?
3. Who finds new products?
4. Who recommends new products?
5. Who approves new products?

☐ **Validate customer's approval process**
1. Who makes the decision -- IT or business users?
2. Who made the decision on the last product?

☐ **Update customer advisory board candidates**

Phase 3c Exit Criteria: Reference story/sales script and 5 to 10 customer visits scheduled. Determine whether you truly understand a customer's pain, and gauge the interest level in the product from potential customers.

Customer Discovery   **Test Product Concept: 2ⁿᵈ Reality Check**   Worksheet 3-d

Goal of Phase 3d: By now, you've presented the product to quite a few customers and listened to how they worked. This phase is a review of the product features versus customer feedback.

> *Author:*   Business Execution
> *Approval:*   All
> *Presenter:* Business Execution, Business Vision
> *Time/Effort:* 1-2 days of authoring by VP Business Execution or Business Visionary, ½-day presentation/strategy meeting with founding team and executive staff and board

☐ **How do your preliminary product specs solve customer problems?**
1. Dead on
2. Somewhat
3. Not exactly

☐ **Re-review feature list and release schedule**
1. Prioritize feature list in terms of importance to the customer
2. Begin to put dates to 2-year release schedule

☐ **What did you learn from your customer visits?**
1. What were the biggest surprises?
2. What were the biggest disappointments?

☐ **Review product spec**
1. Formalize and update the release schedule from Worksheet 1a into an 18-month plan
2. Do your current product plans meet the needs of the market?
3. Do you want to emphasize different features?
4. Is your pricing right?

Phase 3d Exit Criteria: Product feature reality check. Map all you learned from customer visits against your original hypothesis worksheets.

Customer Discovery   Verify: The Problem   Worksheet 4-a

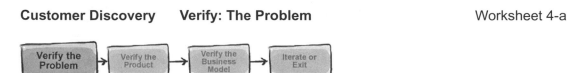

Goal of Phase 4a: You've gone all around the circle. You talked to 5 or 10 customers and *listened to how customers worked.* Then you went back, developed a problem presentation and talked to another 5 to 10 customers to see if your understanding of their problem, alternatives to solve it, and $'s to solve it was correct.

Author: Business Execution
Approval: All
Presenter: Business Execution, Business Vision
Time/Effort: 1-3 days of authoring by VP Business Execution or Business Visionary, ¼-day presentation/strategy meeting with founding team and executive staff

☐ **Problem hypothesis testing: Dead-on, somewhat, or no?**
  1. Did you understand the buyers' real problem?
  2. How did your solution match their needs?
  3. Did you understand the impact on others in the company?
  4. Was your model of how workflow occurred in a prototypical customer correct?

☐ **Where on the "problem scale" were the customers you interviewed?**
  1. Latent problem (you recognize that the buyer needs your product but they don't...yet)
  2. Active problem – Buyer is in pain (the buyer recognizes a need but doesn't know how to solve it)
  3. Visualized problem – Buyer has a vision of how to solve their problem
  4. Home-grown solution – Has cobbled together a solution (the buyer has attempted to solve the problem with piece parts)
  5. Budgeted for a solution – All of the above, and has, or can acquire a budget

☐ **Quantify the problem**
    1. What were the top five problems?
    2. Were you No. 1 or 2?
    3. Measure the problem in dollars or time

☐ **What did you learn from your customer *problem* visits?**
    1. What were the biggest surprises?
    2. What were the biggest disappointments?

Phase 4a Exit Criteria: Customer problem reality check. Map all you learned from customer visits in Understanding your Customer Needs and Reality Check against initial hypothesis worksheets.

Customer Discovery   Verify: The Product   Worksheet 4-b

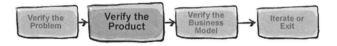

Goal of Phase 4b: In this phase, you summarize everything you learned and see if you have found the right market for your product or if you need to go around the loop again.

Author: Business Execution
Approval: All
Presenter: Business Execution, Business Vision
Time/Effort: 1-3 days of authoring by VP Business Execution or Business Visionary, ¼-day presentation/strategy meeting with founding team and executive staff

☐ **How closely did your product match their pain?**

1. They could see the fit immediately
2. They thought it could be helpful
3. Saw no need

☐ **Feature list**

1. Does the first customer ship feature list match customer needs?
2. Does the 18-month feature list get customers excited?

☐ **Quantify the pain**

1. What were the top 5 pain points?
2. Were you No. 1 or 2?
3. Measure the pain in dollars or time

☐ **What did you learn from your customer *product* visits?**

1. What were the biggest surprises?
2. What were the biggest disappointments?

☐ **Why are you different?**

1. New Market (new users in with no single comparable product)
2. Better features?
3. Better performance?
4. Better channel?
5. Better price?

☐ **Review product spec**

1. Do your current product plans meet the needs of the market?
2. Do you want to emphasize different features?
3. Has the VP of Product Development heard customer issues first hand?
4. Is your pricing right?

Phase 4b Exit Criteria: Customer and product reality check. Map all you learned from customer visits in understanding your Customer Needs and Reality Check against initial hypothesis worksheets.

Customer Discovery   Verify: The Business Model   Worksheet 4-c

Goal of Phase 4c: Rerun financial model based on current market assumptions. Stake in the ground of the vision, preliminary first market and willing customers identified, product and pricing validated by *potential* customers. Are you right or do you need to talk to more people?

> *Author:* Business Execution
>
> *Approval:* Business Execution, Business Vision
>
> *Presenter:* Business Execution, Business Vision
>
> *Time/Effort:* 1-3 days of authoring by VP Business Execution or Business Visionary, ¼-day presentation/strategy meeting with founding team and executive staff

☐ **Customer model**

1. What is the average selling price?
2. Over the next 3 years, how many units will a customer buy?
3. What is the lifetime value of each customer?

☐ **ROI model**

1. Do you understand the ROI for a customer? Revenues? Costs - reduction or containment? Displaced costs? Avoided costs? Productivity improvements? Timesaving? Intangible?
2. Is the ROI demonstrable or provable?

☐ **Market size**

1. If you are creating a new market, what's the size of the closest adjacent markets? Can you be that large? Larger?
2. If you are expanding an existing market, what is its size?

☐ **Service model**

1. Does the product require any 3rd party installation or configuration?
2. How much will this cost you per customer?
3. How much direct support will you need to provide?

☐ **Development model**

    1. How much will it cost you to develop the product?

☐ **Manufacturing model**

    1. How many total units will you sell over the next 3 years?

    2. How much will the product cost to produce?

☐ **Distribution model**

    1. How will you sell the product to your customer?

    2. What will the cost of the distribution channel be?

☐ **Customer acquisition model**

    1. How will customers know about and ask for your product?

    2. How much will it cost to acquire each customer?

☐ **Add it up**

    1. Is this a profitable business model?

Phase 4c Exit Criteria: Financial reality-check time. If you like the market and customer, does this business model make sense? Does it match your profitability needs?

Customer Discovery   Verify: Summarize. Iterate, or Exit   Worksheet 4-d

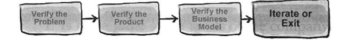

Goal of Phase 4d: You've put a stake in the ground with a series of hypothesis, you've gone out and tested your assumptions about the customer problem, and the product concept and features. Your product and pricing have been validated by *potential* customers, and you have a base of potential first visionary sales prospects. Were you right or do you need to talk to more people?

Author: Business Execution
Approval: Business Execution, Business Vision
Presenter: Business Execution, Business Vision
Time/Effort: 1-3 days of authoring by VP Business Execution or Business Visionary, ¼-day presentation/strategy meeting with founding team and executive staff

☐ **Summarize**

1. What kind of startup are you? (New market, existing market, resegmenting a market?)
2. Rethink *product* positioning – did you learn anything you want to change?
3. Redraw the customer workflow before and after your product
4. Now draw the customer usage map – who are the users?
5. Now draw distribution channel map, year 1
6. Summarize problem verification worksheet 4a
7. Summarize product verification worksheet 4b

☐ **Iterate**

1. Do you understand the market and have customers who can't wait to buy? If not, take everything you learned in Phases 1 through 3, modify your presentations based on feedback, return to Phase 1 and do it again
2. Try out several markets and users
3. Do you need to reconfigure or repackage the product offering? If so, modify your product presentations, go back to Phase 3d (product presentation) and do it again

☐ **Exit**

1. Do customers say that you understand their business problem?
2. Do you understand the organizational impact of the product?
3. Do customers tell you that your product as currently spec'd solves their problem?
4. Has the head of Product Development been in front of customers and understood their issues?
5. Does the financial model work?
6. Have you cultivated at least 5 customers you can go back to and get an order from?
7. If so, you get to try to sell the product in the next cycle – **Customer Validation**

Phase 4d Exit Criteria: Sound business and product plans. Have you learned all you can from customers? Are you ready to sell?

Customer Validation   Get Ready: Value Proposition   Worksheet 1-a

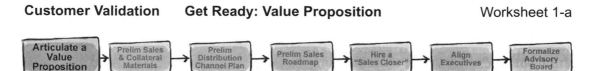

Goal of Phase 1a: Translate everything you learned about customers' problems and what they value about your solution into a Value Proposition (sometimes called a Unique Selling Proposition). This reduces the business to a single, clear, compelling message. It's "why you are different and worth buying." A Value Proposition builds the bond between seller and buyer, focuses marketing programs, and becomes the focal point for building the company.

Input: Customer Discovery: Market Type and Customer Understanding
Author: Business Visionary
Approval: All
Presenter: Business Execution, Business Visionary
Time/Effort: 5-10 days of authoring by VP Business Execution and Business Visionary plus outside writing contractors.

☐ **What did you learn in Customer Discovery?**

1. What were the top 3 problems your customers said they had?
2. Is there a phrase that kept coming up to describe this problem?
3. In understanding how customers worked, where does your product impact them most?
4. How significant is the impact on how customers work?
5. If there are competitors or piece part solutions, what do you provide that your competitors can't or won't? What do you do better?

☐ **Create and craft a Value Proposition (why you are different and worth buying)**

1. How would you alter this Value Proposition by Market Type?
2. Which would result in a clearer differentiation?
3. Which would result in quicker sales?

☐ **Do you have an incremental or transformation value proposition?**

1. Incremental – improve metrics of individual value activities (typically for a new product in an existing market)
2. Transformational – Creating a new market or reconfiguring an entire industry

☐ **Is your Value Proposition emotionally compelling?**

1. Unique (or at least first) in the mind of the customer
2. Understandable in the users' language. Oversimplified message

☐ **Does your Value Proposition make or reinforce an economic case?**

1. Has economic impact
2. Focus on a leverage point in adopters' value chain
3. Impacts the leverage point and is quantifiable in the mind of the customer
4. What's the adoption cost of using your product?

☐ **Does the Value Proposition pass the reality test?**

1. Is your company a credible supplier for this product and claim?
2. Are your capabilities congruent with your reputation and claims?
3. Are your solutions attainable and compatible with customers' current operations? Do they have complementary/supporting technologies in place?
4. Does your product assure continuity? Do you have a product roadmap that evolves from your first product? Does the customer feel a promise of long-term commitment?

Phase 1a Exit Criteria: First pass of a Value Proposition.

Customer Validation   Get Ready: Sales Materials   Worksheet 1-b

Goal of Phase 1b: Before you can go out to sell you need to develop a "Collateral Roadmap" – a guide to all the literature you will put in front of a customer. Then prepare the full suite of prototype sales materials as if you have an entire sales organization.

Input: Customer Discovery: Demand Creation Worksheet and Customer Understanding

Author: Business Visionary

Approval: All

Presenter: Business Execution, Business Visionary

Time/Effort: 10-30 days of authoring by VP Business Execution and Business Visionary plus outside writing contractors.

☐ **Develop a collateral roadmap**

1. List all the key pieces of sales and marketing collateral needed
2. Differentiate where each piece will be used
3. Develop only the material you need for this phase (you'll redo it all based on what you learn)
4. Would this material change depending on Market Type?

☐ **Develop sales presentations**

1. Sales presentation (updated version of presentation used in worksheet 3-d)
2. Technical presentation
3. You may need different presentations depending on the number of people who play a role in purchase decisions inside a company

☐ **Develop data sheets**

1. Product data sheets (features and benefits)
2. Solution data sheets (pain/need and solution)
3. Technical overview with architecture diagrams
4. How would these change by Market Type?

☐ **Develop white papers**

1. ROI white paper
2. Key technical issues if unique
3. Key business issues if unique
4. Others as needed
5. How would these change by Market Type?

☐ **Develop corporate website**

1. Who are you?
2. What problem are you trying to solve?
3. Call for more information
4. How would this change by Market Type?

☐ **Develop pricing material**

1. Pricelist
2. Quote form
3. Does pricing match the proposed sales channel?

☐ **Develop sales demos**

1. Mobile demo
2. Online demo
3. Slide-based "dummy-demo"

Phase 1b Exit Criteria: Collateral roadmap plus complete preliminary sales materials for trial sales to potential customers.

Customer Validation   Get Ready: Prelim Channel Plan   Worksheet 1-c

Goal of Phase 1c: In this phase you develop a "channel roadmap" – a guide to how a product reaches its customer. In this brief you will cover the channel food chain and responsibility, channel discount and financials and channel management.

> *Input:*   Customer Discovery: Channel/Pricing Worksheet and Customer Understanding
> *Author:*   Business Visionary
> *Approval:*   Business Execution
> *Presenter:*   Business Execution, Business Visionary, Sales Closer
> *Time/Effort:* 3-5 days of authoring by VP Business Execution and Business Visionary plus outside sales strategy consultant.

☐ **Understand the channel "food chain" and responsibility**

1. Draw the "food chain" of how you intend to reach your end user (what organizations lie between you and the end user?)
2. Do you understand all the distribution channel alternatives? What are they and why did you discard them?
3. Are you clear about how much demand creation your channel will provide versus your company? If so, is it budgeted?

☐ **Understand the channel discounts and financials**

1. How much will the channel cost (direct expenses or channel discounts)?
2. Are there indirect channel costs (presales support, channel promotional dollars…)?
3. What else is needed for customers to use/buy the product? How do they acquire those pieces?
4. What is the net revenue after channel costs?

☐ **Understand how you will manage the channel**

1. What kind of channel reports will you receive?
2. How will you know what has actually sold to end users?

☐ **Market Type analysis**

1. How would the preliminary roadmap change by Market Type?
2. How would the revenue plan change by Market Type?

Phase 1c Exit Criteria: Complete distribution channel map and plan.

Customer Validation **Get Ready: Prelim Sales Roadmap** Worksheet 1-d

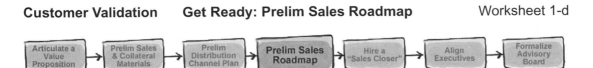

Goal of Phase 1d: In this phase you will develop a preliminary "Sales Roadmap," which consists of four elements: 1) organization and influence maps, 2) customer access map, 3) sales strategy, 4) the implementation plan.

Input: Customer Discovery: Customer Understanding
Author: Business Visionary
Approval: Business Execution
Presenter: Business Execution, Business Visionary, Sales Closer
Time/Effort: 3-5 days of authoring by VP Business Execution and Business Visionary plus outside sales strategy consultant.

☐ **Organization and influence maps**

1. What is the canonical customer organization chart? Is there just one?
2. What are the typical functions in our sales approval process?
3. Who has the problem? Where are they in the decision process?
4. Who are the influencers, recommenders, and decision-makers?
5. Who influences who in the buying process? In what order?
6. Who can sabotage the sale?
7. Who decides the sale?
8. Where is the budget?

☐ **Customer access map**

1. What is the best way into the account?
2. Are there other outside organizations that can help you gain entry?

☐ **Develop a selling strategy**

1. Establish ROI – where/when in the selling process does it matter?
   a. What will be measured? Revenues? Costs - reduction or containment? Displaced costs? Avoided costs? Productivity improvements? Time savings? Intangible?

      b. When will it pay for itself?

      c. Why should they believe you?

  2. Put together org chart, influence map and access map

  3. Create solutions "key pain point"

  4. Develop "optimal visionary buyer" profile

  5. Create a reference story/sales script

  6. Do the economic buyers and recommenders agree that the pain is worth solving?

  7. How many sales calls to get the sale? To who? What is the script for each?

  8. Develop the preliminary sales roadmap

☐ **Implementation plan**

  1. Draft contracts in place

  2. Collateral plan matches selling strategy?

  3. Pricing match feedback?

  4. Presales support/service as needed?

  5. Delivery schedule match Product Development plans?

  6. Tentative step-by-step sales process?

☐ **Market Type analysis**

  1. How would the preliminary roadmap change by Market Type?

  2. How would the revenue plan change by Market Type?

Phase 1d Exit Criteria: Complete but preliminary sales map.

Customer Validation   **Get Ready: Hire a "Sales Closer"**   Worksheet 1-e

Goal of Phase 1e: While the founders have been out talking to customers, and finding interested prospects, the founding team may not include someone experienced in "closing" deals. If not, now is the time to hire a "Sales Closer."

Author: Business Execution
Approval: All
Presenter: Business Execution
Time/Effort: 1 day of authoring by VP Business Execution, 90 days search process, ¼-day presentation/strategy meeting with founding team, executive staff and board.

☐ **Identify need for a "Sales Closer"**

1. Does someone on the founding team have experience "closing" business?
2. Do they have a "world-class" set of customer contacts in the market you are initially targeting?
3. Would you bet the company on their ability to close the first sales?

☐ **If not, hire a "Sales Closer"**

1. A sales closer has a great Rolodex in the market you are selling into
2. They are aggressive, want a great compensation package for success and have no interest in building a sales organization
3. Explicitly do NOT hire a VP of Sales, or someone who wants to build a sales organization
4. Hire someone who is comfortable with ambiguity and change, and lives for closing deals
5. They have to be comfortable with slides changing day to day, strategy being ambiguous, etc.
6. Typical background would be a regional manager

☐ **Market-Type analysis**

1. How would the preliminary roadmap change by Market Type?
2. How would the revenue plan change by Market Type?

Phase 1e Exit Criteria: Sales Closer hired and up to speed.

Customer Validation   **Get Ready to Sell: Realign Execs**   Worksheet 1-f

Goal of Phase 1f: Selling a product implies a contractual commitment between the company and a customer on product features and delivery dates. Before you sell and commit the company to a set of product deliverables, all the players need to revisit the product spec, features and delivery dates.

Input:	Customer Discovery: Customer Understanding
Author:	Technical Execution, Business Execution
Approval:	All
Presenter:	Technical Execution, Business Execution
Time/Effort:	1 day of authoring by VP Business Execution or Business Visionary, ½-day presentation/strategy meeting with founding team and executive staff

☐ **Review and agree on engineering deliverables and schedule**

1. Update 24-month engineering release schedule
2. Agree on the committed features by release
3. Ensure that all changes from Customer Discovery are integrated into product spec

☐ **Review and agree on a "good enough" philosophy for deliverables and schedule**

1. The goal is to get visionaries an incomplete, barely good enough product for 1st release
2. The visionaries will help you understand what features are needed to make the first release a functional product
3. Engineering should not be striving for architectural purity or perfection in release 1.0. The goal is to get it out the door and quickly revise it
4. The purpose is not "first mover advantage" (there is none), nor is it a non-paying alpha or beta test, but customer input on a product they've paid for

☐ **Timing is crucial**

  1. Are you absolutely sure you can deliver a functional product for your early visionary sales?

  2. If you slip badly, a visionary's position in his company weakens and his support is withdrawn

☐ **Review and agree on sales collateral**

  1. Update selling materials to sync with committed releases

  2. Read and approve all sales collateral including presentations

☐ **Review and agree on engineering support for the selling process**

  1. Technical visionary and technical execution commit to sales calls

  2. Key engineers commit to support detailed customer investigation questions

☐ **Review and agree on pricing, integration and post-sales support**

  1. Are you charging enough for the product?

  2. Have you estimated the right amount of time for installation and integration? Are you charging enough?

  3. Have you estimated the right amount of time for post sales support? Are you charging enough?

☐ **Review and agree on engineering support for the integration process**

  1. Who installs and integrates the products after you successfully sell your first few Customer Validation customers?

  2. Commitment and agreement for early engineering support before establishing formal professional services group

  3. One-page summary of integration plan (ownership, timing and details)

☐ **Review and agree on engineering support for initial post-sales support**

  1. Who supports the products after you successfully sell your first few Customer Validation customers?

  2. Commitment and agreement for early engineering support before establishing formal technical support group

  3. One-page summary of support plan (ownership, timing and details)

☐ **Market Type analysis**

    1. Are we still certain about Market Type?

    2. How will that choice affect revenue and expenses?

Phase 1f Exit Criteria: Engineering delivers release schedule and feature list. Engineering agrees the goal is to get a product in a paying customer's hand for customer feedback. All agree that sales to visionaries can be supported by release schedule. Review sales collateral and presentations to ensure they match features and schedules. Agree on sales support, pricing, integration and support.

Customer Validation   Get Ready to Sell: Formalize Advisory Board   Worksheet 1-g

Goal of Phase 1g: Set up advisory board to get visionary customers and industry experts engaged with the company and product. In Customer Discovery you began to think about who might fit on an advisory board, you evaluated potential customers on whether they could add value. Now you will put the pieces together to assemble an advisory board to get you orders.

Input:	Customer Discovery Advisory Board Input
Author:	Business Visionary
Approval:	Business Execution
Presenter:	Business Execution, Business Visionary, Sales Closer
Time/Effort:	1-3 days of calls and meeting by Sales Closer, VP Business Execution or Visionary

☐ **Develop an advisory board roadmap**

1. List all the key advisors that will be needed
2. Differentiate how each advisor will be used
3. Recruit only the advisors you need now
4. Make exceptions for "Brand Names" and "Influencers"
5. Think strategically, not tactically, about the "sphere of influence" and "reach" of advisors
6. Don't believe that you need a "formal" meeting

☐ **Ensure that key technical advisors are on the "Technical Advisory Board"**

1. Technical Advisory Board staffed for technical advice and pointers to technical talent. Later as a technical reference for customers

☐ **Ensure that key potential customers are on the "Customer Advisory Board"**

1. Initially for product advice and unbeknownst to them to get them to buy. Later as a reference for other customers, and as a product conscience

2. Will they make a great customer? Can you seduce them? Do they have good product instincts? Are they part of a customer network?

3. Use them for phone calls for insight and one-on-one meetings w/business and development staff at company

☐ **Ensure that key industry experts are on the "Industry Advisory Board"**

1. Domain experts who bring credibility to your specific market or technology

2. Visible name brands. May also be customers, but typically use to create customer and press credibility

3. Use them for phone calls for insight and one-on-one meetings w/business and development staff at company

Phase 1g Exit Criteria: Advisory board roadmap in place. Customer and Industry Advisory boards assembled.

Customer Validation   Sell: Contact Visionaries   **Worksheet 2-a**

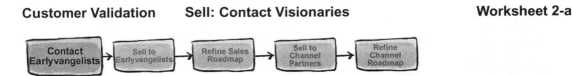

Goal of Phase 2a: In Customer Discovery you visited customers to understand their problems and to see if the product concept solved that problem. Now you want to find "visionaries" and sell to them. Visionaries are the only customers able to buy an unfinished product that has yet to be delivered. They understand they have a problem and have visualized a solution that looks like yours. You may have called on some visionaries in your previous phases, or you may have to find new ones.

Author: Sales Closer, Business Visionary
Approval: Business Execution
Presenter: Sales Closer, Business Execution, and Business Visionary
Time/Effort: 3-8 days of calling by Sales Closer, VP Business Execution or Business
              Visionary

☐ **Find the visionaries**

1. Do they understand their pain?
2. Can they articulate a vision?
3. Were there key characteristics of visionary customers you saw in Customer Discovery that would help identify where you can find more?
4. Targets are not to get engineering alpha tests to technology enthusiasts. They are not customers
5. No free products
6. Betas are *paying* customers. You can give them great terms, but if you can't find anyone to pay, you're in the wrong business.

☐ **Do they have money budgeted to solve this problem?**

1. Now? In six months?

☐ **Make a list of 50 potential customers you can test your ideas on**

1. You are less interested in brand names than in individuals who will give you the time
2. Don't be a title snob

☐ **Get leads of who to call from: (Update from Customer Discovery Phase 3-c)**

1. Investors
2. Founders
3. Lawyers
4. Headhunters, etc.
5. Trade magazines
6. Business reference books

☐ **Begin to develop an innovators' list. Ask others who is the most innovative:**

1. Company
2. Department in a company
3. Individuals

☐ **Create an introductory email (Update from Customer Discovery)**

1. The email should introduce you with a one-paragraph description of the company, a general description of what you are doing and what's in it for them to spend time with you
2. The email should say that you will be following up with a phone call
3. Have the people who gave you the leads send the email.
4. Follow up with a call (see reference story below)
5. 50 follow-up phone calls should yield 5-10 visits

☐ **Update the reference story/sales script from Customer Discovery (why are you calling/emailing)**

1. Focus on the solution (not the features)
2. What problems are you trying to solve?
3. Why is it important to solve them?
4. Say you are starting a company, were referred by X, you are building Y, but you don't want to sell them anything, you just want 20 minutes of their time to understand how they/their company work
5. Give them a reason to see you. What's in it for them?

☐ **Ten phone calls a day**

1. Call until your schedule is booked with 3 customer visits a day
2. Get used to being turned down but always ask, "If you're too busy, whom should I talk to?"
3. For this first meeting you don't care about titles, you just want to gather data
4. Keep hit-rate statistics (any pitch, leads or level better or worse than others?)

Phase 2a Exit Criteria: Updated reference story/sales script and 5-10 customer visits scheduled. Sales Closer leads the effort.

Customer Validation   **Sell: Validate the Sales Roadmap**   Worksheet 2-b

Goal of Phase 2b: Earlier in Customer Validation you put together a hypothetical sales roadmap. In this step, the rubber meets the road. Can you sell 3-5 early visionary customers *before* your product is shipping? The key is finding *earlyvangelists* who are high-level executives, decision-makers and risk-takers. They are not the standard customers you will reach with a standard sales process you will put in place later in the company's life. This is a one-time event you will leverage to build the company.

Author: Business Visionary
Approval: Business Execution
Presenter: Sales Closer, Business Execution, and Business Visionary
Time/Effort: 30-60 days of calling by VP Business Execution or Business Visionary

☐ **Build an organization chart of each target customer and map key influencers**

1. Map key recommenders
2. Map key decision-makers

☐ **Review and execute on sales roadmap**

1. Call on operational side of the company
   a. Qualification sales call
   b. Develop interest sales call
   c. Business discovery sales call
2. Call on technical side of the company
   a. IT inoculation
   b. Technical discovery
   c. Solution capture
3. Statement of work approved
4. Solution approved
5. Negotiations

☐ **Understand pricing goals**

1. Anyone can give a product away; your goal is to sell an unfinished and undelivered product

2. Be flexible on the terms (no payment until delivery, no payment until it works as spec'd, etc.)

3. Be tougher on discounts ("we need a discount because we are your first customer" should be turned around to "you need to pay list price since you get to use it first")

4. Trying to sell at list price is a sanity test as well as test of the customer sales and approval processes

☐ **Keep win/loss statistics on sales calls**

1. Goal is to understand where in the sales process you get turned down (introduction, product presentation, organizational issues, "Not Invented Here" issues, technical issues, pricing)

2. Reevaluate win/loss issues weekly

Phase 2b Exit Criteria: 3-5 purchase orders for an unfinished, undelivered product.

Customer Validation   **Sell: Validate Channel Roadmap**   Worksheet 2-c

Goal of Phase 2c: Introduce the company to potential system integrators, channel and service partners. In a new market no viable transactions are possible until customer base scales, but this begins the partnership dance. In some cases potential partners may be corporate investors.

> *Author:*   Business Visionary
> *Approval:*   Business Execution
> *Presenter:*   Sales Closer, Business Execution, and Business Visionary
> *Time/Effort:* 5-10 days of calling by VP Business Execution or Business Visionary

☐ **Understand system integrators/channel/service partners business model**

1. How do they make money? (By project? By hour? By reselling software?)
1. How does their business model compare to others in their business?
2. What is the minimum dollar size of a transaction that is interesting to them?
3. Draw their business model

☐ **What other companies do these system integrators/channel/service partners work with?**

1. Complementary companies to yours? (If so, call on these companies)
2. Competitive companies to yours? (If so, why would they do a deal with you?)

☐ **Assemble a system integrators/channel/service partner presentation**

1. Your business concept
2. What's in it for these channel/servicepartners?

☐ **Contact and present to system integrators/channel/service partners**

1. Start a dialog
2. Learn about their business
3. Do they hear customers asking for a product like yours?

Phase 2c Exit Criteria: First presentation to value-added integration and channel partners.

Customer Validation   Positioning: Product   Worksheet 3-a

Goal of Phase 3a: While you are getting feedback from customers and partners you continually need to ask, Are you selling into an existing market? Are you redefining/ reframing a current market? Or are you creating a new market? You asked these questions in Discovery - Product Positioning as a hypothesis. In this phase refine this choice and come up with "Product Positioning," then define the customer segment, customer pain points, and competition.

Author: Positioning Resource, Technical Visionary Business Visionary
Approval: All
Presenter: Positioning Resource, Technical Visionary, Business Visionary
Time/Effort: 2-4 days of authoring by Technical Visionary and/or Business Visionary, ¼-day presentation/strategy meeting with founding team and executive staff

☐ **Do you have a new product in an existing market?**

☐ **Do you need to redefine/reframe a market?**

☐ **Or do you want to create an entirely new market?**

1. Is your product/service a substitution for something customers already have?
2. Is it a replacement?
3. Is it a variant on something already out there, but can be "respun" into something new?
4. Is it something totally new?

☐ **Positioning in an existing market**

1. Users are known
2. Market is known
3. Competitors are defined and known
4. Product positioning is paramount

☐ **Competitive product positioning**

1. What are the key features of your product?

2. What are the key features of the leading products in this existing market?

3. What pain points have customers told you they have?

4. How do your product features solve these pain points?

5. How do the features of competitive products solve these pain points?

☐ **If it's a new product in an existing market, define the basis of competition**

1. Positioning the *product* is the basis of competition

2. Picking the correct axes for the basis of competition is critical. For example:

   a. feature/technology axis

   b. price/performance axis

   c. channel/margin axis

☐ **Product messages**

1. Why should a customer buy your product?

2. Develop a positioning statement that clearly articulates the solution to a problem

3. Compare your company to your competitors. What is their company positioning? Are you missing something?

☐ **Who is driving the market?**

1. Are there existing standards? If so, whose agenda is driving them?

2. Do you want to embrace the standards, extend them, or replace them?

3. Are there different global issues from just national ones?

☐ **Positioning in a new market**

1. Users are unknown

2. Market positioning is unknown and critical

3. Competitors do not yet exist

4. Product positioning is secondary

☐ **If it's a new market, assemble the market map**

1. Positioning the creation of a *new market* is the basis of competition

2. List the closest markets to yours (a market is a set of companies with common attributes)

3. Draw the market map with you in the center

    4. Give your a market a descriptive TLA (three-letter acronym)

    5. Why would thousands of new customers believe in and move to this market?

☐ **Do you have some advantage or appeal among any vertical or horizontal market segment?**

    1. Which markets or segments?

Positioning in an existing market you want to resegment

    1. Users are possibly known

    2. Extended market positioning is unknown and critical

    3. Competitors exist if you are wrong

    4. Product positioning is unknown and critical

☐ **If it's a new product in a market you want to reframe, define the basis of how you want to change the market**

    1. Positioning the *change in the market* is the basis of competition

    2. This is driven by some new feature of the product or service that redefines the market

    3. Redraw the market map and show which new feature you offer that drives this. For example:

      • New customers

      • New distribution channel

      • Feature/technology axis

      • Price/performance axis

      • Channel/margin axis

    4. Why would thousands of new customers believe in and move to this market?

☐ **Product positioning**

    1. What are the key features?

    2. How do these features solve the pain points we've identified that customers have?

    3. What pain points have customers told you they have?

4. How does your product solve these pain points?

5. Why should a customer buy your product?

6. Developing a positioning statement that clearly articulates the solution to a problem

7. Compare your company to your competitors. What is their company positioning? Are you missing something?

☐ **Demand creation/lead generation messages**

1. Develop outgoing marketing messages for lead generation

2. Develop sales programs/scripts that sell to the pain points

Phase 3a Exit Criteria: A written description of product positioning. This includes hypothetical product/feature map or market map.

Customer Validation   Positioning: Company   Worksheet 3-b

Goal of Phase 3b: You've decided on how to position the product. Now you need to clearly articulate a company positioning. Revisit the core values, develop a mission statement, unique selling proposition and specific marketing messages for demand/ lead generation.

Author: Positioning Resource, Technical Visionary, Business Visionary
Approval: Business Execution
Presenter: Positioning Resource, Technical Visionary, Business Visionary
Time/Effort: 2-4 days of authoring by VP Business Execution or Business Visionary, ¼-day presentation/strategy meeting with founding team and executive staff

☐ **Review core values of founding team**

1. Not a mission statement
2. Not about profit or products
3. Core ideology about what the company believes in
4. Do you still believe in these values? Are they still fundamental?

☐ **Review company culture model**

1. Star?
2. Engineering
3. Commitment
4. Autocratic
5. Bureaucratic

☐ Company positioning

1. Mission statement – why are you in business?
2. Why is your company different? Why are you special? (This is not about the market or product; it's about the people, team, mission, etc.)
3. Insert market and product positioning as part of mission statement.
4. Compare your company to your competitors. What is their company positioning? Are you missing something?

Phase 3b Exit Criteria: A written description of company positioning Mission Statement.

Customer Validation   Positioning: Present to Analysts   Worksheet 3-c

Goal of Phase 3d: Industry analysts are part of the foundation of credibility that a startup needs – for mainstream customers to feel safe in buying, and as key references for the press. The goal is to meet with industry analysts; get their insight and feedback on your initial positioning (market, product and company); and their thoughts on your product features.

> *Author:*   Business Visionary
> *Approval:*   All
> *Presenter:*   Business Execution, Business Visionary (technical execs if necessary)
> *Time/Effort:* 2-4 days of authoring by Technical Visionary and/or Business Visionary 3-5 days presentation development, 3-5 days presenting

☐ **Contact analysts you've been tracking (from Customer Discovery Phase 2c)**

1. Understand what companies/industries their firms cover
2. Understand what area/companies/expertise the analyst you are calling covers
3. Develop short script of why they should meet with you (what's in it for them, why is your company important)
4. Reference your early customers, and the problem/pain points you solve
5. Set up meetings
6. Ask them how much time you have, what presentation format they like (formal slides, demo, whiteboard talk, etc.) and whether the presentation should focus on technology, markets, or both

☐ **Assemble analyst presentation**

1. This is not a sales presentation
2. Each analyst organization has a view of the market you are in – understand it
3. If you are creating a new market, get the slides that describe their view of the adjacent markets you will affect
4. Presentation will focus on market and product positioning, and details of product features

☐ **Gather analyst feedback**

1. What other companies are doing anything like this?
2. How does your vision fit with market needs? With customer needs?
3. How should you be positioning your product/market/company?
4. How should you be pricing this? How do others price?
5. Who in a company should you be selling to?
6. What kind of obstacles will you face inside a company?
7. What kind of obstacles will you face outside (Funding? Infrastructure? Competition?)
8. What do you think you should do next?

Phase 3c Exit Criteria: Analyst feedback, approval, and wild enthusiasm.

Customer Validation   Verification: Product   Worksheet 4-a

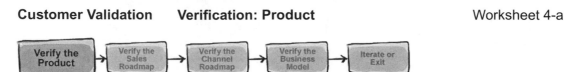

Goal of Phase 4a: You've gone all around the Customer Validation circle "verifying the product," which means showing that you have a product that customers will buy. Review all the objections and feedback you have from customers about the product and the conclusions you have come to about first-release features, subsequent features, and so on.

> *Author:*   Sales Closer, Business Execution
> *Approval:*   All
> *Presenter:* Sales Closer
> *Time/Effort:* 1-3 days of authoring by VP Business Execution or Business Visionary, ¼-day presentation/strategy meeting with founding team and executive staff

☐ **Review product features:**

1. Does the product you are first shipping meet the needs of the market?
2. How closely did your product match customers' pain?
3. Did you lose deals because of missing features?
4. What features stood out as clear "home runs"?
5. Did you lose because your product wasn't important enough to buy until it was a "whole product"?
6. Do you want to emphasize different features?
7. Has the VP of Product Development heard customer issues firsthand?

☐ **Review product delivery schedule:**

1. Did you lose deals over delivery schedule issues?
2. Did you have the right release schedule?
3. Does your plan for future releases have the right features in the right order?

Phase 4a Exit Criteria: Does the Sales Closer believe that other salespeople can sell the product as spec'd in a repeatable manner?

Customer Validation   Verification: Sales   Worksheet 4-b

Goal of Phase 4b: You've gone all around the Customer Validation circle. You assembled your sales materials, found visionary prospects and tried to sell and close 3-5 customers. In this phase you summarize everything you learned from selling.

Author: Sales Closer, Business Execution
Approval: All
Presenter: Sales Closer
Time/Effort: 1-3 days of authoring by VP Business Execution or Business Visionary, ¼-day presentation/strategy meeting with founding team and executive staff

☐ **Prospecting**

    1. How easy was it to get an appointment?

    2. Did customers understand what you wanted to sell?

☐ **Presenting**

    1. Did you understand the real pain the buyers had?

    2. How did your solution match their needs?

    3. Did you understand the impact on others in the company?

    4. Did you need a demo or prototype to sell?

    5. Where the sales materials adequate?

☐ **Customer organizational issues**

    1. Did you identify the right decision-makers?

    2. Did you understand the other key players in the organization?

    3. Did you lose deals because others in the organization objected?

☐ **Pricing**

    1. Did you lose deals over pricing?

    2. Do you have the right pricing model?

    3. What is the average selling price?

    4. Over the next 3 years how many units will a customer buy?

5. What is the lifetime value of each customer?

6. Was there any objection to your pricing? (If not, your product may be priced too low—you should always get a modicum of grumbling.)

7. Besides the absolute price of the product, do you have the right pricing model?

☐ **ROI model**

1. Do you understand the ROI for a customer? Revenues? Costs—reduction or containment? Displaced costs? Avoided costs? Productivity improvements? Time savings? Intangible?

2. Is the ROI demonstrable or provable?

☐ **Distribution model**

1. Are your assumptions about distribution channel correct?

2. What will the cost of the distribution channel be?

☐ **Service/system integration model**

1. Are your assumptions about service/system integration correct?

2. How much will this cost you per customer?

3. How much direct support will you need to provide?

☐ **What did you learn from your customer visits?**

1. What were the biggest surprises?

2. What were the biggest disappointments?

☐ **Can sales scale?**

1. Can other salespeople sell this product?

2. Can they sell it without the founding team calling on customers?

3. How many units can each salesperson sell a year?

☐ **Sales resources required for scale**

1. What pre- and post-sales resources need to be added?

2. How many people need to be on a sales team (salesman, technical presales, post-sales integration, technical support, etc.)

Phase 4b Exit Criteria: Sales/channel reality check. Map all you learned from customer visits in Customer Validation. Sales closer believes that other salespeople can sell the product in a repeatable manner.

Customer Validation   Verification: Channel   Worksheet 4-c

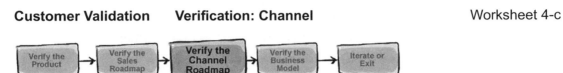

Goal of Phase 4c: Are your assumptions about the distribution channel correct?

> *Author:*   Business Execution
>
> *Approval:*   Business Execution, Business Vision
>
> *Presenter:*   Business Execution, Business Vision
>
> *Time/Effort:* 1-3 days of authoring by VP Business Execution or Business Visionary, ¼-day presentation/strategy meeting with founding team and executive staff

☐ **Distribution model**

1. Can you articulate all the variables involved in using this sales and distribution model?

   a. Sales cycle

   b. Average selling price

   c. Revenue per salesperson per year

   d. Sales team size

   e. Number of salespeople

2. Sales cycle length—If this is an indirect channel, can the channel scale?

3. How will you train and educate the sales channel?

☐ **Other channel costs**

1. Cost of system integration partners

2. Cost of other software partners

3. Other unexpected costs? Stocking costs, store advertising costs, extra pre-sales support?

4. Regardless of the channel, how much direct support will you need to provide?

☐ **Demand creation costs**

1. What kind of demand creation activities (advertising, PR, trade shows, etc.) will be needed to drive customers into the channel?

2. How much will it cost to acquire each customer?

3. Have you accounted for these costs in your business model? (While it may seem obvious, customer acquisition costs need to be less than customer lifetime value. Dollars spent in branding cannot scale a flawed or unprofitable business model.)

4. If this is an indirect channel, are there hidden channel costs (channel incentives) or demand-creation costs such as in-store displays and promotions?

Phase 4c Exit Criteria: Channel reality-check time. If you like the market and customer, does this sales channel model make sense? Does it match your profitability needs?

Customer Validation   **Verification: Financial**   Worksheet 4-d

Goal of Phase 4d: Rerun financial model based on current market assumptions. Stake in the ground of the vision, preliminary first market and willing customers identified, product and pricing validated by potential customers. Are you right or do you need to talk to more people?

> *Author:*   Business Execution
>
> *Approval:*   Business Execution, Business Vision
>
> *Presenter:*   Business Execution, Business Vision
>
> *Time/Effort:* 1-3 days of authoring by VP Business Execution or Business Visionary, ¼-day presentation/strategy meeting with founding team and executive staff

☐ **Sales/distribution model**

1. Sales cycle
2. Average selling price
3. Revenue per salesperson per year
4. Sales team size
5. Number of salespeople

☐ **Whole product model**

1. Cost of system integration partners
2. Cost of other software partners

☐ **Demand creation model**

1. Unique positioning
2. Cost of demand creation (How will customers know about and ask for your product?)
3. How much will it cost to acquire each customer?

☐ **Funding model**

1. How much funding do you need for profitability?
2. How much funding do you need to get to cash flow positive?

☐ **Development model**

1. Additional $s to get to a fully featured product that can be sold by a standard sales force?

2. How much will it cost you to develop the two-year vision of the product?

☐ **Add it up**

1. Is this a profitable business model?

Phase 4d Exit Criteria: Financial business model reality-check time. If you like the market and customer, does this business model make sense? Does it match your profitability needs?

Customer Validation   **Verification: Iterate, or Exit**   Worksheet 4-e

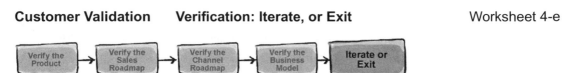

Goal of Phase 4e: This is either the beginning of the end or more than likely just the end of the beginning. You've put a stake in the ground of the vision, preliminary first market and willing customers identified, product and pricing validated by potential customers, and a base of *potential* first visionary sales prospects. Were you right or do you need to talk to more people?

> *Author:*   Business Execution
> *Approval:*   Business Execution, Business Vision
> *Presenter:* Business Execution, Business Vision
> *Time/Effort:* 1-3 days of authoring by VP Business Execution or Business Visionary, ¼-day presentation/strategy meeting with founding team and executive staff

☐ **Summarize**

1. Can you sell the product?
2. Do you need to reconfigure or repackage the product offering?
3. Is the pricing right?
4. Does your business model work?

☐ **Timing**

1. Can you deliver or did you just sell vaporware?
2. If vaporware, at best the company secured a few pilot projects, but as schedules slip, a visionary's position in his company weakens and support is withdrawn. No usable reference is gained. Solution is to shut down selling, admit mistakes, and turn pilot projects into something useful - first for the customer and then as a marketable product.

☐ **Iterate**

1. Do you have customers who bought?
2. If it's a presentation or positioning problem, take everything you learned in Phases 1 through 3, modify your presentations based on feedback, go back to Phase 1 and do it again

3. If it's a product problem, go back to Customer Discovery and reconfigure the product. Use the core technology and come up with another product configuration

☐ **Exit**

1. Do customers tell you with purchase orders that you have a hot product?
2. Did they buy the product as currently spec'd or did you sell vaporware?
3. Has your head of Product Development been in front of customers and understand their issues?
4. Do you have purchase orders from multiple companies?
5. Have you sold all the way through an organization such that you understand the organizational impact of the product?
6. Does the financial model work?
7. If so, you get to try to create a market in preparation for scaling the business in the next cycle – **Customer Creation**

Phase 4e Exit Criteria: Proven that the product is salable and the product features and pricing work. Have you learned all you can from customers? Are you ready to scale?

Acknowledgments

In my 25 years as a technology entrepreneur I was lucky to have three extraordinary mentors, each brilliant in his own field: Ben Wegbreit who taught me how to think, Gordon Bell who taught me what to think about, and Allen Michaels who showed me how to turn thinking into direct and immediate action.

I was also extremely fortunate to be working in Silicon Valley when three of its most influential marketing practitioners and strategists were active. As a VP of Marketing I was strongly influenced by the customer-centric books of Bill Davidow, former VP of Marketing of Intel and founder of Mohr, Davidow Ventures, and consider myself fortunate to have had him on my board at MIPS Computers. Regis McKenna was already a PR and marketing legend with his own firm when I started my career, but his thinking and practice still resonate in my work. Finally, I still remember the hair rising on the back of my neck when I first read Geoff Moore and the notion of a "chasm." It was the first time I realized there were repeatable patterns of business behavior that could explain the heretofore unexplainable.

At U.C. Berkeley Haas Business School, Jerry Engel, director of the Lester Center on Entrepreneurship, was courageous enough to give me a forum to test and teach the Customer Development Methodology to hundreds of unsuspecting students. Professor John Freeman at Haas has offered valuable insight on the different sales cycles by Market Type. Finally my first teaching partner at Haas, Rob Majteles, ensured that my students got my enthusiasm, as well as a coherent syllabus and their papers graded and back on time. At Stanford, Tom Byers, Kathy Eisenhardt and Tina Seelig were gracious enough to invite me to teach with them in the Graduate School of Engineering and hone my methodology as they offered additional insights on new product selling cycles. Finally, Murray Low at Columbia School of Business allowed me to inflict the course and this text on their students in their MBA program.

In the venture capital world in addition to funding some of my startups, Jon Feiber at MDV and Katherine Gould at Foundation Capital have acted as stalwart sounding boards and supporters.

My friends Steve Weinstein, Bob Dorf, Bernard Fraenkel, and Jim Wickett have made innumerable and valuable comments and suggestions.

Will Harvey and Eric Ries of IMVU were the first corporate guinea pigs to implement some or all of the Customer Development Methodology. This book was required reading for every new hire at their company. Fred Durham at CafePress allowed me to sit on his board and watch a world-class entrepreneur at work.

Besides running engineering at IMVU Eric Ries also moonlighted as copyeditor and helped eliminate the embarrassing typos of the first and second revisions.

This book would be much poorer without all of their contributions.

Finally, my wife Alison Elliott not only put up with my obsession with finding a methodology for early stage Customer Development, and my passion for teaching it, she added her wise counsel, insight and clarity to my thinking. This book would not have happened without her.

About Steve Blank

A retired eight-time serial entrepreneur-turned-educator and author, Steve Blank has changed how startups are built and how entrepreneurship is taught around the globe. He is author of the bestselling *The Startup Owner's Manual,* and his earlier seminal work, *The Four Steps to the Epiphany,* credited with launching the Lean Startup movement. His May 2013 Harvard Business Review article on the Lean Startup defined the movement.

Steve is widely recognized as a thought leader on startups and innovation. His book and blog have redefined how to build successful startups; his Lean LaunchPad class at Stanford, Berkeley and Columbia has redefined how entrepreneurship is taught; and his Innovation Corps class for the National Science Foundation forever changed how the U.S. commercializes science. His articles regularly appear in *The Wall Street Journal*, *Forbes*, *Fortune*, *The Atlantic* and *Huffington Post*.

Blank's first book, *The Four Steps to the Epiphany* (2003), offered the insight that startups are not small versions of large companies – large companies execute business models, but startups search for them – and led him to realize that startups need their own tools, different from those used to manage existing companies. The book described a Customer Development methodology to guide a startup's search for a scalable business model, launching the Lean Startup movement in the process.

His second book, *The Startup Owner's Manual*, published in March 2012, is a step-by-step guide to building a successful company that incorporates the best practices, lessons and tips that have swept the startup world since *The Four Steps* was published.

His essays on his blog, www.steveblank.com, and his two books are considered required reading among entrepreneurs, investors and established companies throughout the world.

In 2011, Blank developed the Lean LaunchPad, a hands-on class that integrates Business Model design and Customer Development into practice through rapid, real-world customer interaction and business model iteration. In 2011, the National Science Foundation adopted Blank's class for its Innovation Corps (I-Corps), training teams of the nation's top scientists and engineers to take their ideas out of the university lab and into the commercial marketplace. As of early 2013, more than 400 handpicked teams of scientists and engineers had participated in I-Corps.

Blank also offers a free online version of Lean LaunchPad through Udacity.com; more than 100,000 people have signed up for the class, which is also the centerpiece of Startup Weekend NEXT, a global entrepreneurship training program launched in fall 2012.

Steve is a prolific writer, speaker and teacher. In 2009, he earned the Stanford University Undergraduate Teaching Award in Management Science and Engineering. In 2010, he earned the Earl F. Cheit Outstanding Teaching Award at U.C. Berkeley Haas School of Business. The San Jose Mercury News listed him as one of the 10 Influencers in Silicon Valley. Harvard Business Review named him one of 12 Masters of Innovation. Despite these accolades and many others, Steve says he might well have been voted "least likely to succeed" in his New York City high school class.

Eight startups in 21 years

After repairing fighter plane electronics in Thailand during the Vietnam War, Steve arrived in Silicon Valley in 1978, as boom times began. He joined his first of eight startups including two semiconductor companies, Zilog and MIPS Computers; Convergent Technologies; a consulting stint for Pixar; a supercomputer firm, Ardent; peripheral supplier, SuperMac; a military intelligence systems supplier, ESL; Rocket Science Games. Steve co-founded startup No. 8, E.piphany, in his living room in 1996. In sum: two significant craters, one massive "dot-com bubble" home run, several "base hits," and immense learning that resulted in *The Four Steps to the Epiphany*.

An avid reader in history, technology, and entrepreneurship, Steve has followed his curiosity about why entrepreneurship blossomed in Silicon Valley while stillborn elsewhere. It has made him an unofficial expert and frequent speaker on "The Secret History of Silicon Valley."

In his spare time, Steve is a Commissioner of the California Coastal Commission, the public body that regulates land use and public access on the California coast. Steve is on the board of the California League of Conservation Voters (CLCV). He is a past board member of Audubon California, the Peninsula Open Space Land Trust (POST), and was a trustee of U.C. Santa Cruz.

Steve's proudest startups are daughters Katie and Sarah, co-developed with wife Alison Elliott. They split their time between Pescadero and Silicon Valley.